LABO
AND
SOCIAL DEMOCRATS

Also by Geoffrey Lee Williams and Alan Lee Williams

CRISIS IN EUROPEAN DEFENCE
*THE EUROPEAN DEFENCE INITIATIVE: Europe's Bid for Equality
DENIS HEALEY AND THE POLICIES OF POWER (*with Bruce Reed*)

Also by Geoffrey Lee Williams

THE PERMANENT ALLIANCE: The European–American Partnership
GLOBAL DEFENCE: Defence in a Nuclear-Missile Age

Also published by Macmillan

Labour's Decline and the Social Democrats' Fall

Geoffrey Lee Williams

Visiting Professor of International Relations
University of Surrey
and
Director of the Institute of Economic and Political Studies (INSTEP)
Cambridge

and

Alan Lee Williams

Warden and Chief Executive of Toynbee Hall
and
former Member of Parliament for Hornchurch

MACMILLAN

First published 1989

Published by
THE MACMILLAN PRESS LTD
Houndmills, Basingstoke, Hampshire RG21 2XS
and London
Companies and representatives
throughout the world

Printed in Great Britain by
Billing & Sons Ltd,
Worcester
British Library Cataloguing in Publication Data
Williams, Geoffrey Lee, *1930*–
Labour's decline and the Social Democrats'
fall
1. Great Britain. Political parties: Labour
Party (Great Britain). 2. Great Britain.
Political parties: Social Democratic Party
I. Title II. Williams, Alan Lee, *1930*–
324.24107
ISBN 0–333–46541–5 (hardcover)
ISBN 0–333–46542–3 (paperback)

To the memory of Ada Armstrong

Contents

List of Tables

Acknowledgements

We should like to thank Jill Rathbone who typed the book in its entirety, and we are grateful to Penelope Ford, Janice Williams and Elizabeth Jewell for their assistance in reading and improving parts of the manuscript. We are also pleased to acknowledge Penelope Ford's help in collating the numerous interviews which of necessity this study required. We wish to thank Philip Davies for the index and Keith Povey for his editorial advice. The views expressed are entirely our own.

GEOFFREY LEE WILLIAMS
ALAN LEE WILLIAMS

Introduction

This study, which is divided into two parts, discusses the nature and extent of the collapse of the coalition of interests within the Labour Party which led directly to the emergence of the Social Democratic Party whose initial bid to displace the Labour Party as the principal opposition party failed lamentably in 1987. The book is based on historical analysis and personal interviews with the leading political figures involved in the birth of the new party and the drama of its nemesis in 1988. The book examines in depth the stresses and strains which reduced the Labour Party to a shell of its former self and which, in turn, tore the original SDP to pieces. We seek to show that the bid to break the mould of British politics has, for the time being, failed.

The main feature of the book is its comparative treatment of both parties whose *raison d'être* was brought into question in a period of political volatility and economic change. We have treated the collapse of the Labour Party as a function of the rise of SDP between 1980 and 1988. The real challenge to the mould of British politics came from the right as the left vainly fought to preserve the status quo. We argue that the near-collapse of Labour as a viable opposition party makes the emergence of a new centre grouping in British politics an absolute requirement if the UK is to be prevented from facing indefinite Tory rule. We reveal the extent of the commitment to promote a merger between the Liberals and Social Democrats which was predicated on the basis that David Owen was and is the real enemy of the realignment in British politics.

No sustained account of British politics, however, nor indeed a book dealing with the rise and fall of the Social Democratic Party, could begin without a discussion of the recent difficulties of the Labour Party, which is the party that in the fullness of time the SDP was seeking to replace as the principal opposition party. Once that had been achieved, then the winning of a parliamentary majority was expected to follow in due course. However, the attempt to dislodge Labour as Her Majesty's loyal opposition was not to be an easy or inevitable development and was, in any event, not to be achieved overnight.

Since a minority party or parties seeking to hold the balance in a

1

hung parliament is likely to prove inadequate, there must be a distinctive ideology or *raison d'être*. Ideology in British politics is functional: it is essential to have a label to distinguish one party from another, especially if those parties stand close to each other in attempting to address the need for radical reform. What, then, is the ideology of the Labour Party which the SDP has to undermine or indeed perhaps redefine in the last quarter of the twentieth century? And what part has the split over 'socialist' and 'social democrat' objectives played in destroying the inner core of Labour's distinctive character? Moreover, since the issues of defence and foreign policy were largely responsible for the defection of Dr David Owen in particular, how and why did Labour split over these issues?

The answer to these questions lies in the history of the Labour Party over the last forty years or so and in the course of government over that period. The split over geopolitical issues within the Labour Party reached a crisis point when the domestic consensus also collapsed in the wake of the failure of the Labour governments of 1966–70 and 1974–9. We attempt in Part I of this study to identify the nature of the ideological conflict within the Labour Party as well as the issues which led to the dramatic collapse of Labour's electoral fortunes in the 1980s. Then, in Part II, we describe and evaluate the rise of the Social Democratic Party, as well as its demise and re-emergence in two different forms, and the consequences for British politics, to see whether it can actually challenge and then displace Labour as Britain's radical opposition to the Tories, or whether it becomes merely instrumental in returning a Labour government bent on reversing the Thatcherite revolution.

As readers will discover, about half of the book is about the Labour Party; this is because the Social Democratic Party cannot be understood without reference to the civil war which very nearly overwhelmed the Labour Party after its defeat in 1979.

We seek to show that the strife within the Labour Party does not arise necessarily from the failure of successive Labour governments to implement radical social change of a so-called socialist character. Indeed the Attlee government was quite radical, and is credited with establishing the welfare state, and a large public sector. We argue that Labour governments until 1979 could be relied upon to govern in the national interest as defined by the political values and mores of liberal-democratic societies. In other words, Labour governments operated within the democratic tradition; displaying due regard for the rights of private ownership and of representative government. It was no accident that Labour leaders were often great parliamentarians *par excellence* – Clement Attlee, Aneurin Bevan, Herbert Morrison, Hugh Gaitskell and, more recently, Harold Wilson, George Brown, Richard Crossman and Roy Jenkins. We thus can demonstrate that the Labour Party, socialised by the requirements of the electoral system and the parliamentary system, saw representation in Parliament as the crowning glory of the British Labour movement. It sought power through democratic means exercised in an open manner like any other democratic political party strenuously seeking a parliamentary majority.

We discuss in Chapter 1 how the first post-war Labour government and its successors maintained continuity in British foreign policy in a rather striking manner. Indeed, so much so that Ernest Bevin – arguably Britain's best ever foreign secretary – was described by his critics as a fat edition of Anthony Eden, the most expert foreign secretary ever produced by the Conservative Party this century.

Throughout the post-war period the two main political parties followed a bi-partisan foreign policy which was sustained until the early 1980s. Thereafter the Labour Party broke away from the constraints of traditionalist thinking.

The triumph of the anti-nuclear left was a turning-point in post-war history. The importance attached to a global role and the Anglo-American alliance and more especially the commitment to NATO had been part of the Attlee–Gaitskell–Wilson–Healey realism which was also part and parcel of the ideology of Labourism (see Chapter 1). The rise of the neo-utopianism of the hard-left has played its part in transforming the Labour Party into what is perceived as the most socialist party in Western Europe. This perception does most to explain the rise of the Social Democratic Party.

We describe and evaluate the debate within the Labour Party over defence; however, it is worth stressing that this debate ends in the emergence of a new intra-party consensus provided by the left. Thus most of the critics of this new left-wing consensus are now outside the party. The impact of this change on Labour voters was wholly disastrous. Electorally speaking, defence has become a graveyard for Labour.

To the dismay of Labour's social democrats, the value-change implied in a neutralist stance was preferred by Labour's left to the known preferences of Labour voters whose deep and enduring attachment to the Western alliance has long been a feature of British politics.

The disaffected social democrats within the Labour Party, which included those who stayed loyal to Labour – like Roy Hattersley, John Smith and Denis Healey as well as those like the Gang of Four who formed the SDP in 1981 – denied the need for fundamental changes in British defence policy.

Certainly the Gang of Four denied that Britain was experiencing a broad evolution in popular opinion that required fundamental changes in defence policy of the character favoured by Michael Foot and Neil Kinnock.

The SDP in general, and David Owen in particular, denied the basic premise of the left: that the Labour Party and the Campaign for Nuclear Disarmament (CND) had essentially 'democratised' defence policy by making it a popular issue.

Owen argued that defence policy in Britain since the mid-1970s had merely been 'politicised' following the collapse of the post-war consensus; hence the importance we attach in Part I of this study to describing the crisis within the Labour Party once its more traditional policies were rejected by Conference and the National Executive Committee (NEC).

The rise of the peace movement cannot be described as a genuinely popular movement of dissent. David Owen rejected the elaborate sophistry of widely respected dissenters like E. P. Thompson and Bruce Kent who advanced the claim that the CND was a grass-roots movement of mass protest.

The Gang of Four of the SDP, whose role we describe in Part II of this study, believed that the real source of the defence controversy had a different explanation. From their perspective it was the manifest collapse of the political consensus which became the central problem, not popular opinion.

In fact David Owen has asserted, in various contexts, that protest had had a much greater effect on policy than on public opinion at large.

The possible increased involvement of the public on nuclear issues is simply not to be explained by a democratic revolution in attitudes towards the defence of the realm. The phenomenon has more to do with the attitude of dissident elites who were very active in the Labour Party, as revealed in Part I of this book.

The social democrats who quit the Labour Party identified the Campaign for Nuclear Disarmament (CND) and the activist left within the party as the real phenomenon. They constituted the problem. The rejection of a viable defence policy based on nuclear deterrence and on unqualified support for NATO together with the Anglo-American alliance, had been advanced by highly educated, politically committed, well-organised, and emotionally engaged individuals who had set out to operate from within the wider Labour movement and the Labour Party in particular. It was nothing short of subversion.

The Labour Party had been virtually taken over by the CND, at least as far as its foreign and defence policies were concerned. The party of Hugh Gaitskell, Harold Wilson and Jim Callaghan had become the party of E. P. Thompson, Joan Rudduck, Bruce Kent *et al.*

This outcome simply horrified David Owen, Labour's last foreign secretary. He realised that public opinion tends to be passive on defence issues, at least to begin with; people are inclined, however, to form their opinions based on the stance taken by the parties with which they have chosen to identify themselves for non-defence reasons. Dr Owen knew that a popular consensus is, to a marked extent, a function of political consensus. If, therefore, political views polarise, then general opinion tends to do so. The public may not be the principal source of dissent in defence policy but nor is it simply a passive observer. In his decision to break with Labour and to form a new party, defence played a major part.

David Owen knew as no other political figure did (with the exception of Jim Callaghan) that there are thresholds of public tolerance for deviation from established policy norms. Those who transgress those policy norms will quickly marginalise themselves in the battle for political power – defence then becomes salient enough to adversely influence voting patterns. Thus the newly formed SDP was tough on defence because Owen realised beyond peradventure that the advocacy of unilateral disarmament was deeply unpopular with the electorate.

Of course, we are not suggesting that he took this stance because it was popular: he was in principle utterly opposed to the neutralism and nuclear pacifism of the left. But he also saw that public opinion could become confused over defence. This was likely to occur if the defence issue was not made clear, and the Liberals had, in his judgement, been guilty of contributing to the public confusion over defence.

Clearly this shaped his attitudes towards them once closer collaboration with the Liberals became a fact, during the period of the Alliance. His attitude towards David Steel's dramatic merger proposal following the 1987 general election was affected by the Liberal assembly's irresponsible rejection of the Liberal leadership's support for a British deterrent in the preceding year.

Moreover, the joint SDP–Liberal commission on defence, produced just prior to the 1987 election, was a clever attempt to fudge the issue of defence. This could have discredited the Alliance at a crucial time. David Owen therefore disavowed their conclusions: he was less than pleased with those SDP spokesmen like the clever but prolix John Roper, a former Labour MP, who were prepared to compromise with the Liberals over defence.

There was no need for such a fudge. The SDP, Owen insisted, should stand firmly in favour of Britain's deterrent, though he thought the Trident missile system to be a bad defence buy. He recognised that it might well be too late to cancel it and therefore stood four-square behind a second-strike nuclear deterrent system.

In any event, the great Soviet peace offensive between 1979 and 1983 over the Dual Track Decision (DTD) failed to persuade Western governments to abandon NATO's collective strategy to modernise its long-range nuclear forces (LRTFs) in response to the deployment of the Soviet SS-20s. This decision proved historic: the 1987 Intermediate Nuclear Missile Treaty (INF) was thus made possible. David Owen's analysis was vindicated.

We have stressed throughout this book the importance and significance of David Owen as a national figure. He is certainly the cleverest and toughest politician out-of-power since the days of Sir Oswald Mosley (we do not wish this parallel to be taken pejoratively or literally).

There are, however, striking parallels to be drawn, *mutatis mutundis*, with Mosley's New Party and the formation of the Social Democratic Party (SDP); though there are equally very different aspects involved as well.

Mosley became a fanatic: Owen is transparently reasoned and reasonable. The New Party of the Left formed in early 1931 initially attracted only a few significant political figures and a smaller number of Labour MPs and dissidents. The party promised to break the political mould of the day.

The New Party was joined by John Strachey, W. J. Brown, Robert Forgan and Oliver Baldwin – all Labour MPs. The New Party's manifesto promulgated a plan to mobilise four hundred candidates in the next general election, and appealed for voluntary workers in all constituencies. In a statement written by John Strachey, the party asserted that the 'creation of a new political organisation is a great and difficult adventure which few politicians are willing to undertake, however much they agree with the necessity for new policy'.[1]

The New Party was thoroughly planned. The industrialist Sir William Morris supplied the financial backing, John Strachey the intellectual depth and Professor Cyril Joad much inspiration as its director of propaganda.

There was the hope that the distinguished Cambridge economist John Maynard Keynes would join, together with world-famous playwright Bernard Shaw, and perhaps even Harold Nicolson, the diplomat and politician.

Like the SDP in 1981, on the occasion of the Warrington by-election, the New Party faced its big test at a by-election in Ashton-under-Lyne, a Lancashire cotton town with 4900 unemployed, where, in 1929, there had been a Labour majority of 3407.[2]

Allen Young, the New Party's candidate (a brilliant Glaswegian who had been the political organiser of the Birmingham Labour Party), just narrowly failed to take the seat. The Conservative candidate was in fact elected: he received 12 400 votes to Labour's 11 000, and the New Party's candidate received 4500. This was perhaps less historic than Roy Jenkins's near-win at Warrington some fifty-two years later. But for the New Party in 1929, 4500 votes (without the aid of TV and radio coverage on a national scale) was a considerable achievement. They possessed a more primitive organisation than the SDP; however the 1929 by-election excited interest and support. Moreover, the history of the two respective parties diverge dramatically after this initial thrust. Sir Oswald Mosley's internal rage overwhelmed his capacity for sensible judgement. His attempt to create a new political psychology had an ominous ring to it (he began speaking of a 'national renaissance, of new mankind and of vigour'). Mosley now considered socialism a 'pathological condition'. His rhetoric and his authoritarian streak led to a break with his closest colleagues including John Strachey. The split was decisive; his senior political friends deserted him to return to their former loyalties. The role of leadership figures prominently in both parties.

However, Mosley and Owen bear only a superficial resemblance. While both men enjoyed some ministerial experience, only Owen retained his seat in the House of Commons. The SDP was always more than just an extra-parliamentary party unlike the New Party which failed to attract support and soon ceased to exist. Mosley pressed on to form yet another party which achieved notoriety as the British Union of Fascists.

The New Party was crushed in the 1931 general election (both Mosley and Strachey lost their seats). The SDP has yet to be completely crushed at the polls but faces a very real risk of this in the future. David Owen, like Oswald Mosley, could thus be marginalised.

Owen left the Labour Party because of its attitude towards defence and Europe; Mosley left over the Labour government's rejection of his plan to deal with mass unemployment.

Both were 'doers' rather than 'thinkers', and either one of them would have made an outstanding prime minister. Oswald Mosley tended to surround himself with cronies: strong-arm friends such as Kid Lewis the boxer, Peter Cheyney the crime novelist, and Peter Howard the Oxford rugger player. David Owen is less reliant on cronies but has Rosie Barnes MP, David Sainsbury of the supermarket chain, and loyal John Cartwright MP. Sir Oswald Mosley was admired by and had contacts with his political opponents (such as Harold Macmillan, Robert Boothby, Oliver Stanley and Walter Elliot). Equally David Owen is admired by opponents like Norman Tebbitt, Sir Geoffrey Howe and, arguably, Mrs Margaret Thatcher herself. Both men were admired by women, although Mosley was a womaniser and Owen is not. They both dominated their respective fledgling parties, but whereas the New Party was dominated by Mosley in its very short life, the Social Democratic Party enjoyed a collective leadership (the Gang of Four) for a time. This attenuated Owen's authoritarian tendencies and reduced the impression that the SDP was just another splinter group or minor party (indeed this study reveals the very real support that the SDP enjoyed from a wide spectrum of opinion and of interest in the country). However, Sir Oswald Mosley removed himself from the mainstream of political life when he became an avowed fascist (the black-shirts); his own hubris transformed him from being a charismatic figure of the democratic left into a rather ugly and sinister figure on the far right. He, in fact, became a rather unimportant, though controversial, figure in British politics who enjoyed rather more sympathy among a certain section of the upper class than among the working classes in general. Even his anti-Semitism failed to give him the overwhelming support he was seeking in the East End of London where racial prejudice still exists today.

Dr David Owen in 1989 leads a small party, now the sizeable remnants of the once larger SDP, with which this book is mostly concerned. He possesses Oswald Mosley's charm, ability and ambition to break the mould (Mosley, of course, ultimately wanted to break the system) in order to change society. David Owen is a pluralist and democrat; he represents the wholesome side of British politics. For Dr Owen, empiricism is the ally of freedom, and the doctrinaire spirit is the friend of totalitarianism. Britain was mercifully deprived of Mosley's genius.

This book is a serious attempt to contribute to a controversy about the future of British politics and in particular the future of the non-left opposition to the continued hegemony of the Tory party. We also describe in the first part of the study the melancholy decline of the Labour Party as a party of power. The Labour Party reverts to being a trades-union pressure group offering only organised protest as its electoral appeal fades. The Labour opposition is no longer the alternative government. As we enter the final part of this decade there is no real electable alternative government to the Tories. However, the centre of British politics still holds good as the area from which a sensible and moderate opposition grouping could emerge before the turn of the century, if not before. Britain today may yet be deprived of the opportunity of seeing what contribution, if any, David Owen might have made to the creation of a better Britain. But it is deplorable, as well as regrettable, that his talents may be lost to the nation while lesser figures emerge to represent the centre of British politics. Mr Paddy Ashdown is a lesser figure by far; the likeable Neil Kinnock a man of diminished stature (anyway, his party has vacated the centre ground); and the remainder of the Gang of Four (Williams, Rodgers and Jenkins) are now of little significance. The question remains whether this needed to have been the case. Did David Owen exclude himself or was he excluded? This book suggests the latter rather than the former. Perhaps it was a bit of both. But the nation has not yet seen the end of Dr David Owen. Mr Ashdown may be terribly wrong in describing him as an 'irrelevance'.

Part I

1 Labour's Traditional Image: Support for a World Role

The Labour government of 1945–51 had in no way violated continuity in British policy. Mr Attlee's government pursued a traditional and well-established foreign policy. It was exactly this continuity, this foreign policy consensus, that the 'utopian' and 'scientific socialist' left wanted to break. In its view a socialist foreign policy would be fundamentally different from the one pursued by the Labour Cabinet.[1]

Labour's left wing, divided as it was between the 'utopians' and the 'scientific socialists', however, were split over their attitude to the British Commonwealth. The left were more ideologically motivated than the majority of the party both inside and outside the parliamentary party. The left disliked the unequal and exploitative nature of the Commonwealth epitomised by the concept of a 'mother country'.[2] According to this section of the left, the Commonwealth was not socialist, and could never be so until Britain itself was socialist. They regarded themselves as internationalists, and therefore exponents of true socialism.

The Social Democrats and the Labourites, whom we can identify as in the mainstream of the Labour Party between 1945 and 1979, on the other hand, saw the existing Commonwealth as something wholly admirable and viable.[3] This attitude was strengthened with the manifest failure of Western Europe to embrace socialism and with Europe becoming divided both territorially and politically in the Cold War. The Commonwealth was perceived as that potential 'third force' which would make unnecessary a choice between unreformed capitalism and totalitarian communism. It was hoped that a strong and viable Commonwealth would help prevent 'the splitting of the world into two blocs' and would thus make 'the One World of UNO a reality'.[4] The Bandung Conference of 1955 even gave a certain respectability to this view by strengthening its own part in the transformation of the Commonwealth of the old dominions into the New or Afro-Asian Commonwealth under Mr Attlee's post-war administration. And yet the Commonwealth, so admired by the majority of the Labour Party, never existed as a viable political force in international politics. The Commonwealth remained a loose and diverse assembly of nations.

Despite the markedly different ideological stance between the left and the right and centre, there existed no major disagreement over the ultimate futility of an East of Suez presence. The Labour Party as a whole foresaw an end to it, claiming that the end of colonialism should mean the end of military involvement.[5] Clearly, the arguments which related to India, Burma and Ceylon were also relevant elsewhere; that the countries in the area would never achieve genuine independence while Britain retained a military presence, and that Britain by supporting unrepresentative feudal elites simply imposed neo-colonialism on notionally independent states.[6]

It was the social democratic left, together with the solid right of the parliamentary party, though, rather than the Marxist intellectuals, which tended to gain support from within the extra-parliamentary party. It achieved this by maintaining a distinction between Soviet expansionism, which it would oppose, and indigenous communism, which it insisted it 'had so much better come to terms with'.[7] This opposition to Soviet imperialism, combined with a determination that feudalism and corrupt foreign capitalist or neo-capitalist regimes should not be sustained, aroused some sympathy within a party which itself had struggled to change the status quo. There remained, however, substantial areas of disagreement between the Marxist and social democratic left over foreign and colonial policies.

These areas of ideological disagreement had grown as a result of the erosion of many of the traditional socialist principles and beliefs. So-called 'revisionism' had carried the day with the triumph of the values of social democracy.[8] The principle of collective security had been undermined by the feeble opposition of the League of Nations to Hitler and Mussolini due to lack of support from the Anglo-French governments for tough league action. In addition, the belief that working-class loyalties would transcend national boundaries had been undermined by the unhesitating support given to nation-states in both world wars.[9] And finally the belief that capitalism as such explained the cause of international conflict had been invalidated by the subsequent belligerence and expansion of 'socialist' Russia. The erosion of these principles, however, progressed at different levels within the party and led to conflicting attitudes towards the Cold War.

Whilst the right of the party inside both Parliament and the

Cabinet expounded the value of self-defence and underlined the menace of the Soviet Union, the left, both inside and outside Parliament, continued to champion collective security and to sympathise more with the Soviet Union than with the United States. It also retained its faith in traditional socialist principles, the primary factors being economic determinism and the related notion of imperialism. This analysis revealed that 'all the policies of a nation are directly determined by its economic system', and it consequently pinpointed the USA as the main enemy of socialism.[10] According to the Socialist Union, a body of moderate socialist opinion, the leftist belief in economic determinism had led it to:

the rigid view that there are clear-cut economic systems obeying immutable laws. Compared with these, all that might spring from the different political, social and cultural institutions of a country is of small moment. It matters not if America has free institutions; the fact that she is capitalist has been enough to damn her; and the contrary in the case of Russia.[11]

The conflicting interpretation of the politico-strategic intentions of the USA and the USSR made for very different analyses of the Cold War, and Britain's world role East of Suez was increasingly related to this wider analysis. It was said, by the Marxist or far left, that Britain's world role would increase her reliance on the United States by making her economically dependent on or even a mere client of that country. It complained that the US army was, in 1947, half the size of the British one in proportion to population, and that the inevitable consequence of pursuing a Conservative-type foreign policy was that Britain would become 'a pensioner of America, earning its living by fighting America's wars overseas'.[12] Britain could become an auxiliary of the United States.

The left emphasised the dangers inherent in such a policy:

If America supported by the Labour Government, organises 'collective security' against Russia and uses dollar loans to prop up anti-communist regimes around her frontiers, the Communist leaders can draw only one conclusion. They will assume the worst and stand stubbornly on the defensive until their scientists have made sufficient atomic bombs to redress the balance of military power.[13]

If the Labour government allowed this strategic error to occur, so the critics maintained, an unbridgeable dichotomy would develop between East and West, and any chance of a diplomatic understanding with the USSR would be unredeemably lost. Aneurin Bevan in fact resigned from the Shadow Cabinet on 15 April 1954 over Labour's support for the US policy in South East Asia, and Harold Wilson, later to lead the party, was in total agreement with his colleague's left-wing sentiments on the dangers of America's containment policy.[14]

Both the utopian and Marxist left, moreover, considered the support of non-democratic regimes by the West simply because they were anti-communist, to be ideologically and morally repugnant. Harold Wilson, a tactical member of the left, but in reality a reconstructed revisionist, in an impassioned speech, articulated the left's reservations about the existing policy. 'We must not join with, nor in any way encourage the anti-communist crusade in Asia, whether it is under the leadership of the Americans or anyone else. We must remember that the road to peace in Asia is the way of Nehru, not the way of Dulles.'[15] This posture became known as the 'New Statesman, London, New Delhi' axis.

The left thus believed that Britain's East of Suez role revealed a much wider and more dangerous tendency than Britain's wish to remain a residual imperial power; namely it involved becoming a subordinate partner to the United States in an attempt to build up anti-communist regimes around Russia's frontiers. Such a policy, it was said, would reduce the scope for a third force mediatory role between the superpowers by relating all international conflict to the Cold War. The result would be that 'every small people has to choose between the bleak alternative of anti-communism and communism. We shall sharpen the conflict instead of healing it.'[16] Accordingly the left virtuously insisted that 'The task of British Socialism must be, wherever possible, to save the smaller nations from this futile ideological warfare and to heal the breach between the USA and the USSR.'[17] This could not, though, be achieved if Britain were herself committed to an elaborate global anti-communist alliance system. This was the overwhelming objection to NATO. It was even supposed that a third world war could be prevented if Britain broke with America.[18]

The Left, anyway, argued that Communism could not be confronted or defeated by military means. It saw the Soviet threat as 'in the first instance economic, social and ideological', and argued that 'The most valuable allies of the Soviets are those elements in society which fight against social reforms.'[19] According to the left, it was the general lack of concern for social and economic factors that accounted for Soviet successes. It complained that while 'the under-fed masses yearn for material aid we send them guns'.[20] Aneurin Bevan put the classic view most emphatically:

> The answer to social upheaval is social amelioration, not bombing planes and guns; yet we are making the latter on such a scale that we have no resources left for the provision of industrial equipment which the underdeveloped areas of the world must have, if they are not to go on bubbling and exploding for the rest of the century.[21]

The foreign policy advocated by the left, then, called for the rejection of the belief that British security depended on the military power of the United States, and urged an acceptance of the 'accomplished fact that the defence of the Middle East, as well as of India, Burma and Malaya, is no longer a responsibility of the British people'.[22] It was argued further that 'a break with old-fashioned imperial tradition' was necessary 'if we are to bring our foreign commitments into a true relationship with our economic strength and with our Socialist principles'.[23] The left, of course, over-simplified the East of Suez issue, but their analysis and prescription positively reflected basic values and was not therefore an attitude likely to change in the light of the international environment. Ideological commitment to the left preceded and superseded political realities as understood by the social democratic left of the Labour Party.

It was to be expected that the classic case for social and economic priorities over military ones, based as it was on traditional socialist principles, would gain considerable support and significance from within a party which, when reverting to opposition, had always reinforced and emphasised the role of ideals and downgraded the influence of environment upon declaratory policy.

The official party line was however still very different from the one advocated by the left. The Labour leadership's assessment that the turmoil in South East Asia was due to local nationalist forces seeking to overthrow European rule, and to an 'economic revolution' born out of the Asians' newly found realisation of their wretched poverty, was a conclusion which the left had no reason to controvert.

However, the Labour leadership argued that a British presence East of Suez could not be regarded as a residual method of discharging post-colonial responsibilities, because the Soviet 'threat' in the area had increased. It was this presumed threat which tended to confuse the distinction for the Labour leadership, between non-belligerent reactionary and non-belligerent progressive regimes. If a friendly state were being undermined by Soviet action, overt or covert in character, then Labour tended to resist it regardless of whether it held much ideological sympathy for the regime being threatened. Whilst the Labour leadership declared its support for working with liberal and progressive governments, it argued that it was sometimes compelled to accept 'dubious alliances with reactionary forces', when Britain's security was threatened.[24] The ambiguity in the situation, though, was never really resolved and led to great dissension within the party. It was the eternal conflict between those who wished to change and those who recognised unchanging realities.

Nevertheless, in the main, it was clear that whereas post-colonial considerations dictated to Labour a policy of a phased and relatively rapid withdrawal, Cold War considerations, it was said, made such a withdrawal impossible.[25]

The Cold War in fact had the effect of dramatising the evident divisions within the party. During periods of world tension both wings were likely to fall out with considerable venom. The right of the party, including the Shadow Cabinet, favoured the creation of a universal balance of power; the left, including the vocal elements in parliament and in the party, believed that the only way to prevent a confrontation between the superpowers was to build up a block of neutral powers.[26] While these different approaches were not clear-cut when the international situation was quiescent, an international crisis invariably inspired considerable lobbying on the right in an effort to attract support for the West, and on the left to mobilise those moral forces that supported a third force or neutralist line. These approaches were plainly irreconcilable and, consequently, clashes over Britain's East of Suez role were most acute at times of greatest international tension.

One reason for the abrasive nature of the conflict between left and right in the foreign policy field in general, was that there prevailed within the extra-parliamentary wing of the party the conviction that socialist principles were more operationally relevant within the domestic context than was the case in relation to the external environment where they would inevitably have to be diluted in order to accommodate the interests of other nations.[27] This domestic introspection was justified by urging that a socialist Britain could serve as a model for the rest of the world. As the Socialist Union in its publication entitled *Socialism and Foreign Policy* argued, there existed within the Labour Party no real agreement about the relevance of socialist principles in foreign affairs, and concluded that 'The struggle for socialism has become increasingly to mean the struggle for socialism at home; in foreign affairs the problem has been to survive.'[28] The left was horrified by the logic of this.

Nor would the left condone the use of military power in support of Labour's foreign policy conducted in a hostile environment. This became not only a major bone of contention between the wings of the party, but it also carried overt and far-reaching implications for the East of Suez policy.

Labour's activist left unswervingly adhered to the belief that 'military alliances and armaments were ... the sinister pre-occupation of Capitalist Governments',[29] but experience of coalition government between 1940 and 1945 had indicated that if Labour gained power, or even if it were to behave as a responsible opposition, it could 'less and less dismiss the realities of foreign policy as the concern of Capitalists alone'.[30] As a result, 'Armaments, military alliances and power strategy could no longer be rejected out of hand. The weapons condemned by earlier socialists were now – short of a new world order – perforce part of the Socialist armoury as well.'[31] This realistic attitude and conversion to 'capitalist' ways was never accepted by the ultra-left in the extra-parliamentary wing of the Labour movement. They saw the capitalist military–industrial complex as lying at the heart of international tension and was therefore the cause of the Cold War itself.

Labour in opposition could be expected to become less concerned with Cold War power politics and more concerned with socialist principles, but this change of emphasis was only partially realised. The Korean War, however, was seen by the Labour leadership not only as evidence of aggression by a small communist state, but also as a sharp reminder of the willingness of two great communist powers to support aggression by proxy.[32] Moreover, the challenge in Korea could be the prelude to a Soviet attack in Europe. There was thus a reaction against any half-hearted commitment; this time collective security would have to be supported by the judicious use of armed force.[33]

There are clearly two factors which affected the Labour Party's foreign policy in the early 1950s which ensured that it did not diverge all that much from that of their main political opponents. First, because the Conservatives' basic analysis of the Cold War and of Soviet intentions were not noticeably different from those of the outgoing Labour government, for Labour now to have taken a 'soft' view would have been to contradict its own decisions taken when in power. Second, in this period, the threat to national security was perceived by both rival political elites to be such that it demanded national and bipartisan policies. During the early 1950s a bi-partisan consensus on foreign policy thus existed without any formal agreement ever being overtly necessary. Both major party leadership elites shared the same basic values and beliefs.

Labour leaders, then, saw foreign policy problems in much the same way as the Conservative Party. Ernest Bevin, in his day, had talked about 'power vacuums' and 'Russian expansionism', in a strikingly traditional Tory manner, and now, in opposition, Labour continued to echo the Bevinite doctrine.[34] It is true that the party was still committed in principle to its paramount aim 'to replace the international anarchy by a world order and to build a system in which disputes between states would be settled by arbitration, under the rule of law and not by the clash of physical force',[35] but it did not deny the stark reality of the Cold War, even though it continued to articulate its basic and fundamental socialist ideals. The external environment, however, had to determine policy and not ideology. Indeed ideology counted for less than the objective situation that the country found itself in.

Despite the left's belief that the Labour leadership had abandoned socialist foreign policy principles, the parliamentary left wing was not very active over the East of Suez issue during the 1950s.

Moreover, fortuitously a large part of that faction of utopian socialists who were morally opposed to the use of force, and as such might be expected to oppose the East of Suez role, were also that element most attracted to the ideals underpinning the New Commonwealth. This led to a marked degree of ambiguity in the attitude of much of the party; a toleration of, rather than an enthusiasm for, the use of military power to sustain the Commonwealth was shared by the trade-union movement, then under the influence of right-wing leaders, and was born more out of economic logic than political idealism. The trade-union support for the East of Suez role was based on enlightened self-interest because of the belief that on balance the Commonwealth connection, not least because of the potential markets it offered, was essential to the balance of payments, full employment and economic growth.

However, this attachment to the Commonwealth was enormously strengthened by a suspicion of the trade-union structure in Europe, and by a greatly exaggerated fear of cheap European labour. The trade unions in France were regarded by the moderate and orthodox British trade-union leadership as ideologically aligned with the communists; and where they were not so aligned, as in the case of West Germany, they were regarded as acting in collusion with the employers, in a bid to discipline recalcitrant labour. British trade-union leaders like Ernest Bevin and Arthur Deakin had considerable reservations about trade-unionism on the continent. This somewhat spinsterish attitude towards their colleagues in Europe also reflected the insularity and conservative nature of the Labour movement towards issues in Europe which involved greater *de facto* collaboration with European trade-unionists.

The failure of the trade-union movement to find in Europe a source of inspiration, or indeed a market area where economic growth of considerable magnitude could bring up the living standards of the British working class, reinforced the persistent idea that British living standards depended on Commonwealth trade and investment. It was not until it was realised with incredulity that the French and certainly the West German workers were having a much better deal from their employers than their British counterparts, that superior welfare provisions and sickness benefits existed in those countries, and that wages and productivity were vastly better than in Britain with a much lower rate of inflation, that this anti-European attitude slowly diminished.[36] However, it did not decrease significantly even when Britain took an official attitude towards the Treaty of Rome; over ten years later, of course. And so in the 1950s the trade-union leadership loyally supported the Commonwealth and the use of force in order to sustain it, if this proved necessary. Both Attlee and Gaitskell could rely upon the trade unions' block vote to sustain an orthodox policy East of Suez.

There can, however, be no doubt that the parliamentary critics of Britain's East of Suez role were concerned about the 'national interest'. They firmly believed, for instance, that Britain could not afford the role, or at least should invest its diminishing resources more sensibly elsewhere. They could not however expect to get the same degree of influence over the party in the 1950s as they had exerted in the 1930s. A socialist foreign policy based on pacifist opposition to armaments was, after the experience of appeasement, the collapse of collective security and the subsequent world war, now impossible.

In opposition, Labour could perhaps encourage a return to a more ideological foreign policy, although Bevin's ghost and Labour's experience of office still cast a shadow – Bevin's traditionalism was by now the party orthodoxy. It was clear also that Bevin's policy was the preferred one, because the Labour leadership took the view that the ideology of social democracy was now under as grave a threat from totalitarian communism as had been the case when Hitler threatened the peace of Europe. However, the development of weapons of mass destruction, and the nuclear missile arms race between the superpowers, reinforced the utopian and Marxist left's criticism of Labour's foreign policy consensus.[37] Hence the left embraced nuclear pacifism.

To the pacifist, it was a tentative step towards a disarmed world and the heady ground of world government. To the neutralist, it was the rejection once again of the Cold War and support for superpower politics. To those who feared the growing anarchy of world politics, this anti-nuclear lobby was a means of contracting out of entanglements and obligations. To those fellow-travellers in the party whose sympathy lay with the USSR, it was the critical first step towards the dissolution of NATO, and of all military blocs. And to the trade-unionist, it was an acknowledgement of the importance of domestic affairs. The Campaign for Nuclear Disarmament, a vast umbrella organisation, was not only of relevance for Britain's defence policy.[38] There were far-reaching foreign policy issues at stake in the debate. The seeds of Labour's future crisis over defence were sown.

The Campaign for Nuclear Disarmament was concerned with the future nature and character of Britain's foreign policy, for it attempted to re-define where Britain's interests and allies lay. The utopian and socialist left's enthusiasm for the CND lay in the hope that the Labour Party would pursue a neutralist policy.

Surprisingly, though, even in a rising climate of protest and dissent apparently so conducive to radicalism, the Labour left never really launched a coherent or frontal attack on the world role. This was all the more perverse since all those on the left who supported the nuclear pacifism of the CND were likely also to support the anti-power logic of a 'socialist' foreign policy, and that included the abandonment of the East of Suez role, together with rejection of the Anglo-American alliance, NATO and the Cold War. There was, though, an almost total obsession with nuclear strategy, and consequently the left's direct influence over the East of Suez issue was not as great as its position at the 1960 Labour Party Scarborough Conference appeared to infer. One strand of the CND critique of Labour's policy was the argument advanced by Ted Hill of the Boilermaker's Union that the Commonwealth could institute the core of a third force in world politics led by a non-nuclear Britain.[39] But the left in fact concentrated their efforts on the great domestic debate over socialist principles, and then became concerned with the nuclear controversy. In consequence the world role never became, for any length of time, a major controversy as between the wings of the party, because domestic politics, together with concentration on the winning of political power through elections, tended to defuse passionate interest in concerns affecting the external environment.

Nevertheless, while the left was decidely reluctant to concentrate its energies on dismembering the East of Suez role, it was clear that if the party itself showed any tendency to question that role it could count on considerable leftish support. This was important, for by the mid-1950s there began within Labour's higher echelons, almost in a conspiracy of silence, a questioning which over the next few years was to lead to a full reappraisal of the world role, when significant changes in the external environment forced upon Labour leaders a new perception of realities.[40]

Britain's presence East of Suez made her interests more secure, whether military force was in fact relevant to the problems facing that area, whether the threat to the status quo and local stability East of Suez had been correctly perceived and whether Britain had the capability to act East of Suez anyway. Moreover, there was a more important consideration arising from the cost to Britain's balance of payments of a large presence East of Suez. However, the economic costs were difficult to calculate and could not yet prove decisive in determining policy.

Politically there were increasing doubts about whether Britain gained diplomatic kudos through her presence East of Suez and whether that presence was consistent with socialist morality which rejected so-called neo-colonialism. Did Britain's presence help her economic investments in the area (amounting to a considerable sum) and, if so, did such investments exceed the cost of their preservation?

These questions related principally to the Middle East which had traditionally been of enormous strategic significance for Britain. They had first been raised in the early 1950s when the left as a whole had shown implacable opposition to the retention of a costly presence in Egypt, but they were more frequently posed after the abortive and tragic Suez operation in 1956. As a result of limited military operations in the area during 1957 and 1958, more general criticisms of Britain's role in the Middle East were made.

The truculent Russian diplomatic offensive in Europe 1958–61, however, put the imperial role in jeopardy, for there was no obvious disquiet that Britain might be bleeding her forces on the continent by meeting her inherited obligations East of Suez. It is perhaps too simplistic to assert that Labour's growing anxieties about East of Suez affairs were little more than a rationale for policy decisions taken because of the menacing European crisis, yet it was natural enough for those, on both the left and right of the party, who wanted to buttress European security, to justify a withdrawal of troops from East of Suez with the seductive argument that their presence in that area was no longer necessary.[41] The near-panic the European crisis produced in Labour's divided ranks is perhaps evidence enough that this was in fact the case.[42]

The deep contradiction between Britain's maritime and continental roles, in the form of a competition for seriously limited resources, had become an incontrovertible fact in the late 1950s.[43] It is nevertheless true that each role had its own advocates within the Labour movement throughout that period and that it was not always a straightforward disagreement between the left and the right.

Throughout the 1950s, the heirs of the Bevinite tradition within the Labour Party had consistently upheld the notion that the nation's prestige would be enhanced by sustaining a world role, and that if Britain wanted to minimise the risk of United States' irresponsibility in Asia she must maintain a presence in that area.[44] Another faction within the party, the very influential Eurocentric group – centred on those in favour of British membership of the EEC while agreeing that the United States, although dependable in Europe, might be reckless in Asia – argued that the way to retain influence over the United States was to engender closer ties through defence integration with Europe and to have Britain's independent nuclear deterrent absorbed into a NATO structure.[45] These early adherents to Europeanism, but not a third force Europe, concluded that, if Britain performed a specialist function in Europe, her standing in the United States would also improve. In addition, there existed both a latent but very real fear of Germany and the Soviet Union, as well as a growing awareness of the dynamic economic impact of the European Economic Community, which had now emerged as a major factor in international politics.[46]

Although the influence and balance of strength between the Europeanists and Atlanticists seemed in the late 1950s to be moving in favour of the former, this did not mean the search for purely European solutions, as the parochial nature of French Europeanism was not yet apparent. In any event, the pro-European faction in Labour's ranks was generally anti-Gaullist in outlook. Even if Labour wanted to circumscribe the World Role and to redefine the Anglo-American connection, a universal balance of power with particular emphasis on NATO would still remain as the core element for the leadership. Indeed, apart from the neutralist left, those members of the Labour Party clustered around the leadership on the National Executive Committee and in the Parliamentary Party wanted to limit the East of Suez commitment, and desired to do so largely to strengthen NATO's capabilities against a possible rampant Soviet advance into Western Europe.[47] Why, though, had there been no significant conflict between European and Atlanticist policies previously within the Labour movement? This question relates to the nature of the external environment rather than to different ideological interpretations of policy on the British left.

It was not too demanding for Britain to pursue both maritime and continental roles before 1958. She sabotaged the projected European Defence Community by diplomatic stealth in giving it lukewarm support which made it certain that the French National Assembly would reject the idea. However, Britain was ready with the concept of an expanded Western European Union (WEU) which enabled Britain (and Germany) to make a contribution to European defence under the Paris agreements. Britain preferred an inter-governmental arrangement to a possible supra-national one.[48] Labour went along with that.

The re-arming of Germany, although making a British commitment to Europe necessary, also released resources and men for a more credible continental strategy if any real desire existed to develop one. Conservative governments, however, during the 1950s, did not appear too anxious about being unable to fulfil Britain's 'unprecedented commitment' to the continent. This attitude was quite traditional.[49] There were, after all, not only good economic reasons for not observing this commitment beyond that of a two-division Rhine Army, but also the strategic rationale that deterrence would be weakened if conventional forces were increased.[50] The nuclear threshold had to be kept as low as possible because Britain had no wish to contribute a large army to the defence of Europe.[51] In any case, although Britain did not reach the proposed force levels in Europe, which the NATO Council recommended at Lisbon in 1952, European security continued intact.[52] The Russians seemed preoccupied with events outside Europe, and the United States' deterrent policy remained feasible while her homeland could not seriously be threatened. This position lasted until at least 1960, when the doctrine of massive retaliation was replaced by the flexible response strategy as set out by Defence Secretary Robert McNamara at Ann Arbour in 1962.[53] The Labour opposition accepted this strategy with something amounting to enthusiasm.

Britain's continental role during the early 1950s was not, then, beyond being met by the deployment of existing resources, and the same was true of East of Suez, where commitments had rarely become simultaneously active. The Chiefs of Staff, in the 1930s, and now in the 1950s, feared that both commitments might one day be activated together, but the intrinsic dichotomy between these two roles could persist for the time being.[54] However, as this analysis has made clear, the Labour Party both in opposition and in power, though divided over the question of Britain's external role, was generally predisposed towards accepting the imperial commitment.[55] Labour took the view that existing responsibilities could and should be met. The overwhelming impression emerges that both the left and right within the Labour Party accepted that Britain was still a great power, albeit one in decline.[56] The nation's role East of Suez was not to be disavowed by Labour. The ideology of Labourism was now strongly influenced by the revisionist doctrine which, associated with the social-democratic wing of the party, proved decisive in shaping the party's foreign and defence policies.[57] Labour also remained stoutly Atlanticist in orientation; however, the left's anti-Americanism remained a powerful latent force.

2 Labour and the Defence of the Realm: The Abandonment of Britain's World Role

In the general election of June 1970, Labour was defeated. Mr Wilson, who had presided over the nation's affairs since Labour had first assumed office some six years earlier, returned to the Opposition Front Bench – perhaps to deliberate on the momentous changes in foreign and defence policy which he had both wittingly and unwittingly introduced.[1] In this deliberation he was not alone. There is no doubt about the lasting relevance of his decisions, although some confusion emerged about how they related to a broader foreign policy perspective, and inevitably also criticisms about the way in which they were made. The Cabinet seriously miscalculated its capacity to meet political commitments with diminishing economic resources.

Denis Healey, the Minister of Defence, then, was not entirely to blame for the subsequent failures of his defence policy. He was under extreme pressure from the Treasury's defence ceiling, from the Foreign Office's plantigrade reluctance to cut commitment, and from the government's own anguished failure to achieve economic growth. Then there was the influence of the Prime Minister who favoured a grand strategy with imperial overtones.

Mr Healey was not alone in the difficulties he faced. His inherited responsibilities and commitments were compounded by Labour's vastly ambitious defence strategy. The government as a whole was also set some fairly intractable defence problems, particularly in relation to the East of Suez role. Chronic economic weakness, a Service manpower shortage, the costs and risks of Confrontation with Indonesia, escalating defence costs and greater military capabilities available to actual and potential adversaries, all in some significant way obstructed the formulation of a strong and consistent defence policy. So did the attitude of much of the Labour Party; the Party Conference in particular. The trade unions also strongly influenced the Labour Party Conference, and through the Conference, the

27

National Executive Committee. Of course the NEC tends to take a different view of defence policy from that of the government. The trade unions, despite the challenge of Frank Cousins over the nuclear question in 1960, have, though, generally endeavoured to support the Cabinet over its defence policy. As the right controlled the bloc votes, they carried the day at Labour Party Conferences.[2] The growing influence of the left within the trade unions began to complicate the Cabinet's priorities by 1967, and beyond, but the influence of the trade unions should not be underestimated. Of the twenty-eight members of the NEC, only ten are not directly or indirectly elected by the bloc vote of the trade unions. And it was clear that trade-union opposition was the principal reason for the Wilson's government's abandonment of the Prices and Incomes Policy in 1969–70. The growing left-wing influence within the trade unions and the increase in what the late John MacKintosh described as the populist-socialist influence, contributed to the marked opposition to the government's defence and foreign policies.[3] Indeed, frequent attempts at a well-informed and dispassionate discussion of defence policy simply collapsed into a heated exchange of well-rehearsed argument, which established the continued existence of deep differences of opinion. The hostility of the party to defence matters, additionally the belief that defence goals were of less importance than social priorities, did not make the government's policy-making very easy. The non-doctrinal centre of the party rallied to the government's aid. They regarded the defence policy of the Cabinet as quite appropriate for an essentially non-theoretical Gaitskellite revisionist party.

Above all there was the chaotic and wayward nature of events East of Suez, and the fact that all projections about what might happen if Britain withdrew from the area were impossible to evaluate, since they could plausibly prove true or false according to the variables which any particular scenario might include. There was acute and unexpected doubt about the lessons that could be derived from past and present military interventions overseas. The lesson of the American intervention in Vietnam seemed very different from the lesson of the British involvement in Confrontation (or indeed of that in Malaya between 1948 and 1960) and the East African deployments of limited force.[4]

It was also a complication that as harassed ministers grappled with the East of Suez decision, they must have found it very difficult to evaluate all those pressures exerted upon them, because the World

Role was devoid of real substance. There was no dogma to encapsulate the debate and there were no clear core interests to dictate where Britain's 'national interest' lay. Had the relevance and indeed the significance of the East of Suez role as an imperial responsibility actually disappeared? Was the role no longer an essential element in the containment of so-called global Communism? Did the increasing interdependence and interpenetration of nation-states erode the relevance of military force? These questions were so complex and bewildering because there existed a moral, an intellectual, and sentimental aroma about the role which inevitably led to ambivalence and confusion.

Matters were worse confounded for the government by it so obviously being at the mercy of totally unpredictable events. It is, however, a demonstrable fact that middle-ranking powers are unable to control their environment to any great extent and are to some degree constrained by quite minor changes in the structure of international treaties. Thus even a minor change in the external environment can compel an extensive realignment of policy. It is this which explicates the inconstancy of policy often imposed on states which are rapidly declining in power. 'If I were to identify,' Mr Healey said, 'one single lesson which a minister must learn when he is in office, it is the way in which financial constraints must limit a Government's freedom of choice – even in the richest country in the world.'[5] How much bigger a constraint it must be for the government of a second-rate power, although of 'the first rank', which embraces worldwide commitments.[6]

Nevertheless, despite the complexities and uncertainties faced by the Labour government it did not take the East of Suez decision lightly, and for a considerable time struggled heroically if mistakenly to maintain a position which it thought contributed to international stability, even in the face of mounting opposition. Indeed, the East of Suez role was not universally admired in the country, and even less than respected by an increasingly politicised trade-union movement and in much of the PLP.[7] In standing up to this veritable chorus of opposition, in disregarding the insular predisposition of the Labour Party, and by refusing to contemplate a precipitous wind-up of the World Role, the government revealed a degree of obduracy and resilience, if not courage, which is to be admired or condemned according to political commitment.

However, Labour had to formulate its defence policy against a sombre background and perhaps as a consequence made several

fundamental errors in judgement and revealed some glaring analytical weaknesses. The superficial verdict could be the usual one of 'too
little and too late'. But the Cabinet's rejoinder to its critics was that
Britain's defence policy reached 'the right place at the right time',
and that this is all anyone can ask of a government. But even with the
contention that Britain had reached 'the right place at the right time'
the government could still be condemned because it did not get there
in the 'right way'. Richard Crossman saw it rather in that way.

Patrick Gordon Walker described an alarming process of trial and
error and seemed in no doubt about the unplanned nature of the
withdrawal decisions. 'Faltering enough they seem', he said. 'The
decision appears so reluctant as to have been unintended until almost
the last moment. The Cabinet looks as if it were pushed and coerced
by unforeseen events into an unwelcome conclusion. Factors and
policies that were clearly linked were not correlated.' Later on, he
talked about the 'dilatory progress towards the great decision'.[8] This
impression of decision-making is also confirmed by Crossman and
Brown; indeed by Wilson himself.

Labour followed an unpremeditated, erratic and involved course
and therefore the government was unable to take the long view.
Policy at all levels simply lacked long-term stability, or even coherence. It was clear that policy-making appeared to be somewhat
involuntary and often appeared to be an ill-considered response to
yet another crisis. Labour's policy was in fact a mixture of rational
and calculated primary decisions which then provoked a series of
unplanned and unforeseeable secondary decisions. The government
was involved in an action-and-reaction phenomenon, a capability-
commitment syndrome, induced by the nation's economic plight
which had become progressively worse as world trading conditions
failed to improve. Labour came into power strongly committed to
reinforce the traditional features of British foreign policy: in the end
it weakened them. This outcome was described as an 'act of realism'.[9]

At best, Labour's defence policy was based on a painful realism,
and, at worst, on self-laceration. Labour displayed a curious combination of romanticism and sentimentalism with a penchant for a
contradictory mix of realism and escapism as it shifted from one
policy stance to another. The government at first clung doggedly to
the full range of the nation's commitments and then refused to
augment Britain's capabilities to meet its obligations. In the end it
showed itself more willing to take risks East of Suez than to strain
party unity or to jeopardise its chances of eventual electoral success.

Mr Wilson's priorities carried the day.

Of course, it has been asserted that it would have been absurd for the government to have flouted the views of the anti-East-of-Suez group while simultaneously reinstating prescription charges. It was inevitable that the government not only acceded to pressures it sympathised with, but also came to terms with views which it knew to be inconsistent or even ill-founded. And yet while a government should be responsible to articulated interests, it must not deny responsibility for the ultimate decision. This is, of course, an accepted and traditional distinction, but was the Labour government guilty of fudging important decisions until and unless they were forced upon it by events or organised interests or both?

Above all, the Labour leadership, while in opposition, had imposed a formidable straightjacket on themselves and within which they entombed their ill-fated defence policy. Its much-vaunted 1966 defence review was primarily designed not to reveal where Britain's interests lay and how best to defend them, but instead how best to save money. In consequence Labour's defence policy became wracked with self-imposed contradictions. The government was no longer the master of the nation's strategic interests. It gave the erroneous impression that a defence policy which was economically constricted was necessarily also strategically and politically relevant. Its defence doctrine had been undermined by economic exigency and it was now the saliency of issues rather than their intrinsic importance which obsessed it.

Perhaps this was inevitable, given that Labour adopted an attitude to policy-making where the hope was to keep options open to delay making policy choices and to adopt a permissive attitude towards the decisions themselves. This Wilsonian approach to policy formulation was based upon the Prime Minister's own logic that to choose certain policy options means to foreclose others. To him it was a sum-zero game. While an approach which permits 'decisions to make themselves' may be in keeping with Lord Salisbury's famous dictum, it is appropriate only for a powerful country which can significantly control its external environment. Moreover, such a doctrine requires sufficient capability to limit the damage resulting from the pursuit of perhaps superfluous or obsolete interests. As Britain discovered, the honouring of outdated commitments put an intolerable strain on its economy. That Labour adopted this permissive if not actually passive approach to foreign-policy-making can be attributed to it neither having a coherent set of socialist values which could help shape its foreign policy nor a clear grasp of Britain's 'national interest'. Labour's actual ideology – that is, what we have called Labourism, a synthesis of working-class politics and middle-class revisionist doctrine – lacks a basic coherence, because it attempts to reconcile 'national interests' – whatever they might be – with 'international interests' which can never be properly perceived.

It followed that when the Labour government was faced with the need to make a choice in 1968 it did so not by the process of lengthy deliberation or analysis as to where Britain's interests lay, but through an unedifying process of drift. Above all, though, it was a style of policy-making which generated great diplomatic consternation. Britain projected the image of a volatile, inconsistent, uncertain and dilatory ally. She acted in indecent haste and for mediocre reasons. She demonstrably revealed herself as a nation with worldwide commitments she could not afford and still less sustain, and European aspirations she could not yet define and still less achieve. Britain's indiginity, and not to say impotence, appeared complete.

In October 1964 the top priority of the Wilson government was to save money on defence. With the economic situation that then existed, and the cost in foreign exchange resulting from Britain's global role, this was sensible.

When Healey began his major Defence Review, however, the first question posed was 'What is the best policy we can get for less money?', rather than the more fundamental 'What must we spend?' This emphasis on economy and efficiency, reflecting the mood of the nation and of the politicians, preoccupied defence planners throughout the period of the Labour government.[10]: It was an emphasis on means and not ends.

Defence expenditure could have been reduced once Britain's role for the 1970s had been decided. If the answer to 'What sort of defence policy do we want?' had been 'A European-orientated one', then Britain could have had both a coherent policy to match her foreign policy, and a policy she could have afforded. But the formulation of policy became more difficult when expenditure was arbitrarily fixed before a serious review of commitments and capabilities had taken place.

The policy set out in the 1966 Defence Review could, however, have been afforded if the government had succeeded in running the economy. The Prime Minister's decision not to devalue in 1964–5, and the collapse of the National Plan, however, sealed the fate of the government and of its attempts to stay East of Suez.

Had an attempt been made to cost defence requirements rather than what reduced defence estimates would be allowed from the Treasury, Britain could have had a coherent policy, and money saved for social services.

The important question on which the Defence Review should have been centred, was how much was required to pay for an adequate policy based on a balanced assessment of 'national interests' and commitments. Perceived interests must shape commitments, not the other way round. A policy more in line with British interests was achieved – by a process of trial and error – but *not* through a process of relating ends to means. Therefore little credit can be given to the Cabinet for successfully perceiving what it felt to be in the 'national interest'.

In 1966, following the publication of the Review, Britain gave the uncomfortable impression of being a country with a global role forced on her by commitments that were a legacy of her history and tradition. De Gaulle had, for example, known when to cut his losses. He ended the economically exhausting war in Algeria and then increased the pride of the French by reaching a position of strength following a less ambitious policy. Britain however failed to reorder her external commitments.

The key factor in politics is the timing of a decision; in defence that means knowing when to withdraw. The Labour government seemed to lack the necessary political judgement. They did not show they had mastered 'the art of the possible'.

If Britain's defence policy was to match her interests there should have been a rigorous examination to find out what those interests were in the late 1960s, and what they were expected to be in the 1970s and 1980s. It never took place.

The Review had all the signs of excessive British pragmatism – that preoccupation with 'means' rather than 'ends'. It was no doubt inevitable, with the Foreign Office in a state of intellectual paralysis.

Clearly the Foreign Office was largely to blame for the banal nature of the Defence Review, because it refused to establish a more realistic foreign policy, or even to examine it thoroughly. This alone could keep defence policy its faithful servant.

But the Cabinet compounded the mistakes of the Foreign Office by pretending that economic facts alone should determine policy. The main error of Harold Wilson's government was the prior and absolute commitment to unrealistic goals, which became more and more unrealistic as attempts to manage the economy collapsed. Politicians are by nature optimistic. Wilson's government, however, attempted too much with too little, and failed to find the extra resources needed.

It is difficult to alter policies moulded by hundreds of years of tradition and history, but the Foreign Office had failed to consider Britain's declining economic position. It would have been irresponsible to drop everything outside Europe – like Confrontation – immediately, but the consequences of having to adjust to crisis changes as events got beyond control were worse than the possible effects of a more considered and planned withdrawal. If the job of politicians is to decide between alternative values and policies, and to decide when to do what, then the Wilson Cabinet must be criticised for its inept performance during the first three years of office.

In the crisis following devaluation, the Defence Minister was told to cut all existing commitments except the 'irreducible' commitment to NATO Europe.

This policy was chosen by men in a difficult position, faced by the problem of how best to salvage what they could, and, of course, to remain in power. The Cabinet must keep its non-defence cohorts sufficiently loyal. Their mismanagement of the economy had left them weak, and it was the moment when the left wing of the Labour Party had most influence in affecting defence affairs.

But the real question was still avoided. What were the irreducible limits of military effort required to uphold the nation's interest? Merely to reduce defence expenditure as an end in itself and not as a means to achieving better value for money simply failed to address this question. Saving money on defence is a virtue only if the essential job can still be done. Yet it must be admitted that substantial savings were achieved, and defence resources were often more efficiently used. Under a weaker government the cuts would have been even greater.

With benefit of hindsight it is possible to claim that if the government had devalued sooner – for example, in 1964 or 1965 – then the periodic defence cuts would have been less severe. And if substantial reductions had occurred in Britain's defence commitments and capabilities in 1966, devaluation might perhaps have been averted, or postponed to a time chosen to suit the government and the interests of the nations.

Britain's efforts East of Suez were at last reluctantly abandoned by the Labour government in February 1968. As from 1971 Britain said she would have no further strategic interest in the area east of the Persian Gulf.

The claim advanced in the Review of 1966 and the White Paper of July 1967 that Britain could make an indispensable contribution to peace and stability East of Suez, was not repeated when the government found that the price was too high. Britain had made some contribution to stability by her modest military presence, but that was altering as growing nationalism and the changing pattern of economic and commercial affairs made this of declining value. The policy cost more, and achieved less. For the British, at least, it no longer seemed worth the money.

Britain should have announced her decision to withdraw when Confrontation ended. Aden, together with the Gulf and the Far East, should have been abandoned in 1966, with total withdrawal by 1970 or 1971. This would have given the Gulf and Asian Commonwealth rulers one or two years more in which to cope with the consequences of withdrawal.

Nevertheless, whatever may be said about the way in which the withdrawal decision was made, nobody could deny its importance. It was not only a dramatic departure from the norms of Britain's foreign policy but it also held out Himalayan implications for other nations also. It symbolised not only an admission that Britain's power position had declined, but also a belated acceptance that the Commonwealth and the Special Relationship with America were no longer what they once had been. The historical significance of the decision was all the greater for it marked the culminating point of over a hundred years of change: it was to all intents and purposes an irrevocable decision taken belatedly in the fullness of time. The decision owed nothing to the ideology of socialism as such, but was clearly shaped by Labour's social democratic revisionist doctrine which gave expression to the values of a pluralist liberal-democratic ideology. The ideology of socialism was demonstrated to be functional to Labour in opposition but virtually if not totally irrelevant to Labour once in power. The imperial role was not at first rejected by the utopian and Marxist left of the party because it identified in the Commonwealth the basis of a possible neutralist foreign policy for Britain. When that proved a chimera the left repudiated the imperial role. The revisionist right and the Labourist centre regarded the East of Suez role as the basis of Britain's pretence to remain a great power. When that proved also a chimera the right repudiated the imperial role. This explains why the Labour leadership could embrace the imperial role with considerable enthusiasm and abandon it with alacrity when circumstances forced them to do so. Cultural

Labourism and democratic socialist revisionism within the Labour Party became the dominant ideology of the Labour government, but was not an ideology which encouraged a consistent attitude towards international politics. The myth that a Labour government meant a commitment to a socialist foreign policy – which can never be defined – even in principle, was, however, effectively destroyed. Labour in office indeed differed only from the Conservatives in the slight emphasis it occasionally gave to pursuing national policies which in the long run – and perhaps therefore never – might assist in the restructuring of the international system. Labour simply aspired to play a part in creating an international society of states whose 'interaction' and 'interdependence' would assure world peace.[11] Such a society is, however, an anarchical international society in present circumstances because no real element of government – a central agency – exists. Labour appeared in the 1960s to articulate a somewhat weak Kantian or Grotian belief that expresses what Bull calls 'the element of trans-national solidarity . . . and the element of co-operation and regulated intercourse among states'.[12] This would have appealed to Richard Cobden and John Bright, right through to Arthur Henderson, Harold Laski, George Lansbury and even Ernest Bevin and George Brown. All would have wished to strengthen the element of society in international politics and weaken Hobbesian elements.

However, as events transpired, the Labour Party began to move towards a more utopian 'socialist' perspective in its policies, as the mass membership of the party in effect repudiated Labour's performance in office. The experience of Labour in power between 1964 and 1970 accelerated this change as the Labour Party itself became more socialist and less labourist in its ideology.

The demise of Labour as a party of power rather than one of dogma begins to take shape. In effect the extra-parliamentary party – including the trades unions – turn upon their parliamentary colleagues in a most extraordinary manner. The next decade sees the dramatic collapse of democratic-socialism in Britain. The whole edifice upon which the party's defence policy had been constructed was now in ruins.

3 The Nature of Labour's Historic Coalition

The major source of influence, then, over the Labour Party until the 1970s was the ideology of Labourism which was derived from the four distinct socialist groupings which the distinguished historian of the Labour Party, the late Professor G. D. H. Cole, identified as constituting the doctrinal basis of the Labour Party.[1] Cole clarifies several types of socialism – utopian, scientific, anarchist and evolutionary – but his principal distinction is between utopian socialism and 'scientific' socialism. Labourism, however, mediates 'between nation and class and does so by establishing the general ascendency of nation over class'.[2] The ideology of Labourism is a synthesis of working-class power and middle-class revisionism – an equally contradictory mix of liberalism and collectivism – which was articulated by John Strachey and Anthony Crosland, derived, perhaps, from Evan Durbin.[3] The ideology of Labourism became the basis of Labour's *realpolitik* in its foreign policy during and after the Second World War until 1979.[4]

The utopian socialists are the residual heirs of men like Robert Owen and Robert Blatchford. As Cole wrote, 'where most of the early socialists (the Utopians) differed from the Marxists . . . was . . . in resting their case on arguments of justice and human brotherhood rather than on a conception of class-power'.[5] The 'scientific' socialists, who are also identified in Labour's ranks, are Marxists, who claim that socialism must come about by way of class conflict.[6] However, the ideological character of Labour's domestic policy is essentially derived from Labourism and revisionism of Marxism, which, since the mid-1950s, have become synonymous.[7] This ideology encapsulates working-class interests: that is, a set of attitudes, preferences and feelings of a distinctive group. Labour, as a result of the influence of this ideology, put nation before class. The leaders of the Labour movement aligned themselves – with a few notable exceptions – with all the national symbols of monarchy, judiciary and Parliament.

It is, of course, important to establish the three different and differing perspectives of the Labour Party as they have developed historically.[8] The Labour Party approaches its external and domestic

37

policies from three perspectives: those of trade-unionism, socialism, and government. These differing perspectives have not so far resulted in the growth of distinct groupings, but they have thrown up peculiar problems and unresolved contradictions for the Labour Party, particularly when Labour is in power.[9]

Trade unions are products of capitalism, organisations bent upon the articulation and representation of workers' interests.[10] Clearly trade unions need capitalism as a flower requires water. The trade-union power-base is derived from the rich economic pluralism of Western capitalism which ideologically makes the trade unions seek independence *vis-à-vis* the state.[11] As free organisations, the trade unions are inherently anti-socialist. Free trade unionism and socialism are clearly incompatible, as seen in Poland today – a fully-fledged socialist state threatens to plan the unions out of existence and to cast them into the oblivion of an obsolescent capitalist economic pluralism.[12] Therefore the great trade-union leaders of the past – Bevin and Deakin of the TGWU, Watson of the NUM, Williamson of the NUGMW and Carron of the AEU – were always suspicious and even hostile towards the socialist 'intellectuals' like Harold Laski, G. D. H. Cole and Richard Crossman, including, for a brief period, Tony Crosland, and even Hugh Gaitskell, Labour's first real right-wing leader.[13]

Clearly, in so far as the Labour Party remained a predominantly trade-union party, the ideology of Labourism, somewhat attenuated by revisionist doctrine, remained the essentially distinctive symbol of the Labour Party until the defeat of Labour in 1979.[14] Yet the socialist element within the Labour Party remains, and indeed has grown, because the party needs a set of beliefs and values to distinguish it from the Liberals as well as the Social Democratic Party, and from the more 'progressive' Tories.

The Fabians urged the idea of clause IV upon the trade-union leaders.[15] This commits the Labour Party to take into common ownership the means of production, distribution and exchange, as a relevant ideology for an independent working-class party seeking power with middle-class support. The potential administrators of a socialist commonwealth were to be recruited from the professional classes. This historic compromise resulted in middle-class socialists acquiring their clause IV, and, in the trade union, leaders acquiring the infinitely more tangible weapon of the all-powerful bloc votes of the party conference.[16] The unions proved flexible when the adaptation of working-class interests required the application of socialist doctrine to a limited programme of nationalisation. This proved to be the case with regard to the nationalisation of the mines, and in the support given to the modest programme of socialisation which Mr Attlee's government introduced between 1945 and 1951.[17]

However, the clause IV commitment remained largely notional in the eyes of the trade-union leaders. The trade unions supported Britain's traditional great power commitments with marked enthusiasm and consistency, and, indeed, proved themselves as stalwart opponents of the monarch's enemies at home and abroad. Both the trade-union perspective and the socialist one were well-established within the Labour movement by 1918 – if not before – but a genuinely governmental perspective took longer to emerge and to mature. This was to prove of great importance in the sphere of foreign policy-making. The earlier minority Labour governments before the Second World War were not expected to change things very much. Labour simply lacked detailed internal and external policies.[18] It was assumed with bovine optimism that a Labour government would manipulate the capitalist economy in the interests of the working class in conditions approaching the ideal.[19] In fact, Britain's secular economic decline had accelerated by 1929–31 and the Labour government was forced to make remedies to save the capitalist system, which inevitably brought it into opposition with both its trade-union and socialist wings. Labour's historic contradiction was born. But this contradiction was all but removed after the final crisis of 1931.[20]

However, by 1945, with the arrival of the post-war Keynesian revolution, the Labour Party was able to accept in the short term that a modified capitalist system was just compatible with the 'Socialist' goals to which the party was formally committed. The Labour movement could achieve a workable consensus for domestic and external policies in that more favourable environment.[21] The emergence of the 'managed' mixed economy complemented the somewhat traditional view of 'national interests'. This was seen to be the case after 1945. The stage was set for Mr Ernest Bevin and for the triumph of a Labourist-revisionist foreign policy based upon historical 'national interests' as perceived by successive Labour leaders.[22] This happy compromise collapsed in the mid-1970s.

The nature of Labour's ideology – or at least the various interpretations of it – reflect, then, commitment to certain values which are associated with socialism in its widest sense. There are at least five aims which the Labour Party has been concerned to articulate, promote and introduce within the framework of its legislative programme once it has achieved power. Those five aims have traditionally been concerned with social welfare, the equitable distribution of wealth, the pursuit of the classless society, the belief in the fundamental equality of all races and peoples, and the commitment to a mixed economy with an attempt to establish the proper dividing line between public and private spheres of responsibility.[23] These five aims characterise democratic socialism in Britain.

But in the context of Labour's defence and foreign policies the syndrome of socialism has always appeared less relevant or valid, and no precise 'Socialist' foreign policy has proved possible either at a theoretical or operational level. Labour has found agreement over its external policies even more difficult to resolve than in the sphere of domestic policy, where great difficulties have traditionally frustrated anything like complete party unanimity over long-term objectives and goals.

It appears on the surface that Labour's ideological stance in the area of foreign policy was generally consistent with the ideology of liberal democracy rather than with socialism in any specific sense.[24] Labour's internal debate proved turbulent when foreign policy was raised, but the rationale of the party's defence commitment was never seriously challenged or rejected (despite the 1960 conference at Scarborough which saw Hugh Gaitskell defeated on the nuclear issue), until the fall of the Callaghan government in 1979.[25]

The ideology of socialism as represented by the various traditions from utopian socialism to the ideas associated with social democracy, was functional to Labour when in opposition, but until recently has been almost irrelevant, when related to the national priorities pursued by Labour in office. Socialist ideology proves to be a recessional factor when Labour addresses itself to the conditions prevailing in the international environment, although it is clear that, in office, Labour Cabinets succeed in mobilising ideological support for the fulfilment and pursuit of 'national interests'.[26] If we were to regard ideologies as systems of practically orientated beliefs and attitudes related to social or political groups, then the failure of the 'socialists' to assert themselves (until at least the late 1970s) does need special explanation.

Successive Labour governments since the Second World War have stoutly insisted that the governmental perspective which emphasises continuity in policy and common definition of the public interest, must take precedence over the socialist perspective which reflects a belief in dominant values, such as equality, co-operation, collective welfare or indeed internationalism. The predominant governmental perspective of the Labour Party was reinforced over the years by the attitudes and interests of the trade unions. They, as a powerful producer group, looked towards governments for protection and for the promotion of their interests. Trade-union leaders never fudged the issue of power. They possessed a clear set of attitudes towards government, towards society and towards their members, which revealed a collectivist ideology compatible with socialism, but also reconcilable with capitalism and liberal democracy.[27]

It is contended that indeed only one of the multiplicity of ideological groupings within the Labour Party had ever ignored or rejected the notion of power politics or even took the view that parliamentary power was not worth winning, a contention that the party was not as a whole disposed to support. Early in its history, Labour became a parliamentary party with a large extra-parliamentary wing – the so-called Labour movement. However, the least power-conscious group were the so-called utopian socialists who were rightly accused of not possessing a coherent attitude towards political power or having a specific programme of action which could be implemented successfully.[28]

This group, whatever their shortcomings in the area of domestic policies, were undoubtedly deficient in facing up to the ugly realities of international politics. They rejected power politics as immoral, and were thus more concerned with dispensing with them, because a socialist society would be characterised by features fundamentally different from those of a capitalist society dominated by class exploitation and economic inequality. In some unspecified way, power in its widest sense – that aggregate at the disposal of a minority – would be dispersed or shared among the majority in society.[29] These attitudes derived from those of Robert Owen and William Morris, and were given almost classic expression by parliamentary figures like George Lansbury and Fenner Brockway (later Lord Brockway) in their often eloquent advocacy of the brotherhood of man. To them, socialism was fellowship.[30] The actual influence of the utopian socialists and of the pacifists within the Labour movement – the Christian socialists were a distinct and coherent sect – is difficult to determine. Clearly though, they gave the Labour Party something like an emotional and intellectual distaste for power, particularly that aspect of power related to inter-state relations.[31]

As G. D. H. Cole wrote, 'all the "Utopians" believed that apart from considerations of power, it was possible to affect the future by appealing to reason and conscience'.[32] The belief that the balance of power was an evil exceeded only by war itself, was a view which most utopian socialists shared.

Such attitudes were not shared, however, by the trade unionists – the pristine Labourites – who were the product of industrial capitalism, urbanisation and of political democracy. They, as a powerful producer group, wanted to take part in the political process by the exercise of their industrial and economic power. The establishment of the right to free collective bargaining certainly ensured that they shaped economic decisions taken both by government and private industry.[33] Therefore trade-union leaders acquired a healthy respect for power, especially that embodied in state power. Political power, then, was something to be used for the furtherance of trade-union interests or indeed 'national interests' which union leaders regarded as synonymous with working-class interests.[34] The organic relationship between the trade unions and the Labour Party created the phenomenon of so-called cultural Labourism. These attitudes, when translated into the area of international politics, became powerful arguments in favour of national power, which if necessary should be built up and used for the pursuit of national interests.[35] Mr Ernest Bevin's rejection of pacifism at the Labour Party Conference in 1935 was the forerunner of Labour's commitment to collective security or even national self-defence which after the Second World War led to the Attlee government's commitment to NATO.[36]

Between 1935 and 1949 the Labour Party – or at least the majority of its parliamentary leaders – passed through a utopian to a realist phase in the party's historic evolution in relation to international politics.[37] Future Labour governments would construct a foreign policy based upon perceived national interests. The rhetoric of party conference and the language of socialism together with the idealism of internationalism were downgraded, or retained merely as declaratory principles only.[38] The Labour leadership became committed to the maintenance or indeed expansion of British power in the service of traditional goals of state power – that is, the achievement of national security, economic prosperity and the maintenance of the values of social democracy (based on the assumption that Britain has ceased to be merely a liberal democracy and had become a social democracy after 1918, but especially after the introduction of the Welfare State in the wake of the Second World War).[39] However, such state-orientated attitudes carried with them the suppressed premise that the mixed economy was what Labour had wanted to create and sustain, and were open to challenge by another influential group within the Labour Party.

This group were the heirs to the so-called scientific socialists of the Marxist socialist tradition who represented those committed to a class-war theory of politics. The Marxists were conscious of power; in fact they thought of nothing else. They saw power in its widest sense as a factor to be acquired from those who possessed it, and they regarded state power as the dominance of one class over another. The state was seen as an instrument of class oppression. The capture of the state, in the name of the oppressed masses, would require a power struggle but not one involving overt use of violence. To Labour's Marxists, that power struggle was to take the form of a parliamentary contest for power won through the ballot box and not manning the barricades. This analysis of the class struggle was based upon the central assumption that the course of history was determined finally by the forces of economic development.

As G. D. H. Cole once contended, 'an economic conception of history is equally reconcilable with an evolutionary, or gradualist conception of social development. There is nothing contrary to logic in supposing that, as economic conditions change, political and social conditions change with them gradually, and not by revolutionary upheaval.'[40]

Labour's parliamentary Marxists, from the Keep Left to the Tribune Group, were evolutionary rather than revolutionaries and were never indifferent to the notion of power.[41] The power struggle was the name of the game. They saw perfectly easily that inter-state relations had to be conducted on the basis of power politics. Their interest in a socialist foreign policy, for example, was seen as part of a wider strategy to change the nature of international politics, and to shape a new world order based upon appropriate economic foundations which would then predetermine the nature of the worldwide political superstructure. That political superstructure would inevitably arise upon the basis of an essentially non-market economy.

In practice, Labour's left wing, whether Marxist or not, accepted the mixed economy and argued that the extension of public ownership did not imply an increase in state monopolies. 'It is clear to the serious student of modern politics,' wrote Mr Aneurin Bevin in 1952, 'that a mixed economy is what most people of the West would prefer.'[42] But Labour's Marxists could still agree – though mistakenly – with Richard Crossman's contention made in April 1959, that overall advantage of state ownership and planning had been demons-

trated in the case of the Soviet Union.[43] Mr Crossman wrote in a
Fabian pamphlet that 'in terms of military power, of industrial
development, of technological advance, of mass literacy, and, eventually, of mass consumption too, the planned Socialist economy, as
exemplified in the Communist states, is proving its capacity to
outpace and overtake the wealthy and comfortable Western
economies'.[43] This prediction proved absurdly false, but, as far as
Labour's left wing was concerned, it also perhaps appeared to point
towards what Crossman further argued was an eventual Communist
victory in the Cold War. A major transfer of ownership, by whatever
means, was the central need if the West was to prevail. He ponder-
ously concluded that 'We can predict with mathematical certainty
that, as long as the public sector remains the minority sector
throughout the Western World, we are bound to be defeated in every
kind of peaceful competition which we undertake with the Russians.'
This led to Crossman's egregious prediction that 'when the trend of
world development becomes clear and the Communist victories are
undeniable, a deep revulsion will set in . . . and anger will replace
complacency'.[45]

The left wing of the Labour Party saw a connection between
domestic economic strategy, the question of economic ownership and
social justice – which were in their thinking inseparably linked – and
success or failure in the Cold War which would be won by those states
with valid and popularly supported democratic regimes. Labour's
Marxist left, then, was conscious of state power in the context of both
domestic and inter-state politics.

The third ideological grouping within the Labour Party centred on
what Stephen Hasler has described as 'cultural Labourism', a port-
manteau term to cover an essentially anti-intellectual populism, with
its emphasis upon movements rather than parties. This cultural
Labourism was a synthesis of 'patriotism, anti-communism and
working-class power and interest'.[46] Labourism favoured a marked
national foreign policy, alliance with America, a European commitment (but not a supranational involvement) and the Commonwealth
connection. Cultural Labourism was somewhat chauvinistic, insular
and decidedly populist, if not reactionary, when defining 'national
interests'. Indeed Labourites like Ray Gunter, Robert Mellish,
George Brown and James Callaghan had little difficulty in talking
about the 'national interest', which is a concept that academics tend
to treat with analytical disdain.[47]

Labourites put nation before class, capitalism before socialism (whatever meaning this latter term had for such an anti-intellectual approach), instinct and intuition before theory, and, finally, displayed a virulent anti-totalitarian and therefore anti-communist ethos. Labour under this influence was a party of King and Country in both world wars and loyal to working-class interests.[48] Mr Ernest Bevin embodied these virtues and a few beside. His rugged commitment to certain basic but ill-defined principles was central to cultural Labourism. He was always more than a trade-union leader but something less than an ideologue.[49] He reflected what has been called 'the magic formula for British Labourism', which embodied nationalism, anti-socialism and working-class power.[50] The Labourists were not neutral in the Cold War and never shared the ambition to form a 'Third Force' between 'capitalism' and 'Communism'. That aspiration lay with the utopian and scientific socialists within the party, but it remained an aspiration totally alien to the cultural Labourites and their trade-union colleagues (or brothers, as they were called). The Labourites were not averse to taking power through a parliamentary majority or even to governing with a minority of the seats in the Commons if necessary, and they considered Labour governments just as concerned with upholding the nation's interests as the Tories – indeed they could be more successful than the Tories because they were closer to and more representative of the common people. Professor Peter Wiles contends that populism therefore expresses the conviction that virtue rests with the simple people, who are the overwhelming majority.[51]

The fourth ideological group was composed of the social democrats (later, the Social Democrats, in the 1980s), who were also conscious of political power, and in the post-war period were the elegant advocates of winning electoral power, and who, in the international field, found NATO a more realistic device for collective self-defence than the illusory pursuit of collective security through the United Nations. The so-called right-wing 'revisionists', the Gaitskellites, were also disposed to acknowledge the basic 'ethnicity' of the average Labour voter.

It is arguable that revisionism took over from Labourism in the mid-1950s following the publication of two seminal publications: *The Future of Socialism* by Anthony Crosland, and *Contemporary Capitalism* by John Strachey[52] who was himself a former Marxist. The post-Attlee combination of party leadership – a shift to right of centre – marked Labour's acceptance of the realities of power politics. 'National interests' were paramount both as a concept and as a practical political goal. The traditional socialist commitment to internationalism stretching from pre-1914 days was greatly qualified. And under the influence of Hugh Gaitskell and his close supporters, particularly Denis Healey, the Labour Party faced and indeed removed a basic contradiction in its declaratory foreign policy that had lain at the heart of the party's inter-war foreign policy and which hung like a great shadow over the post-war 'realist' phase of its declaratory policy.[53]

This related to the rejection of the balance of power – hence the bitter opposition to rearmament in the 1930s – and the simultaneous commitment by the party to the doctrine of collective security – which was at once a more nebulous concept.

Also, the revisionists within the party questioned the relevance of proletarian internationalism. They accepted the logic that 'the view that a certain section of society is naturally internationalist is plausible only when it is asserted before that section of society has achieved power', but 'once they rise to power at home, they inherit the concerns for the state's power abroad'.[54] Labour's revisionists could agree with Rupert Emerson that the ethnic group was 'the terminal community – the largest community that, when the chips are down, effectively commands men's loyalties, overriding the claims of both the lesser communities within it and those that cut across it within a still greater society'.[55] The nation to the Labour voter, contended the revisionists, came prior to class; just as George Orwell believed working-class people are 'patriotic because more than any other group they have a vested interest in the nation since they cannot easily leave it'.[56] Chief among the revisionists in the area of foreign and defence policies was a former Marxist, Denis Healey.[57]

The overt commitment to, and the exercise of national power was also reflected in other aspects of Labour's policies which were paralleled in the domestic environment. Internally, this 'national' commitment pointed towards the acceptance of group interests whose constant interaction would require institutional control, which under the Labour government of the mid-1960s led to the tripartite relationship between the government, the trade unions, and industry.[58] Some would see in this the seeds of the corporate state, with its emphasis on national unity and maximisation of state power, and the denial of individual interests in preference to those of powerful pressure groups. Given the eclectic nature of revisionism, it was inevitable that the ideology of social democratism would be drawn from many sources. Indeed, four distinct strands are discernible in social democratic thought, making a strange admixture of thinking drawn from diverse origins, including 'communism, fascism, liberalism and conservatism'.[59]

Thus we can discern in Labour's domestic and foreign policies the impact of concepts of class, of national economic planning, belief in individual freedom and respect for the institutions of state, particularly those associated with parliamentary democracy. These ingredients have given Labour's foreign (and domestic) policy both in opposition and in government (especially strongly in regard to the latter) a distinctly ambivalent nature. It has presented 'a popular, if muddled, view of the world'.[60] And yet despite Labour's manifest commitment to traditional values and to the need for continuity in foreign policy, the fear still persisted that a Labour government would mean the dismemberment of national power through a policy of unarmed neutrality, of pacifism and disarmament.[61]

But, of course, the ideology of social democracy whilst it was in the ascendant pointed firmly in the direction of a protracted clash with the ideology of communism and of Soviet political power in particular. Mr Attlee's government from 1945 to 1951 established the essentially 'Atlanticist' commitment of the British Labour Party as well as that of the globalist perspective of his cabinet.[62] The ideology expressed by the Labour leadership – as opposed to the extra-parliamentary party – was to reveal intellectual and emotional attitudes which virtually encapsulated those associated with the so-called 'cold war' liberals.[63] Such sentiments also reflected the overall view of the social-democratic majority in the Parliamentary Labour Party (PLP) and of successive Labour Cabinets. The ideology of socialism was not considered subordinate to 'national interests'.[64]

But 'national interests' were also considered as subordinate to latent internationalism even if this aspect of policy was somewhat suppressed in practice. As John Strachey argued, 'Britain can serve the cause of peace above all by promoting the emergence of a world authority', to which a Labour government would be committed, and that commitment 'would in fact constitute an almost revolutionary break with any foreign policy which Britain, or for that matter any other nation, has ever pursued'.[65] Strachey recalled that:

During the period of the Labour Government of 1945–51, the Prime Minister sent round a minute to all Ministers defining the basic foreign and defence policies which he desired his Government to promote. They were, first, undeviating support of the

United Nations and, second, a sustained effort to pursue the goals of international disarmament and peace. It was characteristic of Lord Attlee that he saw no contradiction between such a policy and the steady rebuilding of the power of Britain, both by means of participation in such alliances as NATO and by the creation of British nuclear weapons. Nor do I.[66]

Here we see the neat balancing of national with international interests. And it is clear that in regard to 'High Politics' – that is, with regard to external policy – Labour pursued (until at least 1979) traditional policies based upon 'national interests' whose definition was substantially reinforced by the ideology of democratic-socialism.

But some element of the ideology of socialism (as loosely identified in the opening section of this chapter) clearly shaped Labour's foreign and defence policies. In the sphere of 'Low Politics' – that is, with regard to domestic policies – the relevance of ideology was more strongly expressed and felt.[67] Labour found both the internal and external environments difficult to manage, but on balance, even in a period of economic constraint, the domestic environment gave greater scope for attempts to achieve some of the goals of socialism as defined by the Labour movement since 1918. Nevertheless, Labour's defence and foreign policies were not devoid of ideological influence derived from the syndrome of socialism.

And, in fact, Labour's enormously ambitious defence programme which the party had painfully built up in Opposition, especially between 1960 and 1964, contained a number of serious ideological and strategic contradictions.[68] The decision to withdraw from East of Suez, for example, did not arise in the event solely from economic exigency but from those contradictions within the policy itself which events forced to the surface in 1966 and beyond. These contradictions were chiefly to be seen in the area of defence policy, which began to highlight the incipient collapse of the coalition which constituted the essence of the Labour Party and its ideology.[69]

The Labour government between 1974 and 1979 managed to obscure the growing collapse of the defence consensus and with it the passing ascendancy of the social democrats. The relative failure also of Labour's social and economic strategy and the controversy which this created between the left and right began the process which was to culminate in the resignation of David Owen, Bill Rodgers and of Shirley Williams some two years after Labour's stinging defeat in 1979.

4 The Split

Labour's defence thinking, then, comprised of five elements. The *first* was a strong commitment to peace and security through disarmament agreements and arms control which are seen as both means and ends in themselves. Thus for Labour this involved a commitment to international negotiations and détente.[1]

The *second* was an overriding concern for economy in defence. This meant a commitment to a reduction in defence spending based on a tacit rejection of the notion that defence was necessarily a public good. Thus, with the notable exception of the Attlee government which funded the post-war rearmament programme at the height of the Cold War, the 1964–70 Labour government reduced defence spending from about 7 per cent to 6 per cent of the GNP, while giving greater resources to educational and social expenditure.[2] The 1974–9 government reduced expenditure on defence further, to just 5 per cent. However, expenditure increased under the NATO 3 per cent improvement programme in 1979.[3]

The *third* was outright opposition to nuclear weapons in particular, as well as to nuclear power in general. This anti-nuclear pacifism had created immense difficulties for the leadership of the party stretching from the late 1950s through to the 1980s.[4] The resultant internal conflicts within the party were greatly exacerbated by the performance of Labour governments, whose policies appeared to be more consistent with the maintenance of the British nuclear deterrent that the Attlee government had originally brought into existence. The outcome of the tension generated by anti-nuclearism in opposition, and a certain toleration of nuclear weapons and related technologies whilst in power, has contributed to the collapse of Labour's tenuous defence consensus.[5] Labour between 1964 and 1970 strongly supported the UK's nuclear deterrent and gave unequivocal support to NATO's nuclear posture.

The *fourth* element was a commitment to internationalism on defence. This concept had shaped a desire to co-operate with other socialist parties in the Socialist International. Again, given Labour's ambivalent attitude toward the European Community since 1979, there was little tangible evidence that Labour's leaders were capable of playing a constructive role in developing a common socialist programme within Europe or even beyond.[6] Rather, the party had nurtured within its ranks those whose support for unilateralism and neutralism had taken on a rather nationalistic bias.[7]

The *fifth* was patriotism, which is derived from a working-class penchant for xenophobic populist attitudes which are largely at variance with the 'internationalist' commitment of party activists and other ideologues within the Labour movement.[8] The Labour voters' latent patriotism was thus often out of kilter with the declared socialist aims of the party. This was shown to be the case during the more distant Suez crisis and more recently during the Falklands war.[9]

Apart from these five vital but contradictory elements in Labour's value-system towards security and defence in a world living in a state of nature, there lies suppressed anti-Americanism and anti-capitalism. This, the social democratic wing of the party found unacceptable.[10]

From the 1940s to the 1970s American power in Europe was perceived by the leaders of the Labour Party as the prerequisite for the survival of social democracy itself.[11] But by the 1980s this benign and positive perception changed, as President Reagan's America appeared to the left to be less a status quo power than a revisionist power. Whilst revisionism on the left can be tolerated (there are no enemies to the left syndrome), revisionism on the right constituted an unacceptable thrust towards counter-revolution and reaction. However, as opposed to the benign effects of granting America basing facilities during the 1940s and 1950s, perhaps right through to the 1960s, American military developments were in the 1980s perceived as threatening British sovereignty and integrity.[12]

The Labour Party now questioned the very assumption which hitherto underpinned the idea of an Atlantic community: the converging interests of the European–American relationship.[13] However, more crucially, whereas in 1945 defence was the exclusive domain of the right of the party, based on a kind of unofficial belief that the left could do the running with respect to domestic issues and policies – like health, social security and education, to say nothing of economic policy – today, the left claims equal rights to a dominant say in the making of defence policy as well.[14] Clearly, since the fall of the Callaghan government in 1979 (which constituted perhaps the most 'patriotic' Labour government in Labour's history), the left has acquired its own expertise on defence and a preparedness to be specific about what should be an alternative defence policy for a radical (the next) Labour government.[15]

The current evidence seems to indicate that the past record of

Labour governments cannot be regarded as a likely guide to the future. For one thing, they tended, as we saw in the preceding chapter, to be strongly Atlanticist and revealed a strong commitment to working closely with the United States (despite the vitriolic party conference resolutions opposing the Vietnam War) both at a global and a European level in the maintenance of international security.

More significant, perhaps, was their equally strong attachment to maintaining the independent nuclear deterrent which led to the uninhibited repudiation of the 1964 manifesto's opposition to the Nassau agreements concerning the British procurement of the Polaris-missile system. Despite Labour's pre-election pledges, American Polaris submarines operated out of Holy Loch without let or hindrance.[16] Labour also explored the provision of the MLF and Atlantic Nuclear Force. This predictably came to nothing, but the idea was the prelude to joint nuclear planning within NATO at the alliance level that further committed the Labour government to nuclear deterrence.[17]

As early as 1967, the Wilson administration gave early consideration to modernising Polaris to offset the improved Soviet ABM systems. Likewise in 1969, seventy American F1-11 long-range bombers, the government agreed, would be deployed in Britain to strengthen the theatre nuclear element of NATO's flexible response. The Anglo-American alliance was thus reaffirmed.[18] Although both 1974 election manifestos (in line with the 1972 and 1973 resolutions of party conference) committed the party to removing the American Polaris base and disowned any intention of acquiring a new generation of British nuclear weapons, these pledges were simply disavowed in office as the Wilson/Callaghan governments carried through the Polaris improvement programme (Chevaline) on which the Heath government had embarked, despite the risk of enormous cost escalation.[19]

The entire project was kept from the public gaze, and even Parliament was not informed (though the *cognoscenti* could have spotted coded references in the government defence white papers) that Chevaline existed. This was striking evidence that previous Labour administrations were strongly committed to Britain's nuclear programme and indeed to nuclear deterrence.[20] For example, in 1978 the government began provisional consideration of a replacement system for Polaris in the 1990s. And by the time Labour lost its historic vote of confidence in the House of Commons prior to the general election of 1979, it was some way towards accepting the

Poseidon-missile system from the Americans.[21] Moreover, the commitment to seek the removal of the American Polaris base was put on the back-burner and Labour accepted without demur its possible replacement by Poseidon which carried a MIRVed warhead.[22]

The Labour government correctly anticipated and robustly defended NATO strategy, in particular flexible response, including the use of battlefield nuclear weapons with American warheads and American long-range theatre nuclear weapons. Quite properly the government saw the link in the chain of extended deterrence which existed between battlefield and theatre weapons and NATO's front-line conventional strength and the American strategic nuclear forces which guaranteed the alliance.[23]

Also, beyond peradventure, the government supported the drift of American strategic thinking with its growing emphasis away from counter-value and towards counter-force targets as part and parcel of controlled nuclear escalation.[24]

In May 1977 Labour crucially supported the 3 per cent improvement programme to begin in 1979, and participated in, and endorsed, the report of the High Level Group which in May 1978 produced the long-term defence programme. This complex and costly programme included *inter alia* the continuation and expansion of long-range theatre nuclear weapons upon which NATO continued to depend. As part of the improvement process the government agreed in 1977 to an increase in the deployment of F1-11s from 70 to 160.[25]

Given these decidedly Atlanticist commitments, with their marked nuclear orientation, successive Labour governments revealed a sturdy defence of national interests. Government defence white papers underlined the increasing threat posed by the Soviet rearmament programme which renewed European fears concerning Soviet intentions.

At the same time financial constraints were growing, and a major review policy in 1974 by the Defence Secretary Mr Mason led to decisions in 1975 to reduce further deployments outside the NATO area (South East Asia,[26] Simonstown naval base South Africa, the airportable brigades) and in the Mediterranean.

However, the government continued to support a large surface fleet and maintained a sophisticated maritime capability of building three anti-submarine warfare (ASW) carriers. This decision was attacked by the left of the party because it appeared to restore the aircraft carrier as the capital ship of the navy and gave Britain a heightened intervention capability of the kind that Mr Healey had supposedly abandoned in 1966.[27]

Government critics on the right were upset because Labour's Defence Secretary, the robust Roy Mason, had opposed structural reform of the defence effort. Despite cost constraints the government pledged itself to maintain its four distinctive NATO roles within the context of the alliance's commitment to flexible response. These were: to maintain a standing army of over 50 000 plus a tactical air-force in Germany; to make provision for naval and air deployments in the eastern Atlantic; to make some provision for the defence of the UK base itself; and last, but not least, to maintain Polaris for the duration of its effectiveness (thus to run it on till the mid-1990s).[28]

The government's traditional defence posture was placed in the hands of avowed Atlanticists: Roy Mason and Fred Mulley as secretaries of state, Bill Rodgers and John Gilbert as ministers of state.[29] By 1979 defence expenditure was also given a hoist with the 3 per cent programme.

Throughout this period of ultra-orthodox policy the government came under sustained attack from within the party. The most telling and detailed attack was launched by the controversial Defence Study Group appointed by the National Executive Committee in 1974.[30] This was chaired by the formidable unilateralist Ian Mikardo and was completely captured by the anti-nuclear left. One of the authors, with Jim Wellbeloved MP, resigned from the Defence Study Group because of the apparent unilateral bias of the report. It not only questioned the fundamentals of government policy but attempted to advance the outlines of a totally new approach. The report advanced two rather familiar and unoriginal propositions. The first was that there was no real Soviet threat to worry about. The second was that British defence expenditure was therefore far too high and that it should be reduced over five years from 5.2 per cent of GNP to 3.2 per cent.[31] In other words, the Soviet threat was negligible, whether assessed in terms of Soviet ideological intentions or strategic ambitions in Europe or in terms of military capabilities. And apart, therefore, from the illusory threat, Britain's defence expenditure was perceived to be a prime source of economic weakness.[32] Thus the 'cost approach' to defence inevitably dominated the report and a number of alternative policies were discussed, all of which rested on the 'virtuous' assumption that massive defence cuts were a good thing.[33]

The alternative options pursued in the report included, of course, abandoning Polaris (which the group favoured although in ignorance of Chevaline – the savings were modest), reducing the surface fleet and in particular abandoning the multi-role combat aircraft in favour of existing aircraft, using precision guided munitions to enhance NATO's defensive power.[34]

The report, of course, favoured arms reductions in Europe, but not without equivocation. Sometimes the report saw them as a unilateral concession to the Soviets and then argued against an increased German defence effort to offset reduction in nuclear capabilities.[35]

The defence policy thus advocated was essentially a non-nuclear defence of Western Europe with Britain opting to remove all her own nuclear weapons as well as removing American nuclear bases from its soil. The alliance would adopt a policy of 'no first use' of nuclear weapons. The strategic doctrine expostulated can be described as defensive deterrence. This was to be based on a denial capability, exploiting the defensive advantages of precision guided munitions. The principal pillar of pure deterrence with its reprisal capability would be abandoned.[36]

The report also highlighted the presumed negative consequences of high levels of research and employment in defence and put the case very strongly for non-defence transfers. The classic preference for social welfare expenditure was re-stated.

By the 1980s – a period of increased polarisation and conflict within British society – of course, the conversion of employment had become the yardstick of alternative defence strategies.[37]

The report, however, provoked Labour defence ministers almost beyond endurance. Being experienced and practical men they argued that the million-plus jobs in defence-related industries were not easily replaceable, if at all, and were in any event generating a high level of economic activity and promoting equally important social values.[38]

Mr Mason and Mr Mulley respectively defended high defence spending in the light of Soviet military capabilities which were improving in both quantitative and qualitative terms.[39] The Soviets, they stated, were still bent on revolutionary change and possessed only a conditional regard for the status quo in Europe. The ministers defended each of Britain's defence roles, questioned the possibility of swinging defence cuts, opposed a major expansion of the German defence effort, and gravely warned that any major reductions of effort by Britain could easily trigger a general disintegration of NATO.[40]

The bitterness provoked by this report between the government and the extra-parliamentary party marks the beginning of the crisis within the party over defence. Few anticipated that the logic of the report would become the basis of Labour's defence policy in short order.[41]

The pace of events quickened, then, after the publication of the NEC study. In 1978, the annual conference adopted a resolution against basing American Cruise missiles in Britain, in direct opposition to the government's support for the long-term improvement programme and the modernisation of theatre nuclear weapons. This was more than a shot across the bows: it was a calculated challenge to the government.[42]

Mr Callaghan reacted very strongly: his 1979 election manifesto disguised his anger.[43] His manifesto did contain, though, a somewhat elliptical reference to the question of Polaris replacement, but the main thrust of the manifesto was the attempt to relegate defence as an election issue. This strategem exploded into open conflict within the party and was only suppressed in the interests of electoral unity.[44]

The leadership was, in fact, separated from conference by a chasm so deep that it had become unbridgeable.

The Labour Party found itself in a rather curious position as regards defence, given the collapse of its intra-party consensus on policy. The position of the three main groupings of opinion in the party on defence revealed deep divisions. These groupings were, of course, neither exclusive nor internally cohesive at the attitudinal level and profoundly reflected thinking on defence as well as other policy issues dividing the party.

The first group were the Atlanticists or the social democrats, who were largely confined to the parliamentary party (PLP) with a shadowy organisation in the extra-parliamentary party, and were the remainder of the group once so supreme and admired in the leadership and the parliamentary party.[45] The extra-parliamentary body went under the title The Labour Defence and Disarmament Group, chaired by the moderate but formidable Dr John Gilbert.[46] The group was never really supreme in the constituency parties until the fateful and dramatic change in circumstances was able to manipulate, influence or ignore conference. Few of its members ever attended party conference, which was often regarded as an alien hybrid body dominated by the highly politicised and therefore unrepresentative left drawn from the constituency parties.[47] The Labour Defence and Disarmament Group contained those who have had in the past the greatest possible political and intellectual influence in government on defence and foreign policy decision-making (as opposed to the making of declaratory policy), such as James Callaghan, Denis Healey, Roy Mason, John Gilbert and Michael Stewart.[48] It goes without saying that their grasp of defence policy and its complexities was beyond serious question even though there was not complete agreement among them about what ought to be done. Members of this group (like Healey) strongly criticised aspects of the 1979 twin-track decision; but equally strongly supported the retention of American bases in Britain. They also favoured retention of a British deterrent in present but not all conceivable circumstances, and would not opt necessarily for Trident.[49]

A comprehensive statement of the social democratic perspective is to be found in the minority report of the House of Commons' select Committee on Defence report on strategic nuclear weapons policy published in 1980/81.[50] It was signed by John Gilbert, Bruce George and Bernard Conlan (three leading Labour moderates, of whom Gilbert and George are specialists on defence), together with John Cartwright who had just defected to the SDP.[51]

The report favoured retaining Polaris/Chevaline into the next century with new submarines or, failing that, a cheaper deterrent than Trident. It acknowledged that independent use by Britain in a private squabble with the Soviet Union was unlikely to arise but considered that Polaris made a political rather than a military contribution to the alliance. However, it is disputed by some of this group whether a British minimum deterrent using Trident does meet the defensive nature of alliance requirements given that its essential characteristics have shifted from a counter-city to a counter-force deterrent.[52] They saw Trident C4 as unnecessarily destructive for a minimum deterrent, and the construction of the necessary submarines as very damaging to the British defence effort as a whole as well as to the SSN construction programme. This put them very close to the position taken on this issue by Dr David Owen who has made a similar criticism of the Trident D5 purchase. Indeed, Trident D5, the minority concluded, would be even less acceptable, because of its counter-force characteristics, a conclusion, incidentally, with which the majority Conservative report concurred.[53]

The only concession made by these erstwhile 'social democratic Atlanticists' to the vociferous peace movement, largely orchestrated by Monsignor Bruce Kent and supported by Labour's left wing, has been to oppose battlefield nuclear weapons. These Atlanticists saw a striking need for a major structural reform of Britain's defence effort given the runaway escalating defence costs and steeply mounting budgetary pressures.[54] Thus a division of opinion had arisen about the agenda for reform; Gilbert and George, for example, argued in favour of sustaining air and land contributions to the central front at the expense of some diminution in naval provision.[55] Both Gilbert and George basically accepted the logic of the Conservative government's 1981 defence review, highlighted by the alleged experience of the Falklands war, that surface ships are highly vulnerable and should be replaced where possible by shore-based aircraft and submarines.[56] They questioned the traditional logic of the Navy's strategy of reinforcement across the Atlantic for a protracted war (a re-run of the Second World War), on the grounds that allied forces in Germany would not last long enough to make reinforcement possible.[57]

In contrast, Jim Callaghan and Patrick Duffy powerfully argued that the logic of burden-sharing in NATO makes it imperative for Britain to maintain its historic naval role. This capability they argued was a unique British contribution which was not replaceable by other European allies.[58] Thus a British maritime role acted as a nuclear deterrent in the North Atlantic at times of crisis. The expansion of the navy was to be achieved at the expense of Britain's land contribution to the central front. Both groups favoured modernisation of the Royal Air Force with Tornado and increased emphasis on air defence of the UK itself.[59] The present deputy leader of the party, a professed democratic socialist but not a social democrat, Roy Hattersley, a committed European, supported broadly this Atlanticist position which thus retained a voice, but only just, in the leadership of the party.[60]

The official position of the party, as we have noted, was to advocate in principle a non-nuclear NATO. The emphasis was strongly on defensive deterrence through powerful denial capability with the removal of nuclear bases from the UK. However, in his 1983 speech Neil Kinnock speaking as leader of the opposition stressed and reiterated the importance of retaining conventional American bases.[61] He had also sought – with limited success – to restore the credibility of Labour's defence policy with public opinion by tacitly dropping the commitment to reduce defence expenditure, emphasising instead additional spending on conventional forces within a NATO framework which included the forward defence of Germany.[62] His endorsement of NATO's defensive posture was to be constantly reiterated and expanded in this speeches throughout 1986 and the early part of 1987.[63] Mr Kinnock's policy had by 1988 thus moved a scintilla away from the more simplistic position of CND and possibly party conference. In all, he stressed abandoning Polaris and established a case for a unilateral negotiation with the Soviet Union. Thus he took the exact opposite position to that taken by Labour's last Prime Minister, James Callaghan, who rejected the idea of trading in Britain's deterrent in a one-sided concession.[64]

This was later pursued when Mr Kinnock and Mr Healey went to Moscow on their 1986 trip as a future option for a Labour government. The SDP leadership, all of whom were former Labour ministers, greeted this idea with unrestrained derision and contempt.[65] Be that as it may, it is clear that within the Labour Party there was a minority strongly committed to an Atlanticist position, perhaps a majority of the party conference who favoured moves to disengage from NATO, and that the leadership's less extreme position was not widely supported. Mr Foot's last defence spokesman, the late John Silkin, strongly supported a non-nuclear NATO strategy as well as advocacy of a strong British naval build-up.[66] He, too, was strongly unilateralist by inclination and favoured a maritime strategy.

The Callaghan government was more disposed to favour the Royal Navy than its successor, and engaged in a much larger naval building programme.[67] Silkin constantly went further than this in favouring a British global deployment. This stance did not survive Kinnock's leadership. Mr Silkin in any event articulated a socialist perspective with strong neutralist undertones.[68]

The Labour Party was swiftly moving towards disengagement from NATO and towards a socialist/neutralist perspective. The left of the party advocated minimal participation in NATO, strictly conditional participation in NATO, and non-alignment (the policy of CND).[69] Conditional membership implied membership conditional on NATO becoming non-nuclear which, given the strong objections of other member-states and Britain's transparent inability to determine NATO's overall strategy, in effect meant the virtual withdrawal from, or indeed rejection of, the alliance and a consequential policy of non-alignment.[70]

The Labour Party Conference periodically flirted with disengagement but had enjoyed a rather serious affair with unilateralism over several decades. In 1983 it approved a resolution which went further than the 1982 unilateralist motion in opposing all foreign military bases and membership of an alliance dominated by the much-hated Pentagon (and the military-industrial complex) and committed so irrevocably to possible first use of nuclear weapons.[71] This emphasis on a conditional membership of NATO – for this was by implication the meaning of the motion – clearly made it exceedingly unlikely that Kinnock, even if he wished to, could slide towards a policy of near-total commitment to NATO, which a prudent electoral strategy required; hence Kinnock's devious stance over the issue of NATO membership in the 1983 and 1987 general elections.[72] His position on the issue of NATO appeared to be less hostile by 1988, but still subject to qualification since the Labour Party had yet to publish its review on defence which was promised by the end of the year or even later.

The Labour Party by the mid-1980s at any rate could not thus resume either a centrist stand nor even assume a credible Atlanticist position. Thus since 1980 the Labour Party has assumed a distinctive position in relation to defence which placed it in the vanguard of the broader peace movement.[73] This put the social democrats as well as the traditional Labourists in an impossible position, as the melancholy events of 1981 were to reveal. Labour appeared increasingly hostile to NATO and truly agnostic about the EEC. The social democrats within the party who were strongly identified with both these institutions were on the defensive. They could hardly disguise the truth of the position: they knew that.[74]

Labour therefore could find itself in office unavoidably involved in the biggest crisis on defence that the country has ever faced during peacetime. It would have been forced to preside over the demise of the Anglo-American alliance. The chief objective of the CND and the wider peace movement would thus have been realised.[75]

In the short term, then, between 1980 and 1983, the CND-inspired peace movement concentrated on disarmament and in particular opposition to the twin-track decision to deploy Cruise and Pershing II missiles in Britain and Europe.[76] They hoped to tap widespread, but clearly temporary, disquiet about the deployment of Cruise missiles to the UK. During the same period there was an upsurge of criticism of NATO strategy from a wide spectrum of opinion across the board, from the Bradford Peace School to Field Marshall Lord Carver and other worthy 'establishment' figures.[77] What was peculiar to these critics was their opposition to the presumed commitment to the first- or early-use of nuclear weapons by NATO.

None of these schools of thought were exclusively socialist, irenist or social democratic. Proposals for defensive deterrents based on high technology and proposals for heightened conventional forward defence in Germany (requiring conscription to increase the British contribution) can, however, be seen as deriving from social democratic perspectives.[78]

The fullest and the most sophisticated statement of an alternative strategy was the controversial report of the Alternative Defence Commission published in 1983.[79] This report was strongly influenced by leading members of the Labour Party, including two academics, Mary Kaldor and Dan Smith, who played such a big part in drawing up the Labour Party report *Sense About Defence*.[80] There were a few social democrats included on the Commission as well as a number of defence specialists who were very close to the centre-right of the political spectrum. But by and large the decidedly left-of-centre influence of intellectual socialists, like Mary Kaldor and Dan Smith, carried the day.[81] This new radicalism was not derived from the domestic egalitarian perspectives of Tony Crosland nor the humanistic internationalism of Hugh Gaitskell and Hugh Dalton.[82] However, the Commission struck a cautious note and attempted quite fairly to strike a balance between the extremes of unilateralism on the one side and the traditional claims of the pro-NATO Atlanticists on the other.[83]

The report of the Alternative Defence Commission therefore stated the case for NATO from a somewhat orthodox perspective with due emphasis on the potential Soviet threat, but nevertheless concluded in favour of membership of NATO conditional on NATO adopting a non-nuclear strategy.[84] With somewhat greater honesty, in contrast to the Labour Party report it spelt out what this involved:

a policy of no first use of nuclear weapons (to be achieved in one year); withdrawal of battlefield nuclear weapons; withdrawal of long-range theatre nuclear weapons (both to be achieved in three to four years); decoupling from the American strategy nuclear deterrent.[85]

The final requirement of 'denuclearisation' was the most difficult and the one that the Labour Party has grappled with endlessly without reaching a satisfactory solution. A few members of the commission recognised, but most did not, that complete decoupling was indubitably contrary to the rationale of US strategic thinking which had made US membership of NATO possible, and they therefore favoured British withdrawal.[86] The majority never quite accepted this view, because they implicitly recognised that decoupling cannot be completely guaranteed, given that the Americans would retain, or are likely to be urged to retain, well over a quarter of a million conventional forces in Europe.[87]

The military strategy advanced by the commission was one of conventional forces deployed in a strong defensive deterrent role. This was best achieved through a forward defence to save Germany from fighting in a conventional war which if properly supported would extract a 'high entry price' from the aggressor (the imposition of unacceptable casualties).[88] This view was also supported by West Germany's SPD whose new policy stance reflected the idea of a defensive deterrent.

The commission accepted the much favoured defensive war strategy that would eschew as far as possible taking the war into Eastern Europe.

A number of salient ideas emerged from the report which have since shaped Labour's thinking on defence; for example, the very narrow if not reductionist definition of defence which was accepted on the left. That was the belief that the state had only to preserve the territorial sovereignty of the nation against external attack. Clearly such a policy, relying largely on defensive denial capability, would be irrelevant against any sort of pressure that fell short of outright aggression or invasion.[89]

The remaining items were touched on by the report: reserve forces and the rising cost of defence. If conscription was out, the report's proposals in effect demanded much larger reserve forces. But since 1957 – and with Labour's strong approval – the nation had relied on increasingly small professional forces (now about 330 000 and likely to fall below that number), and it was most unlikely that conscription could be reintroduced without a significant change in public and political opinion.[90] It was still even less likely that a Labour government would reintroduce conscription, which would surely be condemned by the left as a threat to civil liberties and the rest. But Labour would either have to spend more on conventional forces or cut back Britain's conventional capabilities to the bone, given the rising costs of defence.[91] Labour faced a crucial choice; the Conservative government attacked Labour's implied commitment to reduce defence expenditure.

Mr Kinnock's response to these well-merited attacks was evident in his attempts to diminish defence as an issue both for the party and the broader public.[92] This tactic was rather undermined, though, by Labour's annual conference, which after the 1983 general election rather perversely approved a resolution which moved Labour closer to an unqualified unilateralist position opposing all foreign military bases and, in effect, membership of NATO as at present constituted. In contrast, the National Executive Committee statement on defence in its policy document *Campaigning for a Fairer Britain* (and also somewhat confusingly approved by Conference), sought a compromise with the right wing.[93] In an attempt to please Healey *et al.*, it re-stated opposition to Cruise, Trident and the 3 per cent improvement programme (but de-emphasised reductions in defence spending) and supported a nuclear freeze and the 'dismantling of foreign nuclear bases in Britain'.[94]

However, on Polaris, an issue which had played such a major part in the 1983 election capaign (barely out of the headlines for a whole week), the compromise conceded something to the multilateralists: 'Britian's Polaris submarines should be included in current arms negotiations. The opportunity is here to wind down the arms race. The government should take it.'[95] Conference rhetoric, however, carried the day. Neil Kinnock, even if he wished to – and he had given no sign of this – could not, like the courageous Hugh Gaitskell, or the wily Harold Wilson, or indefatigable James Callaghan, simply disregard Conference. Moreover, the rules of the game had changed: the left no longer deferred to the right in decision-making in the party. The defection of the social democrats had weakened the position of the moderates on defence. Also, defence had become high politics in Thatcher's Britain and this compelled Labour to give prominence to defence.[96]

The growing schism, then, between government and opposition in relation to virtually everything on the political agenda, had tended to push Labour even further to the left, especially as third parties – namely, the Alliance, both in 1983 and 1987 – now claimed to occupy the centre ground (where Harold Wilson had hoped Labour would stay in perpetuity).[97]

Six factors, then, can be discerned by the mid-1980s which explain the rise of the new utopianism with respect to strategic issues on the democratic left in Britain. (This made the rise of the SDP appear inevitable as well as desirable on the moderate left of British politics.)

First, the systematic incitement of anti-militaristic attitudes which were in fact a disguised form of neo-anti-Americanism.

Second, the left's open-ended commitment to radical social and economic policies which were flagrantly inconsistent with high and sustained levels of defence expenditure. Thus, according to its critics, Labour's commitment to credible levels of conventional capabilities remained a chimera.

Third, the left's deliberate orchestration of deep-seated and protracted opposition to nuclear weapons among the grass-roots of the party, as well as a systematic attempt to spread mass fear of nuclear war which ran counter to the basic requirements of a *deterrent* posture. This took the form of a highly selective opposition to Western nuclear weapons *rather than concern about nuclear weapons in general*.

Fourth, the propagation of a somewhat vague and inchoate internationalism on the left (and among its multiplicity of peace-related organisations) which was directed against pluralist and other societies committed to the defence of national interests. This led to co-operation with other socialist parties in the Socialist International (together with the co-ordination provided by the European Nuclear Disarmament (END) organisation).[98]

It should be noted that Labour's unilateralism in the late 1950s/early 1960s was national in orientation and rather nationalistic in tone, emphasising British moral leadership. Hence Labour's ethnocentrism in the 1950s as revealed in Aneurin Bevan's celebrated remark: 'There is only one hope for mankind, and that hope still remains in this little island.'[99] (Bevan did not of course share most CND positions.) But by the 1980s there was much greater support for a European-wide (or at least West European) peace movement (though Michael Foot still obviously preferred the style of the first wave of unilateralism).

Fifth, the heightening of the xenophobic tendencies peculiar to the European left, which in the case of the British Labour Party revealed a dramatic split between the parliamentary leadership and the party's grass-roots over the Falklands war. The Suez war of 1956 revealed an earlier split which also re-surfaced in 1960 over Hugh Gaitskell's passionate opposition to the CND-inspired resolution that was carried by the bloc vote at the Scarborough conference.[100]

Sixth, the ideologically inspired rejection of a patriotically 'mobilised nation'; this ran counter to the idea of political consensus as part of the pluralist model. In Labour's case this took the form of opposition to the idea of conscription, together with a general suspicion of the armed forces which had been heightened by the use of the army to deal with the troubles in Northern Ireland since

1969.[101] This had spilled over into a concern for civil liberties and opposition to measures to deal with political terrorism.

In Britain, support from the left for the concept of a 'nation in arms' had traditionally been muted. There was some interest in conscription between 1945 and 1951 but little support for ideas about partisan warfare.[102] The Labour Party supported the decision to abolish conscription in 1957 and had since left armed forces off the political agenda (except for defence cuts). Hence there had been no systematic attack – except from the Trotskyist/militant wing of the party – on such conservative institutions as traditionally military staff colleges endowed largely at public expense, or on traditional patterns of recruiting, and regimental traditions which have constrained attempts at a more rational allocation of resources; and most strikingly perhaps, no challenge to the class traditions which are alleged to be found in the British armed forces more than in those of other democratic societies.[103]

It was clear to the social democrats both inside and outside the Labour Party that Britain under Labour would gradually withdraw from NATO, disengage from the Anglo-American strategic connection, reject deterrence based on the threat to use nuclear weapons, phase out the British nuclear force, and seek to reduce the arms burden by reducing the size of the Rhine army, the size of the RAF and Royal Navy, in order to give priority to its extensive social and economic programmes. Therefore the emphasis, as well as the thrust, of British foreign policy would lie in diplomatic not military solutions to threats to European defence. This syndrome, for many, constituted an unacceptable basis for continued membership of and support for the Labour Party. Social democrats like David Owen feared that Britain would cease to play even the role of a first-class power of the second rank. Her role in both NATO and the EEC could therefore become increasingly marginal. Britain's virtual departure from NATO would possibly render the Western alliance totally ineffectual. This would be the prelude to the unilateral decision by the United States to quit NATO itself in order to retire behind 'Fortress America', based on strategic defence. Soviet domination of Western Europe would then become a fact. This prospect was totally unacceptable to the moderate left. Some openly feared that the Scandinavian – Denmark and Norway – members of NATO would be encouraged to retire to a Nordic twilight, living in the shadow of the Soviet power. On the southern flank, they feared, Greece and Turkey would break ranks over NATO, no doubt to face each other as bitter adversaries. The post-war stalemate would be broken: instead of a *balance of power* in Europe the Warsaw Pact power would have achieved a preponderance of power. The geopolitical result of this would constitute the biggest Western defeat in the Cold War. To realists like David Owen and Roy Jenkins this was too big a risk to tolerate.[104]

But if, as one would expect, a Labour government vainly sought to reverse the logic of its declaratory policy and belatedly began to reassert Britain's role in NATO, together with some attempt to return Britain's military power – say, keeping the deterrent or attempting to keep open US bases in the UK – then, given the propensities of the ultra-left in the constituency parties, *direct unconstitutional acts* would indubitably take place, particularly in a crisis situation. In short, the democratic left, which hitherto has always resisted the betrayal of liberal democracy by opposing the encroachments of totalitarian threats from either the left or right (the war against Hitler and the formation of NATO being cases in point), has been penetrated and demoralised by the Marxist anti-democratic left, with their contempt for liberal society and individual freedom; the defence of the West has largely been subverted from within.[105]

The British Labour Party had ostensibly adopted foreign and defence policies which would at the very least make possible the projection of Soviet influence over the whole European continent. Once this had been achieved, the European–American relationship would be at an end. The position of the Labour Party was neatly put by Mr Tony Benn, MP for Chesterfield and a member of the National Executive Committee, addressing a CND rally, who said that the party had a policy of unilateral nuclear disarmament;[106] the argument, which had lasted for twenty-five years, was over. The next question to be resolved, he said, was whether the Soviet Union had intended, did intend, or even would intend to attack Western Europe.[107] He concluded his remarks by saying (which probably above all else lies at the bottom of much thinking on the left) that 'the Soviet Union has never intended to attack Western Europe'. His conclusion was also the party's epitaph: 'the task of the party was to persuade the country that that was so for if the people believed the Russians were coming they would find it hard to get electoral support'.[108]

It is clear that, given Labour's attitude toward defence, the heirs of Hugh Gaitskell, whether democratic socialists or social democrats (at best nominal socialists), could no longer sustain their posture within the Labour movement with a commitment to both NATO and the EEC. Of course, the split between the social democrats and the socialists within the Labour Party reached this crisis point because of fundamental disagreements over the future direction of the party.

5 The Triumph of the Left over Defence

For the greater part of the post-war period, as we have seen, there had emerged a consensus on defence policy in Britain. It was precisely this consensus which Labour now rejected. This had in turn undermined the four sets of values and beliefs which underlay that consensus. These values encapsulated the post-war defence consensus which remained constant until the 1980s. They were:

(1) *Anti-communism* at the domestic level and the containment of communism overseas. For the Labour Party these goals were expressed in a consistent and sustained opposition to communist influence within the party itself and in the trade-union movement. Stalin was never greatly admired – except by a small band of fellow travellers on the back benches of the parliamentary party or by a few 'Stalinist' trade-union officials. Communists could not officially join the Labour Party. There was much fellow-travelling, though, by leading members of the party, from the late Harold Davies to Konni Zilliarcus, both left-wing MPs. Perhaps the most notorious was Tom Driberg MP, who made no denial of his admiration for Soviet-style socialism.

(2) *The acceptance of the concept of the balance of power*. This was heightened by the perception of a Russian threat, and constituted the basis of the Bevin–Healey realism which was to dominate the Labour Party's thinking on defence until the late 1970s. It was evident that after the 1945 Potsdam conference, the wartime grand alliance would not survive. However, there remained a widely held belief within the Labour Party that the Soviets did possess certain legitimate security interests because of the fear of German revanchism. The trouble was that as the German 'threat' diminished the Labour front bench found it hard to persuade the Labour movement that a specific Soviet threat existed. The late George Brown, Labour's former foreign secretary, for example, was called, by his left-wing critics, 'Bomber Brown', because he believed in defence and perceived the Soviet Union as contributing a specific threat to British and Western interests. Mr Denis Healey established himself as anti-Soviet in these early days as a young MP by advocating German rearmament in the mid-1950s. He recommended that party members should read Thomas Hobbes'

Leviathan rather than Karl Marx's *Das Capital*!

(3) *The acceptance and advocacy of Atlanticism.* This rested on an American-led, and arguably American-dominated, defence system. NATO provided such a framework. The origins of Atlanticism lay deep in history: in the dramatic events following the fall of France in 1940, in the Anglo-American meta-political relationship with its roots in the nineteenth century.[1] In the event, Attlee, Gaitskell, Wilson and Callaghan became ardent Atlanticists, even more so than Churchill, Eden and Macmillan. In contrast, Michael Foot, as parliamentary leader and as backbench rebel, possessed none of his predecessor's commitment to the Anglo-American alliance. He did not visit America while leader of the party, an extraordinary but significant error of judgement which his successor Kinnock repaired (though none too happily) in February 1984 and in December 1986.[2]

(4) *The belief in a Eurocentric defence posture based on a strategic withdrawal to Europe.* As we have shown, here Labour governments were not entirely consistent in the pursuit of this goal, because in 1964 the first Wilson government attempted to maintain a strong 'East of Suez' policy in the Indian Ocean, Persian Gulf and Far East, but the post-devaluation crisis of 1967 put an end to this pursuit. The second Wilson government decided on a different stance in 1975, in order to concentrate on an essentially European defence posture. The former policy was overwhelmed by Britain's economic weakness and the sharply rising costs of defence. The rise of defence as a major issue in domestic politics in the 1980s can be traced to a number of factors, each developing in the late 1970s and coalescing into a major political issue in the 1980s. Three principal issues arose: one, the collapse of détente (on which the Labour Party as usual had pinned such exaggerated hopes); two, the onset of the recession, and the growing fiscal crisis; then finally, the change in the strategic climate and the consequent policies of the superpowers.

Soviet defence spending had, for example, increased by a steady 4 per cent per year; 12 to 14 per cent of its gross national product was annually devoted to defence spending. The Soviet Union had relentlessly built up its ICBM force since 1977 (especially its SS-17s, SS-18s and SS-19s), and added to its stockpile of multi-targeted SS-20s at a frantic rate which put the security of Western Europe in question.[3] And, most crucially, behind all of this fearsome weaponry lay the conflict-ridden Marxist-Leninist ideology fired by a quest for security. The Soviet invasion of Afghanistan finally broke the fragile détente of the 1970s.[4]

Against this darkening background three domestic issues arose in British politics: (i) the debate about the future of the British nuclear deterrent; (ii) the controversy surrounding the decision taken by NATO in December (the twin-track decision) to deploy new American missiles in Britain, as well as in Europe, in order to modernise NATO's theatre nuclear weaponry within the strategy of the flexible response; (iii) the controversy associated with the rapid shift of American strategic doctrine in the early 1970s, away from Mutual Assured Destruction (MAD) towards a posture emphasising counter-force targeting (later culminating both in President Reagan's prevailing strategy and the Strategic Defense Initiative (SDI).[5]

The Labour Party, needless to say, split on these issues. This provoked the most serious crisis in the party's turbulent post-war history. The elite consensus collapsed and with it the depoliticisation of defence. By the time that this split had surfaced, the Labour Party was already rent over its domestic and economic strategies as the whole post-war settlement came under attack from the Tories. The gulf between the 'socialists' in the Labour Party and the 'social democrats' was in fact greater than the difference between the Labour leadership and the Tory front bench.[6]

The leadership was now itself in open disarray over the extra-parliamentary party's attitude to government policy in general. This ranged from incomes strategy and economic policy to industrial and public expenditure policy. These issues were worsened by Callaghan's style of firm and positive leadership in the area of defence, as well as his personal conduct with respect to the drawing-up of the de-radicalised 1979 manifesto itself.[7]

Conflict between the conference and the parliamentary party, as well as profound dissatisfaction by the former with Mr Callaghan's abrasive and tough style of leadership, found expression itself in the bitter and protracted debate about reform of the party's structures to increase accountability of the parliamentary party in a situation where conference sought to dominate the parliamentary party.[8] The historic struggle between the Parliamentary Labour Party (PLP) and the National Executive Committee (NEC) had ended in the triumph of the latter over the former. The 'shadow cabinet' was now itself overshadowed by the NEC.

In the internecine struggle which did so much to debilitate the parliamentary leadership, the left sensed victory. They pursued the leadership with venom; this pursuit began as early as 1974, increased in 1977 and reached crisis levels from 1979 to 1981 when the left cited defence as the policy area to which they attached great importance. Dr David Owen was personally denounced and vilified by the left. Mr Tony Benn became the rising star of the extra-parliamentary party.[9]

By 1979, then, defence was the major policy issue. The peace movement was rampant. At the 1980 conference, Labour displayed the real strength of the unilateralists within the party. They had captured the heart and mind of the party.[10] The conference mood was ugly.

Resolutions were passed opposing American nuclear bases, Cruise, Polaris, Trident and any defence policy resting on the threat to use nuclear weapons. Mr Gaitskell's nightmare had become a reality. Labour was now a party of the neutralist left. NATO was about to be repudiated. Mr Bevin's ghost had been exorcised with a vengeance.

At the 1981 and 1982 conferences, further radical resolutions emerged from the far left. These merely reinforced and expanded the unacceptable face of unilateralism to the right wing of the party.[11] This reached its peak in 1982, when conference adopted by a two-thirds majority an out-and-out unilateralist-inspired resolution which thus became part of the party's programme from which the election manifesto would be drawn.

It was scarcely believable. The party's leading role in the European peace movement was, of course, stressed in a bid to hide the stinging defeat of the leadership. It is salutary to recall that most of the anti-unilateralist vote in 1982 came from just two unions under strong moderate leadership: the Engineers and the General Municipal.[12]

The left were now in the ascendant and therefore agreed for tactical reasons not to give prominence to their real goal: to take Britain out of NATO. Thus, for electoral reasons, in a trade-off with the centre and right of the party, resolutions in favour of taking Britain out of NATO were heavily defeated.[13]

Unilateralists and the left urged upon the party a policy of minimal participation in NATO on the Danish, Norwegian and, more obviously, the Greek model, and more recently the Spanish example.

The position of the parliamentary leadership was becoming impossible and it was clear that Jim Callaghan could not hold to his Atlanticist position, and therefore as summer passed into autumn of 1980 he resigned. The Labour Party had suddenly ceased to be 'Labourist', or even avowedly social-democratic in the 'Croslandite' sense (still less Gaitskellite), and became radical *Socialist*.[14]

The leadership contest – bitterly fought – was won by Michael

Foot, a life-long *utopian* socialist, unilateralist and disarmer. He was a charming socialist of the old type and in a sense was the heir of George Lansbury, though he was not actually a pacifist. He defeated Denis Healey who was closely, and from his point of view damagingly, identified with NATO and a *realist* position.[15]

Michael Foot's victory was shocking because it revealed the strength of the unilateralist position within the parliamentary party. His vast personal popularity had helped (he is a superb orator), and it was clear that he gained votes from the centre-right of the PLP who hoped that he would hold the party together as they experimented with 'democratic reform'.[16] This logic proved as feeble as the doubtful premise upon which it rested.

The so-called search for greater intra-party democracy and participation became the order of the day. In the subsequent election for deputy leader, conducted under new rules providing for a broader electoral college including trades unions and constituency parties, Healey was opposed by two unilateralists, Tony Benn and John Silkin. Benn claimed a principled position: he supported the full conference policy on defence, as if oblivious of his membership of the Callaghan government. His stance horrified David Owen, Bill Rodgers and Shirley Williams.[17]

Mr Healey stoutly opposed both Trident and the twin-track decision, with the over-elaborate argument that American nuclear weapons were already numerous enough as far as the Alliance was concerned and that Cruise and Pershing could only add to NATO's escalatory potential which must invite a Soviet pre-emption. This appeared to Owen to be a conveniently specious argument but was typical of the chemical change that appeared to overwhelm Denis Healey's strategic analysis.

The deputy-leadership contest highlighted defence and guaranteed that it remained a major issue in the divided party throughout 1981. The divisive nature of the contest made the position of the social democrats impossible. The writing was indeed on the wall.

Clearly the well-publicised SDP defections which followed this blood-letting in due course dramatised the defence disagreement and weakened the anti-unilateralist strength in the parliamentary party.

Mr Callaghan, however, supported the twin-track decision, so did Bill Rodgers who became Foot's defence spokesman until his reluctant defection to the SDP.

Mr Foot, to the utter dismay of the unilateralists, replaced the deeply disenchanted Rodgers with Brynmor John who was a declared

Atlanticist.[18] His position as defence spokesman became impossible. At conference in 1981 he was refused the right to speak on behalf of the parliamentary party. He was immediately replaced by the left-of-centre John Silkin whose views on defence had the inestimable merit of being suitably, but passionately, vague on controversial issues.[19] Mr Silkin knew little about defence.

By the 1982 conferences, the position of the multilateralists and Atlanticists had become even more desperate. The moderates made the best of a bad job by stressing Healey's role as deputy leader and the conference's votes against withdrawal from NATO together with implicit support for the alliance's nuclear doctrine of early first use.[20]

The dramatic and exciting events of 1982 over the Falklands hoisted strategic issues into the political arena. The party prepared for the general election, preceded by the fullest statement of Labour's revised defence policy in *Labour's Programme 1982*, a general statement of policies approved by the NEC and conference as the basis of the election manifesto.[21]

It revealed the extent and nature of the rejection by the party of its traditional defence policies. Moreover, the superpowers were now to be treated as equally to blame for the deterioration in international relations. The Atlanticist ethos had gone, and with it, the automatic assumption of a convergence of interests between Britain and America. The statement made this transparently clear:

> The erosion of détente since the failure of the United States to ratify the SALT II agreements, with the role of the United States in El Salvador and the Soviet Union in Afghanistan and Poland, linked with the emergence of the new generation of nuclear weapons, has considerably increased the risk of potential conflict. While the United States is equipping a Rapid Deployment Force to impose its will anywhere in the globe, the Soviet Union has intervened directly in Afghanistan and is actively involved in the Horn of Africa. Such interventions are a violation of the rights of the peoples of the world to self-determination.[22]

The superpowers had both suddenly become equally iniquitous.

Labour's defence policy was now without doubt wholly unilateralist. The position which Hugh Gaitskell had so courageously opposed in the autumn of 1960 had become the official policy of the opposition. There can be no mistaking the extent of the changes in policy. Labour was now a scintilla away from becoming a neutralist party. It appeared only a matter of time before it became pro-Soviet.

Mr Gorbachev's appearance in 1985 pleased the Labour Party rather more than it impressed the Communist Party of the Soviet Union. But by then, Labour's own version of *perestroika* and *glasnost* had well and truly arrived.

The statement *Labour's Programme 1982* emphasised non-nuclear, defensive strength within a concept of defensive deterrence. All nuclear bases in Britain would be closed as the first step to a European nuclear weapons free zone, the 3 per cent improvement programme abandoned and expenditures reduced to European levels.[23]

The *Programme* revealed some ambivalence over structural reform within NATO and seemed confused about British defence policy in a variety of defensive roles.[24] No clear distinction was made between deterrence and war-fighting capabilities nor indeed was there any realisation of the interrelationship between them. And yet the manifest contradictions in the party's policy were not the main problem, because in a sense this was not a unique situation for the leadership to find itself in. The main difference lay in the quality and style of the leadership which had neither the will nor interest in restoring a sense of balance and proportion. It was clear which way the wind was blowing. Mr Foot struggled to appear even nominally in command of his wayward troops.

This resulted in the leadership coming under intense pressure from the unilateralists who were now rampant, which further made Denis Healey's position totally untenable. He affected not even to notice.

The leadership's support for the government in the Falklands war further worsened the turbulent relationship between the leadership and the party, now increasingly under the influence of the hard left.

Mr Foot's purist image suffered with Conference, which disliked his support for the multilateralists in the shadow cabinet whose tactics he supported whilst opposing their aims.[25]

The 1983 election manifesto itself gave the unilateralists perhaps nearly all their minimalist demands, though some of the language was devised to obscure the truth of this in order to appease the susceptibilities of the multilateralists who had been compelled to concede too much (their critics suggested that their personal humiliation was exceeded only by their individual loss of honour). Mr Healey was thus reviled by both the left and right simultaneously. His performance fell short of the heroic but he looked exhausted and not a little confused by the turn of events.

Within the manifesto there were *seven* major commitments on defence. These individual commitments were banded together collectively. But each revealed something about the state of the Labour Party. *Four* of these commitments, it was obvious, could be identified as reflecting a consensus within the party – a consensus inspired by and based on successive conference resolutions and party activists' pressure: cancellation of Trident; opposition to and removal of Cruise deployments in Britain; a nuclear freeze; a shift towards the conventionalisation of defence under the rubric of a 'defensive' deterrent.[26]

The four commitments in question reflected a strong attachment to a doctrine for NATO (and for the UK) which emphasised a strategic defence combined with a tactical defence and a negative aim. This, Labour's critics argued, constituted the weakest form of deterrence. *Fifth*, the party promised to diminish defence expenditure in line with the average level for Europe in an attempt to make non-nuclear defence credible by making conventional forces more efficient. How this was to be done, the party did not make clear.

Of course, two further policies did most to divide the party and create for it a major electoral liability. The first was the unilateral scrapping of Polaris. The manifesto was most unsatisfactory because it argued both that Polaris should be 'included' in nuclear disarmament negotiations and that a non-nuclear policy would be achieved within five years. It was confusing, to say the least, to talk of conditional or negotiated reductions on the one hand and then, on the other, to assert that Labour was committed to unconditional abolition of nuclear weapons.[27]

Mr Callaghan (as he then was), Healey and Shore attacked the manifesto during the election campaign and argued that it made little sense to trade in the deterrent without a negotiation to achieve reciprocal reductions with an adversary.[28] This argument was to provide the basis of an attempt to get the Soviets to make concessions to Britain in return for the phasing-out of the deterrent. Yet up till this point, 1983, the only interest the Soviet Union had displayed in the British force was as part of an offer to reduce SS-20 deployment to the level of British and French nuclear forces excluding any American missiles. Clearly, British nuclear deterrent forces could only make more complex the process of arms negotiations with the Soviets, which from a NATO perspective would be unwelcome. From a German perspective, Britain's Polaris force balanced against the SS-20s was a poor swap for American missiles both in numbers and lethality.[29] Labour's sloppy thinking on this question impressed nobody.

Even more confusion surrounded the other commitment: to remove all American bases within five years as part of the policy of going non-nuclear. The right, however, obtained a minor concession in the manifesto's admission that the bases could not be removed 'at once', and 'The way we do it must be designed to assist in the task to which we are all committed – securing nuclear disarmament agreements with other countries and maintaining co-operation with our allies.'[30] This piece of unintended persiflage did little to conceal the deep divisions within the party over asking the Americans to quit providing nuclear bases as part of the West's deterrent system. Worse still, the attempt to find a formula of words to hold the manifesto together as a credible political document fused two quite distinct problems – the securing of agreements with potential adversaries on the one hand, and maintaining co-operation with allies on the other.

The certainty was that Labour would create the biggest crisis ever in NATO's history if it purused its contradictory goals when in power. To confound the problem further – were such a thing possible – the manifesto offered no definition of what it regarded as a nuclear base, because as every schoolboy knows, beyond the clear-cut cases of Poseidon, F1-11 and Cruise bases, all 102 American bases and installations had potentially a nuclear role because they were related directly or indirectly to American nuclear deterrent forces.

The manifesto was fatally flawed in three quite distinct ways. The first was that it offered no coherent or plausible scenario as to how Britain could pursue a non-nuclear policy while at the same time remaining in NATO (although the manifesto did contain an awareness of the now fashionable wisdom on the need to reduce the current dependence on nuclear weapons in NATO's strategy).[31]

The second was that the manifesto chiefly achieved an internal compromise on defence in order to satisfy the various factions within the party, but failed to achieve a set of consistent policies directed both at allies and friends which alone would make the policy remotely viable. Superficial agreement, for example, on some specific policy issues like Cruise, barely concealed vast differences of approach between those who considered the United States to be adequately equipped with nuclear devices (Healey, for example) which coupled the United states to the defence of Europe, and those who wished to decouple the United States from Europe.[32] The gap between these two schools of thought could not be bridged or obscured by clever drafting.

The third flaw in the manifesto stemmed from the obvious fact that, unlike in the past, it was the multilateralists who had made most of the concessions to the unilateralists, which meant that the alternative government had a radically new stance on defence which no observer in or outside the party could regard as a serious position. Intellectually there appeared to be no logic to it. Politically it proved to be disastrous for the party. The social democrats and the traditional Labourists were now at odds with the socialists – the hard left whose influence over the party as a whole was now clear for all to see. The Conservatives exposed this policy to damaging attack. The Alliance ridiculed its simplistic assumptions.[33]

Defence, then, became a major issue in the 1983 election and it cost Labour dear. One poll recorded the Conservatives enjoying a 54 per cent lead over Labour – the highest ever recorded on any issue.[34] Although public opinion surveys revealed some concern about the need for Cruise and Trident, the public remained stridently hostile to the peace movement in general and to unilateralism in particular. Public opinion surveys also revealed the extent of disaffection between Labour voters and party activists on defence. Labour's close identification with the peace movement and the CND has proved to be catastrophic. Thus four years after the events which had led to the split within the Labour Party over defence and which saw the formation of the Social Democratic Party following Labour's earlier general election defeat in 1979, the moderate left were a spent force on the left. The defeat of the right was deeper than a split over defence.

The historic roots of the Social Democratic Party go right back, then, to the inherent split within the Labour movement between the Labourists – that is, those who believed in greater power and responsibility for working people – and those socialist utopians who believed that if you altered or abolished the capitalist system, somehow or another, either through evolutionary or revolutionary means, a more just society would emerge.[35] The shared objective was an ideal welfare state within a classless society.

There were always those who believed both these propositions to be dangerous, superficial and contradictory in themselves: if Labourism triumphed it would mean that the trade unions would decide the priorities, which could only lead to natural mediocrity and the corruption of the real objective of the unions primarily for collective bargaining whatever the nature of the social system. If socialist utopianism triumphed, it would swiftly lead to either Eastern-style democracy, or at best a democracy based on the Yugoslav model. The true seeds of social democracy have owed more to experiments in Scandinavia and to the modern Democratic Socialist Party of Germany.[36]

The social democrats have always survived within the Labour Party as a sizeable minority, at any rate up until the 1970s. Strongly influenced by the writings of Evan Durbin and Tony Crosland, they exercised disproportionate intellectual sway over the party leadership, who were, to a man, social democrats; only Michael Foot and later Neil Kinnock were the heirs to the socialist perspective within the Labour movement. Of course, between the wars, George Lansbury was the socialist candidate for the leadership between the defection of Ramsay MacDonald and the ascendancy of Clement Attlee.[37] However, Crosland's obsession with inequality perhaps made him underestimate the possibility of achieving social change as a result of inevitable economic growth.[38] The central weakness, however, of the Labour government from 1945 to 1951 was its belief in the power of the bureaucracy of Whitehall to deliver democratic socialism through redistribution of income and the devlopment of the welfare state, buttressed by widespread public ownership of public utilities and selective basic industry. The coalition of all these interests co-existed because the leadership of Attlee, Gaitskell, Wilson and Callaghan was conducted on the basis of trial and error with only passing interest being shown in the ideology of socialism.[39] In short, the realities of power compelled Labour to govern within the framework of existing political and economic structures. This meant governing in the national interest and not the trade-union interest.[40] Thus Labour's internal coalition between the socialists and the social democrats survived.

The real challenge to the coalition came with the failure of the Labour government of 1966–7 to contain the corporatist power of the trade unions which the Labour administration of 1974–9 was to further consolidate.[41] It was the crucial issue of incomes policy and Labour's attitude to the European Community which led a number of Labour MPs previously associated with the campaign for democratic socialism to meet together starting from 1968 through to 1979.[42] They had the objective of turning the Labour Party into a Social Democratic Party on West German lines.[43] It was their failure to achieve this which led to the formation of the Council for Social Democracy within the Labour Party from the Manifesto Group. This grouping constituted one of the elements which proved crucial in the formation of the Social Democratic Party.[44]

From the perspective of the democratic socialist traditions, the abuse of trade-union power would inevitably lead to the defeat of a Labour government (as turned out to be the case in 1979). The weakness of the Wilson and Callaghan administrations in dealing with trade-union power within the Labour movement made certain that the ideals of social democracy would be given second place to the interests of militant trade-unionism.[45]

The disillusionment arising from the fact that the Labour government also failed to pursue so-called socialist policies, led to the growth of left-wing extremism in constituency parties whose pursuit of socialist goals had always taken priority over the defence of the parliamentary system itself.[46] Syndicalism (always a latent tradition in the Labour Party) was thus revived: Arthur Scargill became the chief modern proponent of this school.[47] Derek Hatton, the glib Merseyside 'Trotskyist', was the exponent of direct workers' control of local government as a possible alternative to parliamentary democracy, which represented another tradition at odds with a social democratic perspective.[48] Thus the threat posed by Militant Tendency to Labour's moderate image was a growing one. The rise of the Social Democratic Party was made almost inevitable given these pressures and circumstances.

Part II

6 The British Political Tradition in Crisis

Thursday, 26 March 1981, marked what was headlined to be the dawning of a new and exciting era in British political history. The well-publicised birth of the Social Democratic Party (SDP) on that day constituted the first democratic national party to be launched in Britain for fifty years, Sir Oswald Mosley's New Party (NP) being the last real attempt to create a new party in 1931 and Sir Richard Ackland's 1944 Commonwealth Party which emerged during the Second World War being a more recent attempt to challenge the existing parties. There was an air of genuine excitement and drama enveloping the new party which encapsulated the belief that it would palpably change the nature and style of British politics:

> One thing is clear. 1981 was the right year for a breakout. It was as if all that had happened in the preceding years was but a preparation, building up towards the denouement of 1981 and the creation of the new party. Events seemed to conspire not only to give birth to the party but to give it the greatest chance of healthy life. If it doesn't survive and flourish it could not have wished for better growing conditions.[1]

The party's collective but not collectivist leadership which consisted of the 'Gang of Four' – Roy Jenkins, Shirley Williams, David Owen and William Rodgers – seemed to take on the 'character of Martians, just arrived to set the Planet Earth right'.[2] The party was solemnly and fervently committed to 'breaking the mould' of the two-party system and the deeply entrenched class-based politics that had shaped as well as disfigured British political history.

Despite the obvious appeal of the SDP, this was not the first attempt at a legitimate subversion of the traditional order. Other splinter groups had formed from the existing political parties with the same heady hopes of capturing the centre – or indeed the extremes – of the political spectrum and forcing a realignment of the electorate. These breakaway groups were unsuccessful in their bid because they 'tended to be groups born wholly in Westminster, without the grass-roots support that both the Liberals and Labour parties had from their inception'.[3] Those parties that had succeeded were the products of significant secular social and political movements. The Liberal Party had been the offspring of the first phase of the Industrial Revolution, strengthened and sustained by the brilliant rise of the manufacturing and commercial classes. Similarly, the Labour Party gained its credibility and solidity from the emergence of the proletariat as a mass new electorate which came as a by-product of the second phase of the Industrial Revolution, the development of mass production and the spread of the factory system. What becomes apparent from this brief description of British history is that those parties that flowered in response to fundamental social and economic changes had a better chance of succeeding than those that rose merely from the melancholy dissatisfaction of a few ambitious politicians with the existing system. That truth had been demonstrated by the very different careers of Sir Oswald Mosley and Sir Richard Ackland respectively. The fate of the former had become a spectre and the fate of the latter an awful warning.

Would the Social Democrats succeed where other hopefuls had failed? The likelihood of the party's subsequent success was symbolised to a large extent by the country's disenchanted mood and attitude at the time of its creation. It is because of the importance of timing that the year 1981 appeared to gain crucial and particular significance. The crisis-strewn 1970s had signalled the culmination of over two decades of irreversible change in the political and social climate of Great Britain. Such changes provided the now-perfect basis for the emergence of the new party. Indeed, it became increasingly evident from the fall of the Heath administration that the British political tradition was in crisis. Britain's post-war consensus was at an end. In 1955, for example, a perceptive American observer noted with relish:

> There are complaints here and there on many specific issues, but – in the main – scarcely anyone in Great Britain seems any longer to feel that there is anything fundamentally wrong. On the contrary, Great Britain on the whole, and especially in comparison with other countries, seems to the British intellectual of the mid-1950s to be fundamentally all right, and even much more than that. Never has an intellectual class found its society and its culture so much to its satisfaction.[4]

But events had conspired during the 1960s and 1970s to mount a serious threat to the survival of the post-war consensus. In particular, a number of major developments began to take shape. There was a marked and growing dissatisfaction with the two-party system, as is evidenced in the decline in mass party loyalty. There was a diminution of class as an iron-law determinant of voting behaviour. Then, in more recent years, there appeared to be an almost wilful abandonment of the centre ground of politics as both major parties moved ideologically towards their separate and antithetical extremes. It was these three major challenges to the British political tradition that made the emergence of the SDP appear inevitable and timely. As David Marquand wrote shortly after the 1979 general election, which brought Labour defeat at the hand of the untried and seemingly brittle Mrs Thatcher:

> In classical tragedy, the hero is brought down by the interaction between his own hubris and an avenging Fate. By that definition, at any rate, Labour's defeat in the general election can fairly be described as tragic. It is true that Mr Callaghan's humiliation in the two Devolution referendums – the trigger that precipitated the election at the worst possible time for his party – owed less to hubris than to panic. Labour would not have been savaged by the Scottish and Welsh nations in 1979 if it had not run away from the Scottish and Welsh Nationalists in 1974; had it not been so savaged, it would still be in office today. But the results of the Scottish and Welsh referendums, and the parliamentary manoeuvring which followed, were only the symptoms of a much deeper malaise.[5]

Quite so.

That deeper malaise must be seen in the perspective of a 20 per cent rate of inflation and a £4 billion balance of payments deficit in 1974, which some five years later had been reduced to single figures after a futile struggle against a rampant trade-union movement bent on destroying the Labour government's incomes strategy.

Mr Heath's government, elected in May 1970, which had confronted the NUM, turned to the electorate to break the impending deadlock in favour of responsible government. The general election of February 1974 which saw the unexpected return of Mr Harold Wilson to power, was indeed the melancholy triumph of militant organised Labour. Real power already lay with the public sector unions: both the government and the TUC were less important. Indeed, David Rees wrote in *The Encounter* that the first 1974 election had confirmed:

the almost universal conviction in Britain that there is something fundamentally wrong with the country, so great is the reversal of the Antonine mood of the mid-1950s. Superficially, this brooding sense of an endemic, insoluble British crisis which will end God knows where, is manifested by predictions that the existing system will be replaced by an authoritarian set-up by the end of the decade. But these alarmist prophetics have to be seen in the perspective of a 20 per cent rate of inflation, a £4 billion balance of payments deficit in 1974, and a continuing counter-insurgency operation in Ulster that has no obvious military or political solution.[6]

Over the past two decades, then, there had arisen a gnawing national dissatisfaction about the direction in which Great Britain was inevitably heading. The electorate's frustration over the self-evident national economic decline quickly translated into a debilitating cynicism and subsequent loss of faith in the efficacy of consensus politics. Public discontent expressed itself in desertion from the two major parties, as Peter Zentner in his book *Social Democracy in Britain* explains:

> Disillusion over the years found expression in desertion from the major parties. Increasingly, people turned to the Liberals, the Scottish Nationalists, the Welsh Nationalists, or the National Front, or preferred to lend support to pressure groups – from the Campaign for Nuclear Disarmament to Shelter, from Concern for the Aged to Oxfam. At general elections, fewer people voted for the major parties. At by-elections the swing against the party of government became more violent. Fewer and fewer people bothered to vote at all. Many felt disenfranchised and preferred to abstain.[7]

Clearly, evidence pointed overwhelmingly to a decline in the two-party dominance. From 1945 to 1970, the Labour and Conservative parties combined, captured on the average all but 8 per cent of the vote and all but 2 per cent of the seats. The decade of the 1970s saw a dramatic turnaround of party fortunes. In the two elections of 1974, the combined share of the vote dropped to 75 per cent.[8] The Conservative share of the votes decreased by 8.6 per cent, the sharpest loss of any party since 1945; while the Labour Party's support fell by 6 per cent, the worst decline for that party in half a century. The chief beneficiary of the two parties' 'fall from grace' was the Liberal Party, which increased its share of the vote from 7.5 per cent to 19.3 per cent.[9] By October 1974, the Tories had been routed in the great British provincial cities of Manchester, Birmingham, Liverpool and Newcastle. No Tories were returned from Ulster, only sixteen from Scotland and eight from Wales. On this debacle, *The Times* editoralised in the following way:

> In modern times, the Conservative Party has not been so completely reduced to being a party of the English suburbs and countryside. Of course, these are natural areas of Conservative strength, the recent shifts of population have tended to emphasise that. But to be the party of only one aspect of one of the four nations of the United Kingdom is humiliatingly inadequate. If the philosophy, policy and leadership of the Conservative Party cannot appeal to the ordinary urban communities of Britain, the party must be moving towards the danger of permanent minority.[10]

As was noted in 1974 in the context of the dramatic decline of Conservative support in particular and of the two dominant parties in general:

> As if these events were not enough, nationalist movement of long standing in Scotland and Wales have increased their appeal in recent years. These parties advocate national secession from the United Kingdom, and in the British General Election of October 1974, the Scottish National Party (SNP) polled 30 per cent of the votes north of the border.[11]

Britain was about to break up.

This sharp decline in support for the two parties further worsened by the end of the 1970s. However, by the climactic general election of 1979, the proportion of the voters who said they identified strongly with one of the two main parties had fallen to 19 per cent from 40 per cent in 1964.[12] The Tories did well enough to win, but the message was devastatingly clear: instead of a realignment of the electorate between the two parties, the 1970s signified a 'decade of dealignment' away from *both* parties, as Ivor Crewe and Bo Sarlvik suggested in their book of that title. Above all, there was the failure of the British economy, a wretched failure exacerbated by global inflation and the quadrupling of Arab oil prices in late 1973.[13] As Rees observed:

> In this context, it should be noted that the postwar settlement in Britain was based on three factors which worked together to produce national stability, even national complacency. These

factors are reasonably full employment, reasonable price stability, and reasonably restrained collective bargaining. But with the failure of the British economy to expand in the 1960s, this formula has now collapsed, resulting in profound economic and social instability.[14]

The depreciation of the pound sterling, however, was accompanied by a growing breakdown of society's standards in general, as seen by the spiralling crime rate and the mounting indiscipline in the state school system. In a wider sense, the crisis was accentuated by the political weaknesses of these two major parties. In a country which many believe was still fundamentally a conservative one, the ineffectiveness of the Conservative Party in the February and October 1974 elections was a remarkable development.[15]

In June 1970, the Conservative Party fought and won a general election on the broad merits of the free enterprise economy, but in mid-course, during 1972, came the U-turn. Bankrupt corporations were subsidised by the state, and in 1972 a perilous statutory prices and income policy was embarked on. The Industrial Relations Act, long promised by the Tories, tried to regulate the unions. Willy-nilly, the Tories now began to appear as a party of collectivist and overtly interventionist politics.[16] At the same time, by dramatically increasing the money supply in search of 'growth', the inflationary spiral in Britain was given a new boost, hardly a recipe for continued Tory electoral success. In this process, middle-of-the-road support for the Tories dwindled, a disastrous confrontation with the trade unions began to crystallise, while at the same time traditionalist Conservatives looked in vain for proper Tory policies. As a result of the government's power-sharing policies in Northern Ireland, the votes of the Ulster Unionists were lost to the Conservatives in the House of Commons, while in Scotland longstanding grievances against remote Westminster government laid the ground for significant advances by the SNP.[17]

However, conditions for the emergence of a new national party as well as of nationalist parties were further strengthened and enhanced by a major development – the decline in class alignment. Traditionally, class has been the determining influence in voting behaviour in Britain; 'all else,' it has often been quoted, 'is embellishment and detail'.[18] These traditional loyalties, nevertheless, were now clearly breaking down.

David Butler and Donald Stokes, in their book *Political Change in*

Britain, correctly suggested that the class basis of party allegiance began to decline in the 1960s. They cited 'the general affluence of the post-war period; the decline of manual jobs and growth in white collar employment; and the development of the service sector of the economy' as important factors in blurring the old lines of social division.[19]

Clearly, as values are passed on from one generation to the next, such secondary processes become more prey to being displaced. We can properly call this process the 'aging realignment'. This decline in class support (discussed below) was also, then, accompanied by a resurgence of Scots Nationalism and the reappearance of cultural nationalism in Wales.[20] In electoral terms following the October 1974 general election there were eleven Scots Nationalist MPs at Westminster, commanding 30 per cent of the Scottish popular vote. The Welsh managed to gain three seats, with 10 per cent of the Welsh vote. In addition, Scotland could become the model of the future, it was perceived in the 1970s, because she possessed her own historic legal system which provided an effective base for any administrative devolution.[21]

If this resurgence of Scots Nationalism continued, more and more powers would have to be delegated from Westminster to Scotland. A federal solution to the problem might have to be evolved. But if the tide of Scots Nationalism continued to flow unabated, if the SNP won thirty-six or more parliamentary seats, then Scotland could conceivably leave the UK. Such a development would have far-reaching effects, not only on the structure of the United Kingdom, but in international politics.

In the first place, an independent Scotland would have a claim to a very large portion – perhaps a major portion – of the UK's North Sea oil. It was these oil reserves in the North Sea which were presented by both Tory and Labour governments in London as the indispensable factor for British economic recovery.[22] In the event of a Scots secession, no one could say whether Scotland would stay in NATO. There was the future of the US and UK nuclear submarine bases at Holy Loch and Faslane in the Clyde estuary. Presumably, too, in the current era of world politics, an independent Scotland would become a new cockpit of the superpowers with the prize of the virtual strategic control of the eastern Atlantic. The Faroes gap between Iceland and Scotland and through which the Red Navy moves from Murmansk to the Atlantic, is partly controlled from Scots bases.[23]

Labour's defeat in 1979, as has been documented elsewhere, had much to do with its failure to face the challenge of nationalism and the problem of how best to save the mixed economy. In relation to both these issues it is easy to agree with Marquand's measured and scholarly verdict:

> The Scottish and Welsh voted as they did because the case for devolution was put, without conviction, by time-servers and party apparatchiki, who had jumped on to the band-wagon at the last minute, in order to dish the Nationalists, while the case against was put, with verve and passion, by honest men, who put their principles above their party. Much the same was true of the general election six weeks later. The Conservative's arguments for a change of course were crude and over-simplified, reflecting a naive, blinkered and unconvincing view of the world. But they were at least arguments. Labour did not argue. It replied with a display of grandfatherly complacency about the country's existing course, tinged with a kind of weary pessimism about the possibility of change.[24]

This 'grandfatherly complacency' was an all too clear reference to Mr Callaghan's style of government. Yet Callaghan's pessimism, if that was what it was, revealed an attempt to get Labour to face tough economic decisions.

Mr Denis Healey, as Labour's hard-pressed Chancellor, had tried to get his party to face economic realities. The so-called winter of discontent revealed the unreality of the trade-union demands. But as Sir Christopher Soames, then EEC Commissioner for External Affairs, asserted in a speech in November 1974 (well before the dramatic events of the winter of 1978/9):

> it was important that the British should not delude themselves about the sources of their troubles. By far the greater part of them were indigenous and self-inflicted, and Britain was heading for a crisis well before the terms of trade turned dramatically against Britain and other industrial countries.[25]

Sir Christopher said that Britain's troubles went back many years, during which time it had combined a higher rate of inflation, a lower rate of investment, a lower rate of growth, and a bigger number of days lost through strikes than any of its European neighbours.[26] This neatly defined the British disease.

He recalled that, when Britain was first negotiating to enter the European Community in 1961, its gross national produce amounted to 26 per cent of the total gross national product of the Nine.[27] Now it was about 16 per cent, and the government said that by the end of the decade it expected it to be down to 14. Translated into wealth per head of population, and taking the Community average as 100, Denmark and Germany were at the top of the list, in the 140s, and Britain has slipped towards the bottom of the league, in the 70s, with only Italy and Ireland below.

The figures, he said, were 'part of the quantitative picture. In terms of inequality there had been a loss of national self-confidence and sense of purpose, with tolerance giving way to envy, compassion to violence. Those were problems which only the British people, with resolute leadership, could resolve for themselves.'[28] For this crisis of perception and of purpose, the leadership of the two major parties must take some of the blame. The two miners' strikes of 1972 and 1974 showed that the British Parliament was unable to enforce its will over really determined industrial action for political ends.[29]

A Conservative Party unsure of its identity in an era of fast-moving social change, a Labour Party moving swiftly to the left, an emboldened Communist party convinced that 'history' was at last moving its way, pointed to the nature of the growing crisis. Mr Gerry Cohen, a prominent member of the Communist Party's National Executive Committee, wrote in the *World Marxist Review* in November 1973 with real confidence:

> The essence of the Communist strategy in Britain is to strengthen still further the fight for progressive and Socialist policies, and leadership, within the trade unions, to end right wing domination of the General Council of the Trade Union Congress, and to ensure that this advance is reflected in the political field and within the Labour Party . . . It is not so long since the major trade unions were firmly in the grip of the right wing, and were the main prop of the right wing leaders in control of the Labour Party. Profound changes have taken place in the past few years, both in the policies and leadership of the trade unions. Many of the biggest and most influential trade unions, which in the past have wielded their influence and their votes in support of reactionary views within the Labour Party, are now consciously and determinedly using their influence in support of left wing views.[30]

This was by no means a simplistic analysis of the situation.

An official party publication, *Britain and the Socialist Revolution* by Betty Matthews, also asserted that:

The Labour Party can be moved to the Left and the path to such change is through the trade unions. The close connection with the trade unions, which through affiliations, constitute the mass membership of the Labour Party means that the process of building up to a victory of the left in the trade unions, is also the means of winning a victory over the present leadership of the Labour Party ... The culmination of this process would be the election of a Parliamentary majority, committed to a socialist programme as indicated in 'The British Road to Socialism' the CP's official programme.[31]

In fact by chance or design much of Labour's domestic – and virtually all of its anti-nuclear policies – programme was strikingly similar to the Communist Party's 'socialist' priorities by the early 1980s (only after two successive defeats at the polls in 1983 and 1987 did Labour begin to examine more 'realistic' policies).

Ironically, in the event, the most formidable bid to take over the Labour Party came from the Trotskyist left in the wake of the defeat of the Callaghan government. But the growing clash within the party about the management of the economy, under Denis Healey's stewardship between 1974 and 1979, gave the new hard left a growing basis of support. Factionalism was and is an endemic part of the history of the Labour Party. The National Executive Committee became for over a decade a bastion of the hard-and-soft-left. Yet the left has a long history.[32] The Tribune group traces back its descent historically through the 'Victory of Socialism' group of 1958, and the Bevanites of the early 1950s, to the Labour critics of the foreign policy of Ernest Bevin in the immediate post-war years. The members of the Tribune group, whether pacifist, fundamental socialist, or Marxist, were thus a powerful left faction within the PLP with their own internal discipline. Their best-known member was the redoubtable Ian Mikardo, active on the left of the PLP for nearly forty years. The relative, overall strength of the left was seen in the elections for the chairman of the PLP on 14 November 1974. In this vote, Cledwyn Hughes, a moderate, defeated Ian Mikardo by only 162 to 131. The left were a rising force. Soon a militant tendency – a party within a party – would emerge as a major force in Labour politics, as the Underhill report revealed.[33] This report, incidentally, was virtually suppressed by the National Executive Committee.

Serious observers were already vexed. Professor John P. Mackintosh (a brilliant academic and Labour MP) wrote, in *The Political*

Quarterly, in December 1972, about the growth of what he called the new socialist fundamentalism with its emphasis on class politics (this aspect is crucial in accounting for the decline of the Labour Party because of the diminishing importance of class-based politics which becomes quite evident by the 1979 election), which aroused much controversy. He wrote that there were some intractable difficulties for those taking the populist/socialist position:

> The first is that there is no method of solving conflicts between one group of workers and another. If dockers claim the right to 'strip and stuff' containers and thus threaten the jobs of packers dispersed around a number of factories, who is right? The support of the populist/socialist tends to go to the best organised and most defiant group, presumably because they are showing most working-class vigour, but this has no obvious relationship to socialism or to justice. Put in another way, to back those who shout loudest or press hardest is to neglect the weakest and worst paid groups who are often incapable of making a strong case. Another aspect of the problem is that the large general unions, realising that the worst paid workers excite public sympathy, often frame their demands in this light; but if they then also insist on keeping differentials, they are not in fact doing anything to decrease relative poverty. Yet, once again, the socialists who are pledged to support every trade union position have nothing to say about this.[34]

Indeed not!

No wonder, then, that Labour voters were puzzled and dismayed by the attitude of the trade unions towards the Labour government in the winter of 1978/9. Thus the volatility of the electorate was clearly evident in the 1979 election, when only half those voting voted with their 'natural' class party. During that election, the middle class split 3 to 1 in favour of the Conservatives, the working class 5 to 4 in favour of Labour, and the skilled working class divided equally between the two parties.[35]

The Labour Party was particularly mauled by this development. The working class, once the fulcrum of the Labour Party, was falling prey to the deadly and debilitating disease of 'embourgeoisement' – the insidious result of the spread of affluence. As the working class became more affluent and began to adopt middle-class lifestyles and values, they started to question the traditional and hitherto loyal attachment to the Labour Party. Yet this decline in class alignment did not necessarily transfer into a realignment among the parties.

What becomes more obvious was that both major parties as they entered the 1980s found it increasingly difficult to attract a single social class because interests have become so diverse. Now, no one fits the stereotype totally. Such conditions seemed opportune for a new party not deeply rooted in class-based politics.[36]

The crucial development in British politics began with, and was accelerated by, the advent of the Thatcher administration. Hugh Stephenson, in his book *Claret and Chips – The Rise of the SDP*, argues that the essential break in the mould of recent British politics was made by Margaret Thatcher. It was she who took the substantial risk – and who perceived the need to challenge – the conventional mould of consensus politics which had dominated the post-war two-party system. During the 1950s and 1960s, there was a broad agreement between 'the parties on such social democratic principles as the mixed economy and the welfare state'.[37] In 1979 Mrs Thatcher, however, announced publicly that she intended to operate outside the conventionally accepted limits of the political arena and thereby 'she had implicitly made it legitimate for the left to respond similarly'.[38] Mrs Thatcher took her party away from the 'centre ground' of the political arena. She became the most radical prime minister since Lloyd George and the strongest since Winston Churchill. She was willing to defend unpopular stands, and because of that she became known as the 'Iron Lady'. (This sobriquet was also derived from her anti-Soviet stance.) The Conservative Party became divided between the hard-liners, the 'Drys', led by Thatcher, and the more moderate 'Wets'. Mrs Thatcher exploited the rich seam of latent populism which had lain dormant in British politics for a generation.[39] She radicalised British politics.

Similarly, the Labour Party during this period became increasingly dominated by its radical neo-Marxist constituency activists. In 1980, the party demonstrated more than ever its inexorably leftward tendencies. The adoption of an anti-EEC and an anti-NATO stance, and the election of the charming but somewhat unworldly Michael Foot at the extraordinary Wembley Conference in 1980, sent a strong and clear signal to the equally volatile electorate that the hegemony of social democratic influence inside the party was at an end. This insidious infiltration by the extreme left, led by Militant Tendency, became the chief reason behind the breakaway, if not behind the breakup, of Labour moderates and the formation of the SDP.

The public (as expressed in opinion surveys) could sense the latent extremism of the two parties. *The Times* poll of January 1980 found that 60 per cent of the population thought that the Labour Party had moved too far to the left, and 46 per cent thought that the Conservatives had moved too far to the right.[40] Tweedledee had divorced Tweedledum. They then moved away from their more familiar abode. Thus, by deliberately choosing to 'vacate the centre ground of British politics, first the Conservatives and then the Labour Party left a vacant political terrain'. It was as if the 'political seas had parted by magic, leaving the centre ground of British politics free for the first time in recent history'.[41] This abandonment of the centre ground proved to be the most decisive factor in the short run for the future of the SDP.

Ironically, it had been the willingness of both parties to sustain and define consensus politics which had kept the two-party system alive. Indeed, the two-party system had been at its strongest between 1945 and 1974, although it was already presenting a debilitating if inherent tendency to exaggerate the actual strength of the parties because of the electoral system. Although the British political system encourages and sustains adversarial politics with confrontation and polarisation, emphasised by their House seating arrangement, both parties have nonetheless attempted to occupy the *same* centre ground. In the past, so-called valence issues had dominated the political scene over controversial issues. Valence issues are those on which parties and voters are largely agreed upon, like reducing unemployment, support for collective bargaining, securing peace abroad and feeding the hungry. By deliberately choosing to address valence issues, as Stokes explains, the party portrays itself as the 'Party of Good Times'. This way, the party 'wins voters without losing any'.[42] Thus, by pursuing the centre, both parties had hindered the successful establishment of centre parties in the past. The contemporary withdrawal from the centre, however, seemed to have left a gap open in British politics for a fourth party to fill. It was against this ostensibly promising background that the formation of the SDP took place.

Serious challenges, then, to the British political tradition had surfaced in the 1980s to seemingly create the ideal conditions for the emergence of the SDP.[43]

The dramatic decline in party loyalties, the decreasing significance of social class as a determinant of voting patterns, and the abandonment of the traditional centre ground, had combined to give this bid to construct a new party its greatest chance of success. Did the SDP make the best of these conditions? Was the mould really yet broken? The answer to both questions proved extremely disappointing, but the SDP embarked upon its future with more hope than perhaps circumstances subsequently justified. However, for the leading members of the new party the break with the Labour Party was most reluctantly pursued with only David Owen revealing a steely determination to make the break irrevocable.[44]

7 Straws in the Wind: The 1979 Vote of No Confidence

Mrs Shirley Williams, in her emotional but considered letter of resignation from the National Executive Committee of the Labour Party, summed up the feelings of the Labour defectors when she wrote in February 1981: 'The party I loved and worked for over so many years, no longer exists ... it is not the democratic socialist party that I joined.'[1] It was this negative feeling which best expressed the case for the creation of a new party. Moderates had become so heartily disillusioned with the Labour Party that they no longer felt they could work within it to achieve effective change – and still less win parliamentary power. Such cries of disaffection from within had, of course, been a periodic occurrence in the fractious history of the Labour Party. Since its bold inception, the party had been split, as we have noted, between its belief in socialism and belief in social democratic principles. Indeed, was it a party of trade-unionism and really little more? It was created from an improbable partnership between stolid working-class trade-unionists and idealistic middle-class intellectuals. It has never since decided 'whether it is a party of gradual reform in the Liberal and social democratic tradition or of red-hot, full-blooded socialism'.[2] As David Marquand explained, the liberal element in the Labour Party had given the party a reason for its existence:

As everyone knows, the Labour Party started life as an alliance between the trade unions and the Socialist sects which had grown up in this country at the end of the 19th century. What is less often appreciated is that a third ingredient had to be added to the mixture before the party could become a serious contender for power. That third ingredient was the Radical intelligentsia, which had provided the intellectual underpinning for Lloyd George's social reforms before 1914, but which deserted to the Labour Party after 1918, in disgust at the cynicism and opportunism of the Lloyd George coalition. Radical intellectuals did not bring many votes to the Labour Party, but they brought something more important.

95

They could write; they could argue; some of them could even think. Above all, they could and did lay down the intellectual framework within which the battle for votes took place. They asked the questions which the politicians had to answer: and, in asking the questions, they helped to determine what the answers would be.[3]

The history of the Labour Party has inevitably been plagued with bitter and fundamental disputes between socialists and social democrats. There had always existed a potential division between the two factions. What becomes evident is that this time *something* was different. Traditionally, a compromise between the two interests would, for the sake of convenience, prevail, but policies would invariably have more of a social democratic thrust than a socialist one. Over the last fifteen years, the balance of power had shifted. Labour moderates found it increasingly hard to gain a voice in the workings of the party. This time, the social democrats had lost control and foresaw no way of regaining it. Ostensibly, this time the potential split had become irreparable and what had traditionally been a protracted debate had now become a real and unavoidable crisis.

The 1979 parliamentary defeat was a turning-point because it was the last chance for the old Labour coalition to hang together provided they could retain a parliamentary majority. The socialists, the social democrats and the declining number of Labourists (the pristine trade unionists) lived rather more comfortably with each other in power rather than in opposition. Mr James Callaghan had become Prime Minister, following the rather surprising and little-explained resignation of Mr Wilson, and he cleverly relied on a series of shifting pacts with assorted minor parties to preserve his tenuous hold on 10 Downing Street. He had failed to call an election in the autumn of 1978 and six months later he asked the electorate for a renewed mandate.[4] By this time, Britain had been battered and intimidated by a wave of chaotic and crippling strikes and Callaghan had lost the support of the small Scottish Nationalist Party (SNP), which split with him over the issue of home rule for Scotland. That gave the opposition leader Margaret Thatcher the opportunity she needed. She pulled together a temporary alliance of her own and introduced a no-confidence motion.[5]

Before his government faced this challenge, Mr Callaghan had sought to buy time by working out a deal for 'devolution', or limited regional autonomy, with the Scottish Nationalists, who represented eleven vital votes in the Commons. That hope faded early in March when a referendum on devolution in Scotland was defeated. Two weeks later, SNP leader Donald Stewart responded with the first of a small blizzard of no-confidence motions, the Liberals tabled one of their own, and then Thatcher seized the initiative by moving 'that this House has no confidence in Her Majesty's Government'.[6]

Mr Callaghan launched his pre-emptive strike. To woo three Welsh Nationalists, he restored a long-delayed proposal to compensate coal miners suffering from lung disease. He promised payments to miners' widows – and captured the Welsh votes. The horse-trading had begun. Then he went after two Ulster Catholics, who demanded the resignation of Labour's Secretary of State for Northern Ireland, the courageous Roy Mason, and 'political prisoner' status for imprisoned IRA terrorists.[7] That was more than Callaghan could or would want to concede, but he did manage to lure two Ulster Protestants away from the Tories with promises of a possible natural-gas pipeline under the Irish Sea. The Liberals under David Steel rebuffed the government's crude and blatant horse-trading. Labour expected to win the vote in the Commons with a tie, 311–311, which would mean that the Speaker of the House would side with them, since he votes for the government in such situations.[8]

The no-confidence debate was high drama. The high-ceilinged neo-Gothic chamber was packed. Neatly if not primly dressed, Mrs Thatcher stepped towards the dispatch box in front of the bewigged Speaker. 'The government has failed the nation,' she began in that rather throaty monotone now so familiar. 'It has lost credibility, and it is time for it to go.'[9] Amid the usual jeers from the Labour side and cries of 'Hear, Hear!' from the Tory backbenches, the debate got under way.

Callaghan faced the accusation of a long list of failures – on a rampant inflation, on general economic policy, and above all, in dealing with the country's trades unions. Evoking the all-too memorable strikes, Mrs Thatcher called for 'less tax and more law and order', and declared that 'people expect rubbish to be collected, schools to be open and hospitals to be functioning – and they are not'.[10]

Callaghan, radiating heavy sarcasm, taunted Thatcher for hesitating to introduce her no-confidence motion until she had the support of the small parties. 'She found the courage of their convictions,' he said. He won howls from Labour ranks when he ridiculed the minority parties for helping Thatcher bring about an election that could mean defeat for several of their own MPs. 'It's the first time that turkeys have been known to vote for an early Christmas,' he declared.[11]

Pointing an accusing finger at Heath, Callaghan thundered: 'Mr Heath has been removed from the Conservative Party thinking: like . Trotsky he has been blotted out from the photographs in which he appeared with Stalin.'[12] (The Tories, however, had a riposte for that one. Pointing at former Labour Prime Minister Harold Wilson, they shouted 'What about him'?) Callaghan finished with a double flourish. He announced a pension increase – another attempt to sway votes – and he dismissed Thatcher's proposed cuts in welfare spending as a return to 'soup-kitchen social services'.[13]

Switching from the carotid to the jugular, Callaghan accused Thatcher of following discredited policies of confrontation with the unions. It was all good parliamentary stuff. The debate lasted seven hours. When the vote was taken at 10 p.m., the chamber was filled to overflowing, with twenty-five MPs standing in the doors, and after an inconclusive voice vote – both sides were equally loud – the speaker called for a 'division', and the MPs trooped out of the chamber into the 'no' or 'yes' lobby. Seventeen minutes later, the members took their seats to await the results. Thatcher sat calmly, Callaghan, grinning bravely, leaned forward, clapping his hands lightly and nervously. At 10.18 p.m. a Tory whip walked in, beaming and nodding, and an enormous victory roar rose from the Conservative ranks. 'Ayes to the right lobby, 311 votes,' boomed the speaker. 'Noes to the left, 310.' While the Tories danced on the benches and shouted for joy, the Labour MPs sang 'The Red Flag' and 'We Shall Overcome'.[14]

Thatcher's 279 Conservatives had been joined by thirteen Liberals, eleven Scottish Nationalists and eight Ulster MPs. To his 303 Labour votes, Callaghan had added only seven votes from the minor parties. Had it not been for a doctor in Yorkshire, Jim Callaghan probably would have squeaked through. The doctor decreed that his patient, 76-year-old Labour MP Sir Alfred Broughton, was too ill after a heart attack to make the journey to vote.[15]

The last Labour government of this century had fallen; the next one (supposing there is one) would be a real socialist government. The social democrats in the party no longer had a future. Mrs Thatcher won the subsequent election (discussed below). Professor Marquand wrote shortly afterwards that:

As the party had sown, so it has reaped. Mr Callaghan was a much better Prime Minister than I thought he would be. He was more honest, more courageous and had a better grasp of immediate issues. The tragedy is that honesty, courage and even a grasp of immediate issues are not enough – or not, at any rate, at a time of rapid change, when old assumptions have broken down and old paths lead nowhere. But in voting for Mr Callaghan, the party voted for the old assumptions and the old paths; and, once he was there, the forces which had put him there ensured that he would not break away from the implicit ticket on which he had been elected.[16]

Mr Callaghan had become the prisoner of the mindset of the Labour movement – a mystic belief in working-class values and a faith in the inherent good sense of trade-union leaders. As Marquand contends:

> In theory, no doubt, he could have betrayed the tea room in the way that de Gaulle betrayed the colons or Harold Wilson the Tribune Group. But that was a theoretical possibility only, not a real one. Mr Callaghan would not have wanted to betray the tea room in any case; even if he had, he would not have been able to. Just as the hubris of a classical hero was part of his doom, a gift of Fate which he could not escape any more than he could escape the punishment for it, so Labour's hubris in spurning the new ideas at the very point when it most needed them sprang inexorably from the interplay between the character of the party and the character of the problems it faces. Labour spurned new ideas because it knew in its bones that worthwhile new ideas would tear it apart. New ideas do not, after all, appear out of nowhere. They require an open-minded and self-critical climate, in which there are no taboos against free enquiry and no sacred cows which cannot be slaughtered. In such a climate the two great myths of creed and class, the myths which hold the Labour Party together, would be dissolved.[17]

The death of the old Labour Party had been long in coming. Mr Callaghan presided over its death some seventy-nine years after it had all first begun. The brief climax of social democratic influence within the Labour Party had been reached during Hugh Gaitskell's brilliant and turbulent term as leader from 1955 to 1963. Gaitskell had had the support of a powerful group of hard-nosed right-wing trade-union leaders and an influential and able group of revisionist intellectuals. One of the most impressive if not original intellects, Anthony Crosland, in his well-reviewed book *The Future of Socialism*, best explained the philosophy of the Gaitskellite Labour Party:

> It built on the ideas of Keynes and Beveridge, being wholly committed to the goals of full employment and the extension of the welfare state. It established the pursuit of equality as the most important task of a Labour Government but insisted at the same time on the preservation of personal freedom and adherence to the principles of representative democracy. Most important of all, perhaps, it argued that nationalisation should no longer be seen as the principal objective of a modern social democratic state. Rather a Labour Government should concentrate on running a successful mixed economy which could generate the high growth needed to sustain increased public expenditure.[18]

It was this new emphasis on the mixed economy over doctrinaire nationalisation which became the most characteristic feature of modern democratic socialism and the first major source of dissent in the Labour Party. Gaitskell tried to bring about major reforms within the party in hopes of bringing it in line with the realities of the second part of the century. After the stinging defeat in the election of 1959, he made his most courageous but ultimately futile attempt to persuade the Labour Party to drop Clause Four of its Constitution and thus abandon its formal and indeed meaningless commitment to public ownership. This proposal caused a major and hysterical uproar within the party. Although the party was essentially centrist and moderate, many felt – and Harold Wilson was one – that there was no need to provoke such serious disunity and strife within it.[19]

Therefore, the proposal was rejected in favour of maintaining the acceptable illusion – 'whereby Labour in practice was committed to a mixed economy but still managed to keep the purists happy by remaining nominally attached to public ownership'.[20] In the dramatic Conference which followed in 1960, Gaitskell suffered another major defeat when it was decided amidst rising controversy to replace the party's official and traditional policy of multinational nuclear disarmament with a unilateral position. Dismayed by the setbacks, Gaitskell stoutly initiated the Campaign for Democratic Socialism immediately after this depressing 1960 Scarborough Conference. The group was essentially composed of young social democrats with parliamentary experience or aspirations. Among them were Dick Taverne, William Rodgers and Shirley Williams, all of whom would later become instrumental in the creation of the SDP. The Campaign successfully lobbied the trade unions for the defeat of unilateral disarmament and was influential in gaining support for the selection of social democrats as parliamentary candidates.[21]

After the tragic and sudden death of Gaitskell in 1963, the Campaign for Democratic Socialism dissolved, having completed its task. Although their leader was dead, the social democrats by this time were largely in control of the party. The right-wing moderates had successfully weathered the leftward storm. However, the divisive issues of unilateralism and nationalisation that they had so effectively contained in the 1960s would savagely re-surface in 1980 and beyond.[22] By then the right would lack both the will and the resources to fight back. The coalition that had once been the Labour Party was at an end. This fateful breakup pointed towards a systemic change in British politics, and the only doubt that remained concerned how long the demise of Labour and how long the rise of the SDP would take. This over-optimistic approach obscured the real complexities involved in forming a new party.

The experience of the early 1960s had, however, taught the social democrats the importance of mobilisation. In the succeeding years, they would continue to fight the leftward challenge by functioning as a party within a party. The next big dispute came over the question of Britain's membership in the European Economic Community (EEC). Once again, the left and right were seriously split on this issue, with the Socialists by and large opposed to and the social democrats by and large in favour of entry. The strong commitment to the EEC had led sixty-nine pro-Market Labour MPs to side with the Conservative government in the vote on 28 October 1971. This group of Labour pro-Marketeers was spearheaded by most of the same people who had served as the backbone for the Campaign for Democratic Socialism in the 1960s – Roy Jenkins, Bill Rodgers, George Thomson, David Owen and David Marquand.[23] The battle over Europe had strengthened their alliance, which would later become the basis for the formation of the SDP. As early as 1971, then, these moderates could sense a change in the Labour Party that they saw little hope of reversing. Dick Taverne recalled his impression of the gradual transformation that was taking place:

I could sense as early as 1970 what was happening to the Labour Party. I could see at the grass roots a new kind of activist was really taking over. He was more intolerant, he was more Marxist in

general approach . . . I say he because then the Labour Party was
very much male dominated . . . I could see that this activist was not
going to put up with the kind of Gaitskellite approach – which was
the social democratic approach – that had prevailed in the past.
After 1970, it was quite clear that this was not going to have much
more influence.[24]

In many ways, the EEC issue signified the turning-point for these
Labour moderates. Although the social democrats did not have the
hearts of the grass-roots who were more activist and radical, they had
in the past gained support because they largely controlled the
leadership of the party. Loyalty, Taverne emphasised, was their
'strong card'.[25] Over the Common Market issue, however, the social
democrats suddenly found themselves in the minority against the
party. The dispute over the EEC had turned the right wing into
rebels. Being a right-wing rebel was both awkward and impossible,
Taverne admits:

> What I found impossible was not only to be a rebel but a moderate
> rebel. You can always be a left wing rebel in the Labour Party
> because you can always get the support of the constituency,
> activists and the Conference behind you. But you can't be a
> right-wing or moderate rebel in the Labour Party. And the
> Common Market issue drove the moderates into a position of
> being rebels – an impossible position. The radicalism of the
> grass-roots and the awkward position of the social democrats made
> a takeover by the left inevitable.[26]

It became increasingly difficult for the social democrats in the
Labour Party. Roy Jenkins resigned his post as deputy leader of the
Labour Party in April of 1971. David Owen, Dick Taverne and
others also resigned from the Shadow Cabinet as part of a protest
against the party's decision to hold a referendum on the issue of
continued EEC membership, if the party returned to government.
The EEC issue quickly became the apple of discord between social
democrat Labour MPs and their local constituency parties.

The most famous confrontation was in the ancient city of Lincoln
between the brilliant Dick Taverne and the left-wingers in the local
party there. Taverne came under fire for his support of the Conservative Party in the vote over EEC entry. The Lincoln constituency
Labour Party was fervently opposed to Britain's membership in the
Common Market, and in June 1971 passed a resolution calling on all

members of the Parliamentary Labour Party (PLP) to oppose entry. During the following year, the local party voted to sack Taverne at the next election. Taverne appealed against the local party's decision but was turned down by Labour's National Executive Committee, which was moving steadily leftward. Taverne then decided to give up his seat and fight the consequent by-election as an independent Democratic Labour candidate.[27]

Taverne's decision to fight the 1973 by-election as Democratic Labour candidate represented the first time a Labour member fought for the principles of social democracy outside the party. 'I preferred to call myself a social democrat even then but the name social democrat meant nothing to people', Dick Taverne remarked. 'I did a little market research before my decision and half the people questioned said "isn't that the thing they had in Germany before the war?", thinking that social democrat stood for some sort of national socialist movement and the other half thought it was sort of communist. Although I didn't attach the name, I made no doubt about it, my movement was going to be social democracy.'[28]

Taverne's courageous election bid proved to be a dramatic victory. He won with a majority of some 13 000 votes over the official Labour candidate. He received 58 per cent of the vote, against 23 per cent for Labour and 18 per cent for the Conservatives. Immediately afterwards, he set up a National Campaign for Social Democracy which he hoped would be the precursor to a formation of a new party. In his book, *The Future of The Left*, published a year later in 1974, Taverne predicted the inevitable decline of the Labour Party.[29] He proclaimed that the event which took place in Lincoln was not an isolated coincidence but the sign of a growing movement towards a split in the Labour Party and the formation of a new social democratic party in Britain.

The climate was right in the early 1970s for the emergence of a social democratic party. The social democrats in the Labour Party had become isolated over the issue of the EEC, the party was being taken over by the left, and the success at Lincoln had illustrated solid Labour support for moderation. The only setback was that the Labour Party unexpectedly won the 1974 General Election.[30] Victory had created a tenuous bond between the two factions, as Taverne confirms:

> The split was never likely when Labour was in Government because in Government the more sensible forces assert themselves.

The figures who are the abler ones are likely to be more amenable to the signs of the times and thus generally make up the administration . . . It is the left wing that are blind to these facts . . . There is in Government a great tendency for everyone to move together whereas in opposition the tendencies are much more divisive. In Government, it is the administration which matters, so the Party becomes less important and so it was in 1974. Thus, the moment of truth was postponed.[31]

A convincing argument can be made that the split would have taken place in the early 1970s had Labour not been re-elected. A poll was taken during this period by *The Times*, which asked, 'If there was a party led by moderates like Roy Jenkins, Shirley Williams and Dick Taverne, plus the Liberals, would you vote for it?', and twelve million people said 'yes'.[32] There was an enormous amount of support for a third party even then. There still is. A new movement within the Labour Party was developing. The momentum had been slowed down by the surprising electoral victory but its major thrust continued to push towards a split.

Determined to halt the growing influence of the left, the social democrats set up three groups during the five years of government: (i) the Manifesto Group of Labour MPs (1974); (ii) the Social Democratic Alliance (SDA) (1975); and (iii) Campaign for Labour Victory (CLV) (1977).[33] In December 1974, right-wing MPs countered the left's attempts to take over the Parliamentary Labour Party (PLP) by establishing a Manifesto Group within the PLP.[34]

The Manifesto Group, as its title suggests, set out to ensure Labour government's adherence to the manifesto on which it had been elected, and to prevent dilution by Conference decision or pressures from the left to introduce new and contradictory policies.

The Social Democratic Alliance (SDA) was launched in June 1975 under the influence of the formidably intelligent Professor Steven Haseler, and had as its primary aim the reverse of the growing hold of the far left. The SDA diminished much of its significance, so its opponents alleged, by insisting on an 'almost hysterical witch-hunt against the Left, which alienated many leading social democrats'.[35]

It was the Campaign for Labour Victory, reminiscent of the group which had launched the Campaign for Democratic Socialism, that received the most broadly based support and was considered the most important of the three groups which campaigned for social democracy in the mid-1970s. The CLV gained credibility from the endorsement it received from leading Cabinet moderates like Shirley Williams, Bill Rodgers and David Owen. The Campaign developed out of a meeting chaired by William Rodgers, following the disaster of the October 1976 Party Conference at Blackpool.[36] During this conference, the left seized control of the proceedings and overrode both the new leader, James Callaghan, and the deputy leader, Denis Healey. In many ways, the CLV represented the 'last-ditch' attempt of the social democrats to save the Labour Party.[37]

After 1977, the situation inside the Labour Party began to worsen as it became increasingly obvious that Callaghan's government would be labelled a failure. The Liberal–Labour Pact of 1977–8, which successfully kept nationalisation off the agenda and freed the government to pursue a reduction in public spending and a stricter incomes policy, gave encouragement that perhaps a split was not inevitable. This victory was quickly overshadowed by what was eventually termed the 1978–9 'winter of industrial discontent'.[38] It was actually a long-drawn-out nightmare, since, during that period, Britain was hit by one major strike after another. The trade unions had rebelled against the Callaghan government that had ignored Conference decisions against incomes policy. The unions were alienated by a Labour leadership they no longer trusted, and supported a left that appeared more amenable to their cause. The breakdown in co-operation between the leadership of the trade unions and the Labour leaders sent a powerful message that disaster was impending.

With the demise of the Callaghan government came a revival of the left and demands for more radical policies. The left entered the 1979 General Election firmly, if not irreversibly, in control of the Labour Party. They already dominated the annual conferences, and now they controlled the National Executive Committee with a majority of seventeen to twelve on the centre right. In addition, the failure of the government helped to persuade many trade unionists to their side as well. The whole atmosphere became more negative as frustrated moderates hoped for the party's defeat in the next election.

Although divisions had existed in the past, events had conspired during the preceding decades to somehow make this time different. As the Labour Party entered the 1980s, it was set on a course towards inevitable decline. 'Experience suggested,' William Rodgers, later Vice-President of the SDP and member of the 'Gang of 4', stated, 'that this time the Labour Party could not be saved.'[39]

. . . partly because the Party was moving to the left and partly because of its strong institutional links to the trade unions which were not going to be broken. The trade unions were increasingly unpopular and were thus becoming an incubus around the Labour Party's neck. People like myself, Shirley Williams and David Owen were becoming more and more isolated. We were now in the minority . . .

Though we hadn't changed in our convictions the Labour Party had moved steadily to the left and was no longer a responsible alternative to the Conservative Party. All trends had indicated that the Labour Party was suffering from 'terminal decline'. Although it could enter 'periods of remission', in the long run its movement would inevitably be downward.[40]

A party divided between a growing left and an isolated right, the increasing unpopularity of the trade unions, and the scent of 'terminal decline' combined to create the perfect ingredients for a breakaway. The time for action had arrived.

8 The Birth of the SDP

The story of the birth of the SDP begins with the climactic General Election of 1979. The defeat of Labour in that election represented the party's worst showing in fifty years. Labour's share of the vote showed a striking drop from 39.2 per cent in the October 1974 election to 36.9 per cent in 1979. Speculation had become reality – the Labour Party had embarked on its journey towards electoral decline. During the next two years three different forces would come together to create the new party: Roy Jenkins in Brussels, the democratic Labour groups like Steven Haseler's Social Democratic Alliance (SDA), and the 'Gang of Three' – Williams, Rodgers and Owen. The appalling results of the 1979 General Election and the sparking of these three forces made the formation of a new party inevitable:

> With a right-wing and unpopular Tory Government in power, Labour bound to move to the left in opposition, Shirley Williams out of the House of Commons, and Roy Jenkins watching it all from Brussels and waiting to come back, you had a pretty combustible combination.[1]

Shortly after the May election, the first of the forces made his move. Leading moderate and former Deputy Leader of the Labour Party, Roy Jenkins, on his return from his four-year post as President of the European Commission in Brussels was invited to participate in the Dimbleby lecture series. In his lecture entitled 'Home Thoughts From Abroad', which was delivered on BBC television on 22 November 1979, Jenkins elaborated on his impression of British politics since his departure from the political scene. It was in this broadcast that the idea of the creation of a new centre party was first seriously cast into the public domain. Jenkins called for an escape from 'the constricting rigidity – almost tyranny – of the present party system'. He cited that economic and social changes had taken place in Britain, but had occurred within 'the skin of a political system which has in its essentials remained the same'. In response to the leftward infiltration of the Labour Party which was 'likely to produce a result unacceptable to the majority of Labour MPs', Jenkins argued for a 'strengthening of the radical centre'. His answer to the internal disputes in the Labour Party was clear:

The response to such a situation, in my view, should not be to slog through an unending war of attrition stubbornly and conventionally defending as much of the Old Citadel as you can hold but to break out and mount a battle of movement on a new and higher ground.[2]

It was his prediction that 'such a development could bring into political commitment the energies of many people of talent and goodwill who ... are alienated from the business of government, whether national or local, by the sterility and formalism of much of the political game'. Jenkins truly struck a chord. The response to his plea was immediate. He received thousands of letters within weeks which gave him every indication that the troops had been waiting to assemble.[3]

The second force, the Democratic Labour groups, quickly mobilised. The momentum was building. The Social Democratic Alliance (SDA) proved to be the most effective. Soon after the 1979 election, the SDA branched out into a federation of small local social democratic groups around the country. It even changed its membership requirement to include those who were not in the Labour Party, so as to attract those who had by now been expelled from the party. Within a year, the SDA commanded forty such local groups which made up a total of some 2000 members. They even threatened to put up their own candidates against Labour left-wingers. The SDA and other Democratic Labour groups provided the troops; now what was needed was leadership.

The third force proved to be the most reluctant. The 'Gang of Three' were deeply embedded in the leadership of the Labour Party and at first they were unsure if a breakaway was the necessary answer to their unhappiness. Both Bill Rodgers and David Owen were in the Shadow Cabinet, and Shirley Williams, despite her loss of a seat in the 1979 election, was still quite involved in the party's National Executive Committee. Although there were frequent meetings between the 'Gang of Three' and Roy Jenkins to discuss the prospects of a new party, the 'Gang of Three', during this early stage, were resolved to try to save the Labour Party from within. Shirley Williams was perhaps the most firmly committed of the three to staying in. At a meeting of the right-wing Manifesto Group, in May 1980, she said that the idea of forming a new social democratic party was nonsense: 'I am not interested in a third party. I do not believe it has any future.' Bill Rodgers was a lot less apprehensive. In a speech that he gave in South Wales a week after Jenkins's presentation, Rodgers gave the Labour Party one year to save itself:

> Our Party has a year – not much longer – in which to save itself. A year in which to start repairing its ramshackle organisation and to get some money in the till. A year to start winning friends amongst the men and women – almost thirty million of them – who did not vote Labour last time. A year in which to start proving that it is a credible alternative to the harsh and divisive government of Mrs Thatcher.[4]

Rodgers's ultimatum was the first public statement by one of the 'Gang of Three' that their patience was wearing thin. His message to the left was clear – 'You straighten up or we get out . . .':

> A party of the far left – in which Tribune members would be the moderates – would have little appeal to the millions of voters who reject doctrinaire and extreme solutions . . . I do not believe that many of us would want to be a passenger on such a gravy train to disaster . . . If the hard-line leaders of the left want a fight to the finish, they can have it. But if as a result they should split the Party, they should not suppose that the inheritance will be theirs.[5]

The following year was the moment of truth. The battle began at the Labour Party's Special Conference in Wembley on 31 May 1980 and ended at a similar conference in the same place eight months later. Events would transpire to bring all three forces in line. The end result was a dramatic breakaway.

During the 31 May conference, the left cast the first stone by rallying enough support for the endorsement of a policy document called 'Peace, Jobs, Freedom'. The document committed Labour to an anti-EEC and pro-unilateralist position. David Owen was booed off the podium for his defence of multilateralism. Owen was deeply influenced by this ugly experience. Largely because of his encouragement, the 'Gang of Three' then issued a joint statement to the public that they would leave the party if Labour adopted withdrawal from the EEC as its official policy.

Anxieties mounted when the left-dominated Labour Commission of Enquiry endorsed the principle of mandatory re-selection of MPs and consented to favour an electoral college to elect the party leader. It was the last endorsement which struck the sharpest chord. Selection of the party leader in an electoral college meant that the leadership would become more accountable to the trade unions and left-wing constituency than to Members of Parliament.

Noel Tracey, in his book *The Origins of the Social Democratic Party*, argued that the question of representative democracy was one of the most immediate causes of the split in the party. The Social Democrats' dilemma was that 'with little or no support in the constituency parties or the trade unions, the only way they could continue as before was on the basis of their "autonomy" from any form of Party control and now that was reduced if not removed'.[6] In response to this threat, the 'Gang' wrote a letter to the *Guardian* on 1 August 1980. This letter was very important because in it 'the Three' implicitly stated their terms for remaining in the party:

> If the NEC remains committed to pursuing its present course and if, consequently, fears multiply among the people, then support for a centre party will strengthen as disaffected voters move away from Labour. We have already said that we will not support a centre party for it would lack roots and coherent philosophy. But if the Labour Party abandons its democratic and internationalist principles, the argument may grow for a new democratic socialist party to establish itself as a party of conscience and reform committed to those principles. We are not prepared to abandon Britain to divisive and often cruel Tory policies because electors do not have an opportunity to vote for an acceptable socialist alternative to a Conservative Government.[7]

. Despite this announcement, they still hoped they would not have to carry it out. They, the 'Gang of Three', still felt themselves to be 'socialists' struggling to maintain a Gaitskellite posture for a party which was moving rapidly to the left.

The Labour Party Conference at Blackpool in September 1980 was the final straw. In the conference, major constitutional changes were proposed and passed. All MPs were in future to be subject to re-selection procedures which meant that any Labour MP, even Ministers, out of line with party policy were liable to be thrown out by local constituency activists. In addition, it was decided that leaders of the party would be elected by an electoral college representing the party as a whole.[8] On policy issues, the Conference voted for the Alternative Economic Strategy, import controls, withdrawal from the EEC, unilateral nuclear disarmament and the closing of US bases in Britain. The split became irrevocable when Michael Foot was elected as the new Labour leader over Denis Healey. Denis Healey, a moderate, was considered the obvious successor to Callaghan. Had

Healey won, most social democrats would have felt obligated to give him a chance to save the party. But by this time the left's support had hardened: Foot was elected on the second ballot by 139 votes to Healey's 129 votes. With Foot at the helm, the 'Gang of Three' finally became resigned to the fact that redemption was not imminent.

Preparation for the new party began soon after. The 'Gang' was joined by Roy Jenkins to become the 'Gang of Four'. After a series of meetings, it was decided that they would announce their intentions after the second Special Conference at Wembley in January 1981. During that Labour conference, plans were made for the implementation of an electoral college to choose future party leaders which would give the trade unions 40 per cent of the vote, the Parliamentary Labour Party (PLP) 30 per cent and local parties 30 per cent. On 1 January 1981, immediately following the Special Conference, the 'Gang of Four' issued their famous 'Limehouse Declaration', so named because it was drawn up at David Owen's house in the dockland area of Limehouse, East London.[9] The declaration stated that the 'need for the realignment of British politics must now be faced' and set up a Council for Social Democracy to serve as a prelude to the formation of a new party. It was in this declaration that the 'Gang' first made mention of the 'moulds' they intended to break:

> Our intention is to rally all those who are committed to the values, principles, and policies of social democracy. We seek to reverse Britain's economic decline. We want to create an open, classless and more equal society, one which rejects ugly prejudices based upon sex, race or religion.[10]

Things took off with breathtaking speed. The day after the announcement of the Council for Social Democracy, nine Labour MPs joined it. Letters and donations began to pour into the Council. On 3 February 1981, the *Guardian* published the 'Declaration of a Hundred' which listed one hundred leading supporters of the Council. Within five weeks of the Limehouse Declaration, more than 25 000 letters urging a breakaway were received. Opinion polls compiled between the end of January and the end of March showed support running between 23 and 31 per cent in favour of a new social democratic party on its own, and at between 38 and 40 per cent for a Liberal-social democratic alliance.[11] The response was much better than the 'Gang' had anticipated and hastened the formation of the new party.

The fact that a new party was needed became unquestionable.

Social democrats foresaw no salvation for the Labour Party. Although there was a growing bond and meeting of minds between Roy Jenkins and Liberal leader David Steel, most social democrats had dismissed the idea of joining the Liberal Party. Dick Taverne's reason for not joining the party best explains the perception that many had of the Liberal Party:

> Why then did I not join the Liberal Party? Because I could never quite see the Liberals breaking through on their own. They had a smell of failure associated with them. They had been in Opposition since 1920. So the Liberals were no longer associated with power. And that still holds true today. If there is a difference between Social Democrats and Liberals it's not in philosophy but in attitude. The Liberals are less realistic in formulating policy and the Social Democrats, having had experience in Government, are more practical and realistic. The difference between the two is in approach.[12]

Obviously Taverne was drawing a distinction between joining the Liberal Party and merging with them.

Mr Christopher Brocklebank-Fowler, Conservative for Norfolk North-West, who created a dramatic scene by crossing the floor of the House of Commons to join the new party, chose the social democrats for similar reasons. One would expect that the Liberals would have provided a more natural home for a defecting Tory. But no. Mr Brocklebank-Fowler's decision was based mostly on the greater credibility of the new party: 'It comes partly from their greater political weight and experience as individuals. They have four recent Cabinet ministers, whereas no Liberal MP for more than 30 years has had experience of office.'[13] Even Liberal leader David Steel during this period expressed his support for a separate party. He felt that there would be a greater potential to break the hold of the two existing major parties on British politics if a new social democratic centre party came into being, working in alliance with the Liberals, than if the Liberal Party was merely enhanced by a few prominent figures like Jenkins. In his view, 'Two parties together would offer a wider potential attraction to the centre ground of electoral support.'[14] Although both sides saw a need for a separate party, they also knew even at this early stage that an alliance was the only way for both to survive simultaneously. The logic of a future merger between them had received an early disavowal.

At nine o'clock in the morning, in the Connaught Rooms, on

Thursday, 26 March 1981, the 'Gang of Four' assembled to formally launch the Social Democratic Party. The official breakaway from the Labour Party had been made and reconciliation in the future did not look likely. One political pundit equated the Social Democrats' departure to the burning-down of one house and rebuilding of another:

> We ran out of the burning house, clutching our valuables, some of them already singed. Now that we have built ourselves a new house, those valuables remain the centre-piece of its various rooms, though we are acquiring new furniture all the time as more and more people come to live with us and especially as they come from other houses than the Labour ones, and from the tented camps of the floating vote.[15]

The journey to the Connaught Rooms was both long and painful. But this was only the end of the beginning. The real journey was yet to begin. (Few foresaw that it would be so brief a journey before the dramatic split of 1987 destroyed the 'Gang of Four'.)[16]

Now that the party was officially launched, the struggle for stability began. The politics of stability involved the questions of membership, policy and organisation.

During the first few months of its existence the SDP attracted an enormous amount of support. Within ten days, the Social Democratic Party numbered 43 588 members. The response was extraordinary. People came in droves, as if the frustration of years had been unblocked by the announcement of a new political party. When asked in an interview what kind of strategy was used to lure supporters, Vice-President William Rodgers quickly responded, 'We were pushing at an open door':

> As Britain changed socially and economically, so people were looking for an alternative. When we launched our party, we were in a sense pushing at an open door. For ten years people had said we need a new party of the centre, or 'centre left' as I like to call it. So we came along and offered them what they had been wanting for quite some time. The fact is that people were waiting for us when the party came.[17]

Who were these 'people in waiting'? The evidence shows that the SDP had tapped an untouched resource. Contrary to many perceptions, the SDP was more than a 'Mark II Labour Party' – home only to Labour defectors. The new party was made up of almost two-thirds 'first-time party affiliates'. David Owen, in his perceptive article 'The Enabling Society', cited this large entry of first-time party affiliates as evidence 'that there was a definable philosophy of social democracy that was unrepresented by any party in British politics and that would provide the electoral basis for a totally new party'.[18]

The growing composition of the party was representative of a progressive, metropolitan middle-class liberalism (with a small 1). The membership of the SDP was overwhelmingly middle-class – academics, journalists, civil servants, scientists, teachers, doctors, lawyers – all joined in great numbers. Even a League of Social Democratic Lawyers was founded. True to the notion that social reform movements are started by the intelligentsia, the SDP was plagued with a host of distinguished professors, young college activists and noted authors. This rich and talented resource, Dick Taverne considers, was to be the most valuable in terms of policy-making. Soon party meetings resembled university seminars rather than traditional political meetings. This, in fact, proved to be something of a mixed blessing, as anyone attending a senior common-room meeting will appreciate.

Ian Bradley, noted *Times* journalist and specialist on the SDP, went so far as to re-name the party 'Socially Distinguished People'. In an article with that title, Bradley revealed the findings from a questionnaire conducted by London Weekend Television in 1981 which was sent to nearly 10 000 SDP members in twenty-two area parties across Britain. The response he received from 5568 replies only reinforced the much-held image of the SDP. The membership of the Social Democratic Party, he surmised, was 'predominantly young, male and middle-class with an almost total commitment to the European Community and a strong desire to curb the power of trade unions.[19] Of those who replied, two-thirds were male; 57 per cent were under the age of 45, with a larger concentration in the 25–34 age group; and 57 per cent were in professional and managerial occupations, compared with only 16 per cent in the British population as a whole. The figures showed a staggering social bias in the SDP's membership. Not only were the majority of the respondents middle-class professionals, but only 7 per cent were in the working class, compared with 53 per cent in the country at large. It became increasingly clear that the party which set out to, as Shirley Williams has often said, 'break the mould of class-based politics', had become a distinctly middle-class club itself.[20]

This image of the SDP was further portrayed by its leadership. The party, largely the creation of the personalities and styles of the 'Gang of Four', had also taken on their traits. All four are rooted in a middle-class Oxbridge background. Jenkins (the most intellectually able) and Rodgers were former grammar school boys, the sons of a Welsh-miners' MP and a Liverpool Corporation clerk respectively. Moreover, David Owen (the most decisive and dynamic) and Shirley Williams were the products of public schools, with Owen raised as the son of a well-to-do general practitioner and Williams brought up in the upper-middle-class family of writer Vera Brittan and her husband professor Sir George Catlin. Similarly, all four were Oxbridge graduates. Jenkins, Rodgers and Williams went up to Oxford while Owen went to Cambridge University.[21] It is not surprising, then, that they all had a similar view on political issues, and practice the same style of politics. This made it easy for the four to form a temporary collective leadership for the party. For a time the most immediately striking feature of the party was its lack of a single leader. During the interim between the creation and the organising of the party, the SDP was run jointly and equally by all four. In an article she wrote for *The Times*, which was published the day the party was launched, Williams prided the collective leadership on challenging the 'conventional pyramid structure of the old parties'.[22] She described it as having 'great dividends: complementary experience and complementary knowledge of a wider range of government departments and subjects than any single leader could ever have'. This assertion overstated the case for collective leadership and therefore must be seen as an attempt to forestall a power struggle. Even though the party members voted later to choose an official party leader, David Owen, the SDP was still somewhat influenced by all four (until the split in 1987).

The chief problem with the party's membership was that it lacked a clearly defined interest. The sort of non-class, non-interest based party the SDP was developing had no established roots in British politics.

Despite the many problems the trade unions created, the Labour Party's link with them did give it a definable basis and interest to represent. Similarly, the Conservative's link with big corporations gave it a financial as well as ideological basis. The SDP failed to attract large donations from private industry and it was unable to capture the wholehearted support of a powerful interest group. Ironically, in the party's attempt to appease all, the SDP failed to give to itself a real and definite identity. This inability to establish a distinct identity during this early stage would later become one of the party's major weaknesses. The search for an identity was crucial and a decisive factor which impeded the SDP's success. As has been asserted, nobody can underestimate the importance of establishing an interest:

> Although I think we have established ourselves as a serious party, one thing we have not done and I think is a precondition for our success is to carve out a real identity for ourselves in terms of interest. We are viewed as a middle-class party attracting professionals and intellectuals. We are not identified sufficiently with powerful interest groups which in British politics is a prerequisite for support. We must decide quickly which interest we do represent.[23]

This was profoundly true; however, important interest groups were not initially attracted to the SDP.

The image the SDP established, then, during the period 1981 to 1987 was to haunt them indefinitely. A superficial examination of its membership and its leadership revealed the party to be strongly middle-class. This truly did not appear to be the stuff from which radicals are made. During the years to follow, the SDP would confront major difficulties in its attempts to overcome its image as the 'party of the claret drinkers'.[24]

Shirley Williams during one of her classic moments of periodic introspective vacillation and agonising self-doubt declared openly that a new Jenkins-type centre party would have 'no roots, no principles, no philosophy and no values'. After the launching of the party, she was frequently reminded of her statement and subsequently asked 'Where are the policies and what are the principles of your new party?' Many critics charged the party with a lack of policies.[25] Their case was strengthened by polls of SDP members that showed that they were also unsure of what their party stood for. The leadership saw themselves, as Rodgers commented earlier, as the party of the 'centre-left'. But what did that mean and was it true? Where were the detailed policies on housing, education, taxation, industrial democracy, reform of the House of Lords, to name a few? If the portfolio's detailed policies did not exist in the first weeks of the party's existence, the leadership had ready explanations, referring to the disease, 'manifestoitis', which plagued the other parties. Instead, they emphasised that policy had to involve the membership, and this, they added, would take time. David Owen said, somewhat characteristically, when a woman demanded to know what was in the new party's manifesto:

> Look, love, if you want a manifesto go and join one of the other parties . . . The members will be involved in making our policy. We are not going to spoon-feed them. That would be dictatorial.[26]

The irony of his prognosis was not lost on his critics when he became party leader.

Nevertheless, the SDP did have some policies, even if at this stage they were only sketched in broad outline. The first tentative spelling-out of the SDP policies was in a statement entitled 'Twelve Tasks for Social Democrats', which later became the basis for its brochures. In the economic sphere, the party called for a mixed economy – an economy based on a mixture of publicly and privately owned industries. In addition, the party supported an investment programme with a flexible income policy. Although the specifics were often muddled in the rhetoric, the SDP was clear about what it did not want – neither the monetarism of the Conservative government nor the Alternative Economic Strategy of import control and more nationalisation advocated by the Labour Party.

Socially, the SDP was committed to shaping Britain into a classless, multi-racial society – free from discrimination on the grounds of race, sex or religion. Largely due to the influence of Shirley Williams, the party put as a major plank in its policy recommendation on argument for a 'better deal for women'.[27] This would appeal to women who made up half of the British electorate. In all these intentions, the SDP was inherently advocating an equal opportunity for all. Paradoxically, the party's insistence on equality would be hindered by its support for decentralisation. Part of the party's policy called for greater community control. The net effect of decentralisation of government and welfare services is to increase inequalities. The leaders of the SDP were only dimly aware of this contradiction in policy and were slow to realise that some intervention by central government was necessary to ensure equality. They argued, however, that theirs would be a different and better kind of intervention than before. But why this should be so was not a straightforward question.

Another very important part of the SDP's policy was their demand for fair elections. Here the logic was clear-cut. They proposed constitutional reform which would replace the present 'first-past-the-post' system of the British electoral structure with one of proportional representation (PR). Under a proportional representation system, they contended that everyone's vote would count. Britain would then be true to the doctrine of 'one man, one vote'.[28]

The strongest and most clearly defined part of the SDP's programme was its stance on the EEC, mulitlateralism and NATO. It was disputes over these issues which finally led to the split in the Labour Party and the formation of the SDP. Undoubtedly, the party's leaders and activists were fervently committed to Britain's continued membership in the EEC. Most of the ones in Parliament at the time voted against the Labour Party and in favour of entry during the crucial vote in October 1971. In the poll conducted by London Weekend Television mentioned earlier, members of the SDP overwhelmingly pledged their support in favour of the Common Market. As Table 8.1 illustrates, 92 per cent of the 5568 SDP respondents were opposed to withdrawal from the European Economic Community.

Table 8.1   attitudes of SDP members on major policy issues

	In favour %	Against %
Withdrawal from the European Communities	7	92
Incomes Policy	89	9
Government investment aid for certain industries	79	19
Unilateral disarmament	22	76
Legislation putting employees in the board room	73	25
Curtailing trade-union immunities	72	24
Leaving nationalised/private industry frontier where it is now	72	26
Leaving private schools as they are	28	72
Assemblies in English regions	31	67
Outlawing the closed shop	67	31
Reducing tax relief on mortgage-interest payments	32	64
National assemblies in Scotland and Wales	56	41
Wealth tax	63	34
Raising tax to pay for higher public spending	55	41

Source: The Times, 30 November 1981.

The table also reveals the enormous dislike (76 per cent) most of them felt for unilateral disarmament. The SDP's overall plea was for international co-operation.[29] They were very much in favour of NATO, EEC and similar multilateral attempts. Underlying this stance was the attitude and realisation that Britain cannot do it alone. Isolationism is self-defeating. It was the party's belief in internationalism which became the dominating ethos of SDP policy. Most believed that this plank would be the overriding factor in encouraging people to join.[30]

It was realised from the beginning that the SDP could not 'break the mould' alone. It became increasingly obvious to some – though not to Owen – that there would be no place in British politics for four political parties. Discussion had taken place even before the formal creation of the SDP about the possibility of an alliance with the Liberals. Opinion polls showed enormous and growing support for an alliance. Gallup polls published in the *Daily Telegraph* asked: 'If the new SDP formed an alliance with the Liberals so that a candidate from only one of these parties would stand in each constituency, how would you vote?' The results of these polls, done before and after the launching of the party, are reproduced in Table 8.2.

Table 8.2   Support for the Alliance

	Mar 19 %	Apr 2 %	Apr 16 %	May 14 %
SDP/Liberal	46	48.5	45	40
Labour	27	24.5	28	28.5
Conservative	25	25.5	25.5	28.5
Other	2	1.5	1.5	3

Source: Daily Telegraph (1981).

The polls made it equally as evident that alone neither party would have much of a chance. Various opinion polls showed that the Liberals and the SDP separately would only command between 15 and 19 per cent of the voters. The message was eminently clear: the prospect for either of the two parties to form a government was 'Together or Never'.[31]

Despite the obvious choice, the two parties at first were reluctant to accept their options. Many Social Democrats were eager to form their own identity and didn't want to be tied to the stereotypes associated with the old political parties. Rodgers explained that the 'hardest part in organising the party has been establishing and maintaining an easy working relationship with the Liberals':

> We are a new party. Literally, two-thirds of our members have never been members of a political party and they are very open-minded, eager to be efficient and very prepared to be persuaded. The problem is that the Liberals have been there for very many years and they have become settled in their ways. Some

of them are not very anxious in winning power. They see the Liberal party as a party of protest mostly. They have the very hard task of giving way to us, to enable us to fight as many seats as they have.[32]

Many Liberals, as Rodgers suggested, resented the emergence of a new political actor; 'they had laboured long in a strong political vineyard . . . to stand aside for someone else just at the moment when it looked as if there might after all be some harvest was difficult'.[33]

But was the only real barrier to the forming of an alliance psychological? The Liberals and the SDP were, after all, largely agreed on ideology. In some key areas like the EEC and the economy, they had similar programmes. A partnership between the two parties seemed as natural as it was advantageous. Now all that was needed, some argued, was to overcome these attitudinal barriers.

Although there was uncertainty and opposition among the grass-roots, the leadership of both parties knew that success depended on an alliance. David Steel, the Liberal leader, and Roy Jenkins, then SDP leader, were agreed on the idea from the start. Activists, like Dick Taverne, had also acknowledged the choices. In an article he wrote for *The Times*, Taverne described the choice as 'Unite or Die'. He urged all concerned to realise that the difference that the Alliance could make was the difference between life and death, especially for the SDP:

> We must all realise that in the longer term there is no room for separate Liberals and SDP. Under our present electoral system their separate survival is inconceivable. The odds against a third party are formidable, against a fourth they would be insurmountable . . . It follows that unless the SDP swallows the Liberals or vice versa the two can prosper only if they become one party or remain permanently allied by such close ties that they are one party in all but name.[34]

Reservations were thwarted by the nature of the situation; by the middle of 1981, all had considered the options and decided to give both parties their greatest life chance. Although the allocation of seats and the formulation of a joint policy statement had not been worked out, the Alliance was formally approved by the Liberal membership at their annual conference in Llandudno in September 1981. Both parties were committed to making the Alliance work. It was not long before the Alliance entered its first race.

Indeed, by the end of 1981, the SDP was well on its way towards gaining some stability. The SDP ship was, someone asserted, packed with passengers, had a direction and a sturdy superstructure, and now it was time to test the waters. This nautical line perfectly illustrated also the risks of hidden obstacles just beneath the surface which could scupper the whole ship, and the fact that the crew were known to occasionally mutiny or even to desert ship without regard to the interests of those on the bridge.

But when the excitement and aura of newness was removed, the real questions came into focus: Could the SDP or the Alliance really win? Would the opinion-poll results actually translate into votes? Had the SDP a real future, either as a part of a new merged party or as a separate entity?

An examination of the 1981 by-elections and the General Elections of 1983 and 1987 soon made it apparent that the future was far from assured. Important lessons were learned. Yet events continued to outpace the formation of the party. Even before the Alliance was formally cemented, it was brutally hurled into a political contest. News broke that a seat in the Warrington constituency would soon be vacated by veteran Labour MP Sir Tom Williams, who had just accepted the appointment of circuit judge. The by-election that would result would be the first opportunity for the new party to prove itself. The SDP was eager to keep up the momentum their formation had created. They were disheartened, however, by the gloomy prospects. Warrington was not an ideal seat to fight, being a Labour stronghold in the North West. To win would be almost impossible; even to put up a good showing seemed very unlikely. But to pass up this opportunity would discredit the party. To back away from a confrontation with Labour would spell defeat! There was no choice. The SDP would have to fight.

In the light of the unfortunate prospect, the SDP came out in full force. It was decided that they would have their best chance if one of the party leaders would stand as candidate. The choice fell on Shirley Williams but there was also very considerable support for Roy Jenkins, since polls had favoured both of them. Mrs Williams, after much typical procrastination, decided not to stand, despite the fact that at least one opinion poll carried out by the *Sun* newspaper suggested that she could win the seat with a sizeable majority. The spotlight quickly turned to political heavyweight Roy Jenkins. Jenkins courageously accepted the challenge and the Alliance prepared for what the media billed as the 'by-election of the century'.[35]

The Alliance was not the only party shaping up for the battle. The Tories hoped to avoid the humiliation of coming in third, while the Labour Party viewed the campaign as the perfect opportunity to avenge defectors. Well-known party affiliates from all the major parties appeared at rallies held in Warrington. The Alliance put on a most impressive performance. Leading Liberals like David Steel and Cyril Smith, showed overwhelming support for their new allied friends. The contest at all times was a bitter clash directly between Roy Jenkins and the Labour candidate, an ardent CND supporter, Douglas Hoyle. Underlying the acrimonious surface fight between the candidates was the much more important battle between Labour and SDP ideology. The SDP campaign centred around the extremism of the Labour policies, and Labour emphasised the SDP's lack of policy.[36]

The results of the July 17 by-election would go down in electoral history. Although the SDP lost, they were considered the real victors. Their display of determination and resolve had turned a 'safe' Labour seat into a marginal one. The new party, whose membership in Warrington at the start of the campaign had numbered only thirteen, had moved up from literally nowhere into a close second place. Jenkins lost by only 1759 votes. He dramatically described the results as 'my first defeat in thirty years in politics. And it is by far the greatest victory that I have ever participated in.' Labour received 48.3 per cent of the votes, compared with 61.6 per cent in the previous election. Moreover, the SDP garnered 42.4 per cent of the vote, compared with the Liberal's weak 9 per cent showing the previous time.[37] The Warrington by-election was an odd sort of victory – but a victory nonetheless. It was this initial success which perhaps indicated that the SDP was not just a mere aberration. The Warrington by-election was perceived as a 'watershed for the SDP' – first, and most important, it appeared to put an end to doubts about whether the party was capable of making the transition required to move from a political 'happening' into an effective political force, where it counts: in the ballot box.[38]

Warrington provided the short-term impetus to carry the Alliance into two more decisive victories. On 26 November 1981, Shirley Williams, who had recovered temporarily from her bout of introspection, was returned to the House of Commons as the first elected Social Democrat. She won an impressive victory in a by-election at Crosby, previously a 'safe' Tory seat. She managed to turn a 19 000 Conservative majority into a 5000 majority for the SDP. In 1979 a local Liberal had polled 15.2 per cent of the vote, but now Shirley Williams polled 49 per cent. This was due in part to the nationwide reputation of Williams, but more significantly pointed to the strength of the united forces of the Alliance.[39]

During the previous month, on 22 October, Liberal candidate Bill Pitt won the first Liberal/Alliance seat in Croydon North West. With the backing of the SDP, Pitt was able to overcome the defeat he had suffered three times before. The Liberals quadrupled their vote to 40 per cent (but Pitt's improbable rise to fame proved somewhat short-lived as he lost his seat at the next General Election).[40]

The results of the 1981 by-election at Warrington, Croydon and Crosby had a similar ring. As Table 8.3 reveals, the most important lesson learned from this initial success was that the strength of the Alliance was a crucial factor in the success of both parties. This did not point, however, to the alleged advantages of a merged party, since this implied a possible takeover of the SDP by the Liberals, whose shallow history was hardly likely to lead to a sound marriage between two such disparate partners.

Table 8.3 By-election success

	Warrington (16 July 81)	Croydon (22 Oct 81)	Crosby (26 Nov 81)
Alliance vote	42.4%	40%	49%
Increase over Liberal vote in 1979	33.4%	29.5%	33.9%

Were these successes, then, signalling a new realignment of the British electorate? Peter Zentner, in his book *Social Democracy in Britain*, supported this hotly contested proposition. He argued that by-elections revealed the true feelings of the electorate:

Arguably, parliamentary by-elections became the clearest indicators of how the electorate actually felt. Then votes were registered on equal terms between the parties, for to vote for either major or minor party would have no bearing on the government of the day, and people could afford the luxury of voting exactly as they felt.[41]

The SDP successfully survived the first round, but the big test was yet to come. If Zentner was right, then the task ahead of the SDP was to influence voters to display those feelings when it really counts – during the General Election. This became the real impediment to future success. Yet 1981 appeared to be a big success for the Social

Democratic Party; by the end of that year, there were 39 Alliance MPs in the House of Commons and 27 were members of the SDP. Only two, however, were elected under the SDP banner. Jenkins was elected at the Hillhead by-election shortly after Williams's stunning victory at Crosby. The future looked promising. Support for the Alliance during these early months rose to as much as 48 per cent, compared with the usual 15 per cent for the Liberals hitherto. Such a show of support, if repeated at a general election, would have produced a majority SDP/Liberal government. This prospect was enhanced further by the extremism of the Labour Party and the overwhelming personal unpopularity of Mrs Thatcher as revealed in public opinion surveys published before the Falklands war.[42]

There occurred, however, a dramatic turn of fortune. Support for the Alliance quickly diminished. A fall in support that was as equally rapid and almost as massive as its rise, occurred between the Glasgow Hillhead by-election in March 1982 and the brilliant capture of Port Stanley by British forces three months later. In retrospect, Shirley Williams's win at Crosby proved to be the peak of SDP support. From the turn of the year onwards, both support for the party alone and for the Alliance began to drift downwards at the rate of about 1 per cent a week. The ebb of support threatened to become a torrent. By the middle of 1982, support for the Alliance had fallen to about 23 per cent. Critics charged that such a decline was inevitable. They argued that the initial appeal of the SDP was based on the personality of its leadership and the sheer uniqueness of being involved in a fashionable movement rather than on policies and values. Once the novelty had disappeared, the true supporters were revealed. There was much truth in this, hence there was a frantic rush by the Alliance to save its dwindling base. Jenkins's win at Hillhead in March 1982, many thought would regenerate the earlier momentum. The impact of Hillhead was quickly nullified by the Argentinian invasion of the Falklands one week later. Thatcher's courageous and brilliantly successful handling of the Falklands crisis denied the Alliance the opportunity to regain its appeal. The government's popularity soared. SDP membership tailed off and the Alliance never recaptured its 1981 level of support. The downward run had commenced. It was never to be reversed.

The success of the Falklands crisis became, of course, the major determinant of the General Election of 1983. More than any other issue, it created the mood for the re-election of the most unpopular and yet the most courageous British leader in post-war history. David

Butler and Dennis Kavanagh in their book, *The British General Election of 1983*, explained the importance of the Falklands invasion in boosting support for the 'Iron Lady':

> The Falklands invasion proved to be the turning point in the political history of Parliament . . . British troops showed notable bravery and skill; the British public, as they watched the reports on television, could share proudly in a brief revival of imperial glory. And there could be little doubt that Mrs Thatcher had been, in fact as well as name, the victorious leader. She had managed operations . . . and taken hard decisions without hesitation. Her strident cry 'Rejoice, rejoice . . .' caught the mood of the great mass of public.[43]

The Election of 1983 was, then, a decisive victory for the Conservatives. They received 42.4 per cent of the votes and 397 seats in the House of Commons. For Labour, the election signalled demise, producing the party's worst showing yet. Labour received only 27.6 per cent of the vote, compared with 36.9 per cent in 1979.[44] The 1983 election produced a 'mixed bag' of results for the Alliance. Although the party did not perform nearly as well as earlier polls predicted, it was able to attract 25.4 per cent of the vote – an improvement on the Liberal 1979 vote by 11.4 per cent. This translated, however, into only 23 Alliance seats, of which 17 were Liberal and 6 were SDP. This was a wretchedly poor showing for the SDP who boasted 29 MPs in the previous Parliament. In the reshuffling, the party saw the loss of seats for leaders Shirley Williams and William Rodgers. The glimpse of encouragement that helped it recover from the darkness was the Alliance's consistent second-place polling in 313 seats.[45]

Two things become apparent from the results of the 1983 Election: the growing realignment of the British electorate, and the complete and manifest unfairness of the electoral system. Both these developments carried important implications for the SDP and the Alliance. The 1983 Election showed further signs of an increasing realignment of voters that began in the 1979 election. If there was one clear loser in the 1983 election it was the Labour Party. Over a third (37 per cent) of Labour's 1979 support deserted the party in 1983. As Table 8.4 shows, the Alliance was the main beneficiary of the swing of votes.

In 1983, 22 per cent of the 1979 Labour voters supported the Alliance. For every three that switched to the Alliance, one went to the Conservative Party and one did not bother to vote. The Alliance

Table 8.4   The flow of votes from 1979 to 1983

	% 1979 vote				
	Con	Lab	Lib	Did not vote	Too young
% 1983 vote					
Conservative	77	7	14	22	28
Labour	4	63	9	12	17
Liberal/SDP	13	22	72	14	20
Other	—	1	—	—	2
Did not vote	6	7	5	52	33
	100	100	100	100	100

also benefited from a slight swing in the Conservative vote. It was the Conservatives that they posed the greatest threat to in the future, because in two-thirds of the 397 Conservative-held seats, the Alliance ran second.

The 1983 election also reinforced the declining class alignment. Once again Labour lost out. The working class, the traditional Labour stronghold, was becoming increasingly defiant. For the first time, Labour's share of the trade-union votes fell below 50 per cent. Only 39 per cent of the trade unions voted Labour, as compared with 55 per cent and 51 per cent in 1974 and 1979 respectively. Professor Ivor Crewe summed it up: 'The Labour vote remains largely working class; but the working class has ceased to be largely Labour.'[46] The Alliance received 29 per cent of the trade-union vote, while the Conservatives received 31 per cent. Labour's rout worsened among the skilled working class, such that the Conservative Party received 40 per cent over the Labour's retainment of 32 per cent. In addition to signalling the further decline of Labour, the realignment that the results of the 1983 election pointed to renewed hope for the Alliance at the next general election.[47]

However, one of the biggest issues tossed into the public arena was the manifest unfairness generated by the electoral system. The 'winner – takes – all' doctrine, inherent in the British 'first-past-the-post' system, produced such disproportionate results during 1983 that many people began to question its value. The Conservatives gained 61 per cent of the 650 seats with only 42 per cent of the vote. This was a drop from its 1979 percentage of votes (43.9 per cent) by 1.5 per cent, but in terms of seats the Conservatives increased their majority from 43 to 144. The Alliance was especially hurt by the electoral system because of its widespread distribution. Unlike the Conservative Party which has a large concentration in the Southern region, or the Labour Party with its concentrated vote in the Northern industrial region, the Alliance was generally evenly spread out. Thus, although the Alliance received only 2.2 per cent of the votes less than Labour's 27.6 per cent, it won 186 fewer seats. This was a ludicrous and outrageous outcome, and the *Sunday Times* commented that the 1983 General Election had produced 'a new order of unfairness'.[48] The *New Statesman* calculated that even if the Alliance had won 32 per cent of the vote and beaten Labour for second place, it still would have generated only thirty seats. The public was bombarded by reports from the media and pleas by the Alliance regarding the extreme injustice of the electoral system. In a fully proportional system, the Conservatives would have gained approximately 120 fewer seats, Labour 20 fewer and the Alliance 140 more. Such an outcome would have produced a 'hung parliament'.[49] Instead, the current electoral system produced the biggest one-party majority in almost fifty years. Although Conservative and Labour were the two top parties, they commanded the majority support in less than half of the constitutencies: 57 per cent of all 1983 votes were anti-Conservative and 72 per cent were anti-Labour. The results of the election, needless to say, cast serious doubts on the rationale and legitimacy of the electoral system. Established to give the government-of-the-day a working majority in the House, the electoral system now seemed to have defeated its purpose. Changes had occurred in the British political tradition such that the system was now surrendering enormous control to a government that was disliked by the majority of the electorate.

During the aftermath of the General Election of 1983, it became necessary for all the political parties to assess their position. The Conservatives were bestowed with the hard task of avoiding the economic and political mistakes that had produced the unpopularity of its previous administration. For Labour, the problem was how to reverse its steady and possibly irreversible decline. The dilemma it faced was whether to sacrifice hard-won left-wing policies in the hopes of recapturing the centre-ground. For the Alliance, the task ahead was to define its direction. The Alliance had entered the 1983 election on the optimism of earlier polls; the impact of that election had forced them to face the reality. Each party separately had to decide its destiny. Could the SDP regain its 1981 momentum? Would the Alliance ever govern? Events between 1983 and 1987 proved to be decisive; it soon became clear that a third Conservative victory might have to be the essential prerequisite for the emergence of the Alliance as the loyal opposition. Labour would have to be destroyed as a parliamentary party. The actual outcome of events proved even more complex than these apparent truths foreshadowed.

The first electoral results, however, produced a sense of realism. It made it evident in the long run that certain environmental changes were essential to the success of the SDP. The reality that the Social Democrats came to acknowledge was that without proportional representation, a close stable alliance and a conducive political atmosphere, their future success could not be assured. The future fate of the SDP, then, depended largely on the combining of these three factors. The last two factors proved both difficult and elusive. If by success the SDP meant the prospect of forming a government or forcing a 'hung' Parliament, then these were the decisive issues. It was this reality that now confronted the Social Democratic Party. Yet a profound systemic change could only come with a fundamental change in the electoral system. The trouble was that neither the Conservatives nor Labour had the slightest interest in electoral reform.

9 The Chimera of Electoral Reform

One of the key factors in the SDP's possible success rested in its ability to secure proportional representation. As David Owen best expressed it: 'The hope of our alliance must lie with those millions of people who have no vested interest in the present system and sense it is failing them.'[1] As the 1983 election results revealed, the electoral system unduly penalised third parties. Although the Alliance captured 25.4 per cent of the votes, it received only 3.5 per cent of the seats. Because of the even distribution of its support, the Alliance had to win a far greater percentage of the vote in order to secure a significant number of seats. A mere 2 percentage points could sometimes mean 100 more seats. As David Butler once put it, a 'party's fortune can move extraordinarily fast from famine to feast'.[2] This unfairness of the 'first-past-the-post' system stood as a major barrier against the Alliance achieving any substantial electoral success. The problem of electoral reform involved two questions: What kind of PR? What is the likelihood of getting it? The second question remained the most imponderable and difficult one to assess.

There were two forms of proportional representation most often recommended as suitable: (i) the German system, and (ii) the Irish system of single transferable vote. Both of the systems prevent the waste of votes cast for non-winning candidates which occurs in the present British system. In Germany, the electoral system is a mixture of the British 'winner-takes-all' system and proportional representation.[3] Under this system, the voter has two votes, the first being for a constituency representative, while the second is a vote for a party. The voter is free to give his candidate vote to one party and his party vote to another party. Constituency representatives, as in Britain, would be elected from the total of first votes, but in Germany the constituency representatives fill only half of the seats. The other half of the seats will be determined by the total votes cast for a party by the electorate. The number of constituency seats which each party wins from the first vote would be subtracted from the total number of seats to which it is entitled, using the criterion of proportionality. Thus, if there were 100 total seats and a party received 20 per cent of the total vote and only received one seat from the constituency vote, then it would be entitled to four of the remaining seats. The Germans also attach a threshold of 5 per cent of the total vote to stop the proliferation of small parties. The additional seats a party wins are filled from a list of candidates predetermined by the party from the leading constituencies in which that party polled second during first votes. Critics argue that this system would produce a hierarchy of MPs between those chosen by a constituency and those appointed by the party. They emphasise the unfairness and lack of accountability of the list system. Dick Taverne and other advocates of PR point out the flexibility such a system would allow. It would give people who lack the prestige, ability or money to engage in a campaign but who would nonetheless make a great contribution in Parliament, the chance to serve in the House of Commons. The most attractive feature of this system, as most proponents stress, is its similarity to the present British system and the relative ease with which it could be implemented. It is for this reason that most opponents, like the Tories, would, if forced to choose, select this system.

The system of PR officially favoured by the SDP and the Liberals was the Irish system or the Single Transferable Vote (STV).[4] This system, which has worked quite well in Northern Ireland, aims to minimise the influence of the party in the election of MPs. Vernon Bogdanor, in his book *What is Proportional Representation?*, suggests that the STV operates so as to maximise the use of as many votes as possible.[5] The implementation of the STV in Britain would require multi-member constituencies. Constituents would, therefore, elect not one but, say, five members to Westminster. The voter would be asked to rank the candidates in the order of preference. If a voter's first-preference vote cannot be used to help elect a candidate – either because the candidate for whom the first preference vote is cast has no chance of election, or because the candidate has more votes than needed to win a seat – then instead of the vote being wasted, it is transferred to the voter's second choice whose election it might help to secure. This process is continued until all seats in the multi-member constituency are filled. Each elector thus has a single vote as in the British electoral system, but that single vote, by contrast with the British system, is transferable in accordance with preferences which the elector has marked. Bogdanor explains that 'the proportionality of the system is derived from the fact that to win a seat a candidate needs to win enough votes to equal a quota. Since each candidate needs one quota to win a seat, the "cost" of a seat for each candidate in terms of votes should be the same. Thus STV should, in theory, yield perfect proportionality.'[6] The reasons for the Alliance's support between 1983 and 1987 for this system were obvious. It became apparent that in multi-member constituencies, all three of the major parties would succeed in winning at least one seat in almost every part of the country. This would avoid the large concentration of party support in certain regions.[7]

The Alliance emphasised the beneficial effects upon the workings of government, since parties would be less likely to favour the interest of one sector over another. Another advantage of the STV system, which the Alliance stressed, was the personalisation that it breeds. Dick Taverne argued, 'it puts personality back into politics; you don't just vote for the Party, you vote for the individual'.[8] It was clear that the overriding reason why the Alliance supported this system was that it best achieved their objective – gaining influence and control in Parliament.

The most important issue was whether PR could be secured. What was the likelihood of the electoral reform? Ironically, the only sure way of securing PR was if the Alliance were in government or in a position of influence. The prospect of that occurring would be heightened as if PR were already installed, as earlier results have shown. Thus, the irony was that in order to break the mould of the two-party system, the SDP had to break out of an electoral system designed to ensure its permanency. Jeremy Joseph, author of *Inside the Alliance*, dramatically described the dilemma:

> The difficulty was that the mould appeared to have an inbuilt mechanism designed to ensure its survival as if it knew that it was under attack. Like a Roman fortress perched high on a hilltop, it was capable of mounting a formidable defence . . . Morally the mould had been broken, but legally it remained very much intact.[9]

Although there was a growing awareness among the public of the injustice created by the electoral system, the implementation of PR was wholly in the hands of the political party in power. The discussion of electoral reform was nothing more than a discussion of self-interest. The likelihood of PR was therefore dismal under a Conservative government. They do very well under the current system and would not willingly choose to change it. The only foreseeable way of securing PR was if the Alliance could produce a 'hung parliament'. If at the next election the Alliance could generate a significant number of seats, it could threaten to block the formation of government unless PR was implemented. By holding the balance of power, the Alliance could exert enormous pressure on the government-of-the-day. At the very least, it could request a referendum on the issue to let the voters decide. Taverne described the scenario necessary to secure PR:

> The only way we can get PR is either to become the Government, which is possible but unlikely, or to hold the balance of power with a strong influence. If next time instead of 23 seats we got 30 and held the balance, we would still not be in a position to dictate to anybody. But if we were to secure 80 seats, we would have to have received about 37% or so, probably much more than Labour. With many more votes than Labour but still with many fewer seats, it would be so absurd that people would not tolerate the system any more. We would be in a position to say 'We will not bring down the government only if you give us PR. Otherwise we will force a new election.' Under those circumstances, I do not think anyone could resist giving us PR.[10]

Such was the optimism about the outcome of the next election.

Although there were varying interpretations of the likelihood of electoral reform, the bottom line was that the initiative to adopt PR must be made by the Alliance. The Alliance would generate enough leverage to command its adoption. The stakes were high but the payoff would be guaranteed success. Because of the necessity of coalition government as a result of PR, the party in the centre would enjoy a pivotal position. Zentner equates the power that the Alliance would obtain under PR to Communism – 'once in power, it is forever':

> In one important respect, the Alliance grouping is like Communism: once in power, it is forever. But where Communism does this by abolishing elections and installing a dictatorship of the proletariat, the Alliance would achieve permanent government through the introduction of PR. For under PR, the party of the centre is almost guaranteed a place in government.[11]

Indeed, PR was identified as an essential factor in the long-term success of the SDP. Its adoption depended on the Alliance's capability to break through the established system. There was no chance of achieving that unless the Alliance stayed essentially intact.

But a crucial question was raised here: did support for the Alliance exist because it consisted of two political parties rather than one? Success in the short term, it was perceived, depended on the formation of an Alliance and the avoidance of conflict. Electoral success, it was decided early on, demanded a united front. The mixed results of the 1983 election, however, forced a serious reassessment of the situation. Studies of the election results revealed that one of the main reasons the Alliance lost support was because of its lack of a clear and coherent identity. The electorate was confused about what the Alliance actually meant. Was it one party or two parties? Did it have one leader or two leaders? The problem that had to be tackled was a question of image as well as of substance. After the 1983 election, the Alliance faced three choices, which some four years later assumed historic significance: (i) to dissolve the Alliance and pursue separate identities; (ii) merge into one party; or (iii) turn the Alliance into a real union – a marriage in every sense but with the possibility of divorce still an option. The actual decision taken became the source of internal conflict and of agonising doubt, but, for David Owen, the decision remained in his view the correct one.[12]

The first option was largely dismissed. Most people agreed that a breakup would be self-defeating: neither party had a chance separately; even under PR, a breakup would spell disaster. The Alliance was in reality a kind of coalition between disparate parties with different ideologies who were condemned to be partners but were not indissolubly intertwined.

The initial success at Warrington, Crosby, Croydon and Glasgow Hillhead had shown that victory was possible when the Alliance was united. Both parties performed better when their forces were combined. Even under PR, Taverne believed, a breakup would be disastrous:

> Far more important is the fact that even under PR, a fight between the two parties would ruin both. Each party would need double the resources because it would not have enough money or manpower to fight as effective a campaign separately as they can do together. Moreover, the electorate would be confused. Why should one support an SDP candidate rather than a Liberal or vice versa, if the policies of the two are much the same?[13]

Thus their bond now somewhat limited the possibility of an early breakup before the next election. Experience had also suggested that the first option, termination of the Alliance, would be self-defeating and must be dismissed in the short term. In 1983 the decision to opt out of the alliance was not really on, except in a hypothetical sense.

The second option open to the Alliance was a merger of the two parties, such that they would be one party with one leader. There were many calls for merger from both sides after the 1983 election (which, of course, by 1987 became too hard to resist for the majority in both parties). Taverne pointed to the confusion caused by having two leaders. The typical question post-1983 was Who would be the Prime Minister? He (Taverne) would have opted for a merger as the most logical progression after the 1983 election, but acknowledged that parties do not behave logically. Another option he proposed was the formation of a federation in which there would be two constituent elements but a united national organisation – one leader and one programme. Similarly, some Liberals as well wished to see a merging of the two parties. The then President of the Liberal Party, Alan Watson, in an interview, expressed his optimism about the relationship within the Alliance but revealed his desire to see a merger. Watson reluctantly added that such prospects were very unlikely without Jenkins at the helm of the SDP (indeed a prophetic remark!):[14]

> Personally, I am very optimistic about the way things are going with the Alliance. I would have liked to have seen a merger of the two parties after the last [1983] election ... But those prospects were thwarted by the resignation of Jenkins as SDP leader and the illness of Liberal leader David Steel during that time. The merger was impossible without those two personalities. The SDP has been taken over by David Owen who makes no bones about it – he wants the SDP to have a separate identity.[15]

Indeed, David Owen stood as the major obstacle in the way of combining the two parties. Owen strongly argued, as do many others, that such a development would be welcomed by the two old parties. He explained that they would find it 'far easier to narrow an Alliance Party down into a small centrist band of opinion, but far harder with a two-party alliance to weaken both the distinctive traditional Liberal appeal and the distinctive new Social Democratic appeal which we have built up since our foundation'.[16] This was a powerful and compelling argument. Although there were good arguments on both sides of the issue, it was assumed that because of the differing beliefs, attitudes and subtle differences of posture and of style, merger as an option could only be dismissed unless and until the Alliance was no longer threatened by a larger party to its left, namely the Labour Party.

What prevailed after the Election of 1983 was the adoption of the third option which carried the Alliance into the Election of 1987. It was agreed that the Alliance would be run like a common-law marriage, with perhaps a touch of sin about it. An exerted effort was made to sharpen the image of the Alliance. The Alliance in order to be successful had to present itself as a union, in every sense of the word; but as a union and not in a merger of their separate identities.

Despite this approach, between the 1983 and 1987 elections, the Alliance was not totally effective in achieving a harmonious united front. There was an enduring tension between the leadership. Many Liberals considered Owen to be arrogant – which clever men often are. Such sentiments were also shared by many within the SDP, especially by Bill Rodgers and Shirley Williams who had become tactical allies of Owen. They now regarded him with the gravest suspicion and reserve. His biggest and most numerous critics though were to be found within the Liberal Party. The Liberals were never able to love Owen.

There came in short order some internecine and bitter disputes over defence policy, with a considerable number of Liberals advocating a unilateralist position. This reached a critical point at the Liberal assembly in September 1986 when a pro-unilateralist motion was passed in defiance of the Liberal leadership, which virtually repudiated the stand taken by the SDP only a few weeks earlier at its annual Conference. By August 1984, the Liberals, then, were saying 'We can't go on in this present form.'[17] The Liberal Party's leading election strategists concluded in 1983 in a confidential document, 'A Strategy for the Liberal Party', that 'the nature and direction of the Alliance with the SDP must be resolved unambiguously within the early years of this Parliament and that to delay longer will be devastating'. The document stated that it was impractical for the Alliance to carry on in its present form – 'the strain of a negotiated relationship of so-called equals is a debilitating distraction, both locally and nationally, to effective campaigning'. There were some well-merited doubts as to whether the marriage could last much beyond the next election, especially if the Alliance failed to make its long-awaited breakthrough. Party leaders however, insisted that such disputes inside the Alliance were a natural occurrence in the early stages of the development of any similar arrangement. They countered these insinuations of irretrievable breakdown in the Alliance by reiterating the closeness of their partnership, relative to the internal conflicts which plagued the other two parties. William Rodgers contended:

I think that our Alliance has worked remarkably well and achieved more than anyone believed possible. Despite some internal disputes, we have a much closer partnership than the left and right wings of the Labour Party. There is far less between David Steel and David Owen than between Denis Healey and Tony Benn in the Labour Party or between Mrs Thatcher and James Prior in the Conservative Party. So it is a remarkably successful partnership but it does require a great deal of hard work.[18]

This was true as far as it went, but it tended to underestimate the actual policy differences between the Liberals and the Social Democrats on crucial issues of the day; also it tended to play down the very real dislike the two Davids felt for each other.

Could, then, the marriage last? This question assumed importance as the Alliance prepared for battle in the next general election and for the inevitable by-elections in between. Despite the internal disputes within the Alliance, the realism of their situation made it work. The reality was that both sides could not succeed separately. If either partner wished to influence Parliament, then they must work together. The encouragement given by their second-place position in 316 constituencies gave added reason for sustaining the partnership. The possibility of a hung parliament was the motivating force that ensured the maintenance of a stable Alliance between 1983 and the summer of 1987. Both sides were readily prepared to compromise to make the marriage work, since there were real prospects for them to gain influence given a parliamentary deadlock. It was this possibility, coupled with the reality that only together was success for both likely, that could make the marriage last. Necessity forced them to do all in their power to convince the public of their credibility. With each successful by-election and each good electoral showing, the Alliance, so ran the argument, moved closer and closer towards establishing themselves as a serious and capable contender for government. Whether the marriage lasted, or whether it broke down after the next election with the Alliance stuck with about 20 per cent of the popular vote, there were other factors that both helped or hindered the likelihood of the SDP gaining influence. In many ways, success for the SDP was affected by external forces beyond their control.

The success of the SDP depended as much on the actions of others as on their own efforts. Just as the SDP's formation came at an opportune time when both parties had left a void in the centre ground, so their future success depended, to a certain extent, on the continuing 'extremism' of the other two parties. The Alliance itself avoided, however, the extremism of the centre to which certain sections of the Liberal Party were and are prone. Given that it retained a sense of balance by adhering to a realistic set of strategic, political and social policies, then it benefited from certain changes in the political environment. More so than any other external factors, the future of the SDP depended, then, on the future of the Labour Party. Dick Taverne asserted: 'In a two party system as we have without electoral reform there is a certain enormous bias against a third party that something has to go fundamentally wrong with one of the major parties for the third party to have a chance to succeed.'[19] As the 1983 election revealed, the Labour Party received 27.6 per cent of the vote, only 2.2 per cent more than the Alliance, but received some 200 more seats than them.[20] The future of the SDP, then, depended to a great extent on the continual disintegration of the Labour movement. The prospects of this happening, most evidence suggested, were not inconsiderable but difficult to assess in advance of the election campaign itself, which in 1983 was indeed a remote probability.

It is easy to point to the continuous drift leftward of Labour policies and leadership. Moreover, they still retained the essential ties with the unions, which had become considerably more and more unpopular. During 1985 and 1986, though, the Labour vote pulled up considerably during Kinnock's honeymoon and dream-ticket period of leadership. His calculated and devastating attack on the Militant Tendency at the Labour Party's annual conference in the autumn of 1985 greatly increased his personal popularity. Most polls showed support at between 27 per cent and 30 per cent, as well as above this from time to time. Rodgers viewed this as just a 'period of temporary remission – the slide will still continue'.[21] Taverne made a similar prediction, stating, 'although the Labour Party is presently staging a kind of recovery, the fundamental problems – namely the takeover of the left and the influence of the unions – are still there. The odds must be very heavily against Labour in the next election.'[22] Of course, as the election approached, the position of the Labour Party improved in early 1987 with polls which gave it support equal to the Conservatives – indeed at times they appeared to be pulling ahead. However, the defence issue with Labour's commitment to unilateralism and its flirtation with neutralism generally weakened their position. Labour members also cast some doubt on the ability of their party to reverse its leftward course, at least by the next election. As earlier evidence showed, Labour was the overall loser in the General Election of 1983. Austin Mitchell, in his book *Four Years in the Death of the Labour Party*, correctly said in the 1983 election that the opposition, not the government, was the election issue.[23] The election, he stressed, could only be understood in terms of its dominant pattern: 'Labour's demise'. What happened to the party was not 'a sudden loss of faith but the end of a long process of decline and disintegration'. The same external conditions that were a prerequisite for Labour's reversal were also important for the SDP's success. But it was not merely a question of Labour's incipient disintegration which affected the SDP and its Liberal ally. There remained the single biggest factor in British politics: Mrs Thatcher herself.

The SDP's success could be facilitated by a conducive political atmosphere. Not only did it depend on the decline of Labour but on the continuation of factors that led to Labour's demise. The British political tradition would have to continue to be in crisis. This crisis was not and is not the crisis of Marxist mythology, but something at once more specific and peculiar. Moreover, the Alliance had to capitalise on Labour's breakdown. Success depended to an extent on the further erosion of party loyalties, the decline of class alignment and an increase in the floating vote. It was difficult to assess the situation properly, as both Owen and Steel discovered, because even if they could exploit these factors to their advantage, the time-scale over which each of them developed was variable. In the short term, most experts undoubtedly foresaw a further decline in traditional alignments by party and class. Bo Sarlvik and Ivor Crewe, in their book *Decade of Dealignment*, admitted that the 'SDP's ambitious objectives [of breaking the mould] involves assumptions about the modern British electorate for which our research undoubtedly offers some support.[24] The two authors demonstrated in their study a gradual dealignment and slowly growing volatility in the British electorate. Between a normally spaced pair of elections, the proportion of their panel respondents who switched parties or moved in or out of abstention ranged from 34 per cent to 42 per cent. This evidence could be the makings of a conducive atmosphere for the success of the SDP and the Alliance to flourish. This depended, as Owen argued, on the ability of the Alliance to improve its identity. The floating vote was not just waiting to fling its support to the Alliance. As Crewe and Sarlvik asserted, 'British electors nowadays might be more detachable but they are also easily re-attachable.'[25] Indeed, the risk of a Labour victory could see a return of the disaffected Conservative vote, and heightened electoral prospects for Kinnock could see a return of disillusioned Labour voters. Both major parties would thus gain. This was nearly true. In many ways the factors that were crucial for the success of the SDP were intertwined with each other. It was important to have PR but the likelihood of getting it required that they beat the electoral system at its own game. No better way to do that than to present a united Alliance. Similarly, threats to the Alliance were caused by the frustrations with the system itself. The likelihood of success could only be strengthened by the right political atmosphere. But even that offered no guarantee unless the Alliance was able to capitalise on it. It is important, argued Owen, that the SDP acknowledged the reality of its dilemma.[26] The plight of a third party or even fourth party involved many interlocking factors. An understanding of this fact and an establishment of strategies to overcome them would bring the SDP much closer to achieving its goal. Here, though, basic errors of judgement were made by the leaders of the SDP and Liberal Party respectively. Neither party leader could agree on whether Kinnock or Thatcher was the real enemy. It is now clear that in the run-up to 1987 the Alliance was not within an ace of breaking the mould of British politics. Almost all the evidence shows that the mould had only been cracked. The SDP's aim to break the mould of class-based politics was curiously enough largely discredited by its own membership which was and has resolutely remained overwhelmingly middle-class. More importantly, the SDP's efforts to break through the two-party system had been destroyed by the realisation that in order to break the mould it had to achieve victory from within it, but after 1983 this seemed barely conceivable. Tony Cooper, the local Chairman of the SDP for the Derby constituency, where only a few years previously buoyance and optimism thrived and now fewer than fifteen members attend its monthly meeting, gave vent to this disillusionment:

> We set out to change the system, but we have to win under the old system which means being the kind of party and the kind of organisation that we entered politics to destroy.[27]

The dilemma that the SDP and the Alliance faced was that it must beat the system at its own game. Thus far it had not been able to do that. Crewe and Sarlvik blamed the party's inability to break the mould on its lack of a real electoral basis. Instead of creating a new social and ideological constituency, they saw the SDP as only having attracted, at least temporarily, part of the large volatile, potential Liberal vote which their studies reveal to have existed for years.[28] The SDP's failure in the mid-1980s to mobilise a distinctive electoral base, they say, was because its 'appeal appears to be negative and diffuse, rather than positive and specific; to be based on its leadership, style and sheer novelty rather than on policies and ideology'. As Sir Alfred Sherman argued in 1985, the hunger for fresh thinking which gave the SDP its initial opportunity had declined. He suggested in his authoritative article, 'Why the Mould is Still Intact', that the novelty and excitement of the new party allowed it to brush over the substance that counts – policy. He tellingly accused the leadership of the party of having no new and innovative ideas for solving age-old problems. He therefore implied that the SDP had only given a new name to old solutions and ideas. Unless it could obtain substance then the mould will remain intact:

> The Party's newness was taken to justify its leaders' reluctance to re-examine their own past. In their former incarnation, they had played a major part in shaping the Britain they now deplore. Unless they are willing to identify how, where, when and why they went wrong, how can they find remedies? Those who will not ask the question cannot hope to find the answers . . . If the SDP has lost the will to question received ideas and generate new ones, the demand remains. The jackpot is still there to be won.[29]

This analysis was basically right: the SDP had not produced a new radicalism; only David Owen's attempt to define the conditions of the new market economy had suggested an approach. Owen apart, the Gang of Four had nothing to offer except stale and repetitive arguments still rooted in the politics of the 1960s.

Although evidence shows that the mould has not been broken, it cannot be denied that it has been cracked. The breathtaking speed with which the SDP took off posed a definite threat to the existing order. Its formation into an alliance with the Liberals and the results of early opinions and by-elections made the old parties perk up and take notice. Although it was unable to sustain its high momentum into the election of 1983, it was able to come in second in some 316 seats, most of them in traditional Conservative strongholds. It was able to pull 25.4 per cent of the popular vote, only 2.2 per cent less than Labour.[30] The obvious injustice in the 'first-past-the-post' system caught the attention of the public, when the SDP's close showing only gave it 3.3 per cent of the seats in the House of

Commons. This achievement sent shockwaves throughout the political system: they proved to be shockwaves whose intensity soon died away as the parliamentary battle assumed its basic two-party stance, despite the best efforts of the Alliance, and of David Owen in particular, who brilliantly seized every opportunity to heighten his party's profile.[31] This inevitable preoccupation with the short-term issues, from the dramatic Westlands–Heseltine drama to the controversies associated with security and the whole question of the British economy, tended to obscure the matter of electoral reform which was at best rather a dull issue.

What were the prospects for the future of the SDP? If the Alliance was able to present itself as a united partnership bound in every way but name, and if the political atmosphere proved conducive, then taking the most optimistic view the most likely outcome was that it would force a hung parliament. Both Rodgers and Taverne somewhat incautiously predicted that Alliance would win 60–80 seats at the next election and about half of those would be SDP seats. Even if the Alliance was unable to garner that many seats, Rodgers said that success in the future would come, if we keep marching forward:

> The very fact that the Alliance has increased its membership from 23 to 60 or 80 seats will be seen as a major revolution. Even if we don't get that many and only get 40 to 50 seats, it will be seen as a major development. All we need to do is keep marching forward. And if we keep marching forward the amount of ground we actually cover is not important. The fact is that we are moving forward and I take the view that we, the Alliance, should be the government of Britain within the next 10 years.[32]

If William Rodgers's prediction was overly optimistic, as it clearly was, one thing was for sure that any long-term success that the SDP might achieve would be in large part due to the interaction between the three factors – electoral reform, an effective Alliance and a conducive political climate. The adoption of PR gives the only real hope of the centre of British politics ever actually governing. Yet by the end of 1985 electoral reform was to all intents and purposes off the political agenda. It was clear that it was now a long-term question. For whatever the outcome of the next election – whether it resulted in a Conservative victory (as it did), or a hung parliament producing either a coalition with the Tories or with Labour (though David Steel has made it plain that the Liberals would not serve under Thatcher in any circumstances) – the passing of a bill to introduce a change in the electoral system would not be given any priority. For more pressing matters would arise. The SDP in the meantime was grappling with the intricacies of Alliance politics, whose principal liability was the tension – both creative and negative – between the two Davids, who felt obliged to maintain their respective party structures as distinct and distinctive entities. The next general election was, however, swiftly approaching.

10 The Beginning of the End

After the 1987 Greenwich by-election, David Owen radiated confidence. There had been a stupendous victory for the Alliance. Rosie Barnes appeared to be tailor-made for the circumstances; telegenic, she oozed confidence and charm tempered by sound common sense. Her apparent inexperience was an asset not a handicap: she was not tainted with a past record to defend. Her market research background gave her the confidence to express the middle way in simple terms. (This was to prove less beguiling when she did a straight-to-camera party political broadcast during the general election campaign, when the thinness of her material was only too apparent.) Clearly her racy style of speaking caught the imagination not only of Greenwich, but of people elsewhere. She was catapulted overnight into national prominence, right into the central policy-making bodies of the party.[1] She accepted this allocated role as if she were born to it. It is interesting to speculate whether any of the former MPs who were now SDP members could have won that by-election with the same margin of votes. Clearly, the SDP would have won in any case because the tide was temporarily running in its favour; she alone might have been the only candidate capable of producing such a stunning result.

The Labour candidate was also tailor-made, although for Labour disastrously ill-fitting! Mrs Deirdre Wood was judged rather harshly as she clearly did represent a segment in the Labour Party which Mr Kinnock preferred to hide. There is no doubt that her political position was consistent with that held by the majority of the London regional Labour Party. She was catapulted into near-oblivion, which in the following general election was undeniably confirmed. The Conservative candidate was a worthy local councillor with city connections that did him no good since there were a number of city scandals circulating at the time. Although, of the three, he could claim to be the longest-standing resident of the area, he lived in the fashionable Blackheath end of the constituency. He was forced onto the defensive and his lack of experience and charisma led to the Conservative Party being crushed. There isn't any doubt that had he been the Conservative candidate in the general election, in a seat where the tide was running in favour of the Conservatives, he would have joined the ranks of many other run-of-the-mill Conservative

143

MPs. He was potential Thatcher cannon-fodder – a reliable foot-soldier.

Greenwich was ripe for the taking. On its riverside banks, it contained a fairly large thinking vote – young professionals, civil servants, probation officers and social workers, many of whom had been disenchanted for a long time with the simplicities and suppressed anti-democratic tendencies of the left. These included the teachers whose dispute at that time with the government benefited Rosie Barnes and did not attract them to vote Labour. In spite of the moderate and reasonable record of the previous MP, the late Guy Barnett, in what was thought to be a strong Labour seat, David Owen had every right to feel confident about Greenwich, as Woolwich and Bermondsey had already fallen to the Alliance, and once the Alliance won a seat, it seemed to hold on to it. If this pattern could be repeated nationwide, it would be sensational. The outlook was good given these indicators.

But David Owen was aware of the local factor, the 'loony left', that was delivering by-election votes to the Alliance, and he was also aware that when it came to the general election there would be regional variations, and that the Conservatives were in an extraordinarily strong position with Labour trailing in the opinion polls. He recognised that in the Labour heartlands of the North, Labour's grip would be maintained, especially in Scotland. The great opportunity for the Alliance was in the Home Counties and in the West Country. He felt that his neighbouring constituency in Plymouth should go SDP and that the Liberals, correspondingly, should do well in the West Country. On the other hand, he perceptively realised that if Labour did come back rather more strongly, this might tempt a lot of Conservative voters who had voted for the Alliance to return to the Tory fold. Furthermore, the arguments that would have to be deployed in the election campaign for the desirability of a hung parliament were perhaps too sophisticated for the man-on-the-street raised on the two-party system.

He was privately critical of the way in which the seats had been allocated between the Liberals and the SDP. The Liberals seemed to have the more likely seats while the SDP had some very tough seats to fight. He expressed himself strongly over the way in which Liberal caucuses had challenged the selection of experienced SDP candidates, even turning down any help in a local government by-election from an SDP member unless he wore a Liberal badge. All this was to augur badly for the future. It suggested that any future merger would become a takeover.

In spite of many meetings between the parliamentary and extra-parliamentary leaders of the Alliance, the strategy for the 1987 election campaign was not sharply or clearly defined. The manifesto agreed by both parties reflected this ambiguity. It was pedestrian in tone and devoid of any real contemporary theory as to what the Alliance stood for, beyond being more moderate than the Labour and Conservative parties. Nowhere was the weakness to be more evident than in the one area that should have been the Alliance's strongest point: defence policy. The cobbling-together of a defence policy based on the Anglo-French nuclear deterrent hid from the electorate the fact that the Alliance was not in agreement as to how an independent British nuclear deterrent could be maintained in the 1990s and beyond.[2] There's no doubt that David Steel's views were shaped by the need for accommodation with Liberal activists inside and outside parliamentary ranks and people such as Paddy Ashdown (the member for Yeovil, and future leader of the Social and Liberal Democrats in 1988), who had boxed themselves in in favour of solutions they knew to be absurd but which were acceptable to party activists. The hard decision on the replacement of Polaris was avoided: the Alliance was to be anything but tough on defence given the Liberal party's stance.[3]

Although David Owen opposed Trident and perhaps would have preferred keeping Polaris at least until the end of the 1990s, he was of course pragmatic, understanding that there were some circumstances in which the Alliance would have to support the retention of Trident, particularly if they found the point of no return had been reached in terms of expenditure and deployment.[4]

It was this emergence of the old politics reminiscent of the cavorting of the Labour Party that gave the opportunity to Mrs Thatcher to attack the Alliance's ramshackle defence assumptions in the early stages of the campaign. She cut through them like a knife through butter, and badly wrong-footed David Owen, whose overheated reaction merely confirmed in the eyes of the electorate his uncertainty about the real prospects of Anglo-French nuclear arrangements.[5]

The Conservatives had no difficulty in traducing the policy and ridiculing the two Davids for their trip to Paris to sell the idea to the French – who had listened with polite disdain to their fresh-found enthusiasm for a second centre of deterrence to be held in trust for Europe. The French were quick to point out that any new arrangement that didn't include the Germans in at least accepting this policy would be doomed. Mrs Thatcher had no difficulty in identifying the Alliance as therefore being opposed to the necessary modernisation of Britain's nuclear deterrent, and she plausibly claimed that it was only the Conservative Party that was unambiguously in favour of an independent British nuclear deterrent even if it was based on an American system and technology. If defence was a disaster area for Labour it was also a real problem for the Alliance because the policy appeared to be a fudge. This impression was reinforced by the Alliance's joint commission's report on defence published just before the election which added to the literature of observations on the subject. The SDP's John Roper, a former Labour MP, who defended the document, must have felt that he was on familiar ground.[6]

The two Davids were clearly not comfortable with each other; both felt constrained by the other's presence. They therefore came across in television appearances as Tweedledum and Tweedledee, united by only the lowest common denominator. This damaged David Steel less because that was what was expected of a Liberal leader, but damaged David Owen more because he had built up an extraordinary reputation in a short time from a narrow political base, and was then the most significant political figure apart from the Prime Minister herself. Clear, incisive, aggressive and with little humour, he had a cutting edge which the electors warmed to. He had also had the advantage of being able to arouse seething anger from his former Labour colleagues, which helped to define his position in exactly the way that was required. This terrific advantage was thrown away by the two-leader approach. It minimalised the effect of both of them. The election campaign was dogged throughout with differences of opinion between David Owen and his campaign advisers, particularly on the Liberal side where his appeal to Conservative voters created a deal of distrust and scepticism.

We know enough from the material published following the election (particularly the commentary written by the former Liberal president, Des Wilson, who has provided us with a blow-by-blow account of the arguments over which party the Alliance would favour in a hung parliament) to leave the firm impression that the Liberal end of the Alliance favoured some kind of deal with Neil Kinnock in the vain hope at that time that he would espouse PR and abandon his unilateralist defence policy. Mr Kinnock in fact rejected the former and continued strongly to espouse the latter: this stance was unlikely to fundamentally change in the future (despite his more ambiguous statement on BBC TV in 1988 in which he appeared to qualify his support for unilateral nuclear disarmament).[7]

David Owen's consistency of purpose as well as his personal resolve were largely obscured during the campaign by David Steel's ill-judged preference for a possible deal with Labour if the electorate opted for the delights of a hung parliament. The Alliance in fact could not decide whether it wanted to achieve outright power or seek to hold the balance in the new parliament. However neither David actually appeared to know which outcome his party either expected or preferred.

Looking back at the election campaign and considering these contradictions, the Alliance campaign was not all bad. It lacked passion and eloquence but nevertheless maintained a degree of momentum which could have carried the Alliance further in its election quest had it not been for the Labour leaders' skilful public relations packaged campaign which so worried Mrs Thatcher. Doubts began to be raised in Tory central office halfway through the campaign as to whether it was wise to have blunted the Alliance campaign so early on, thus giving Labour a real chance to recover and present a genuine threat to Mrs Thatcher's majority. But, in fact, as Labour's prospects improved, so did the anxiety of the electorate, who now began to fear the return to parliament of the most extreme Labour government since the party was established seventy-five years before.

We need not spend time analysing any further the reason why, faced with this prospect, the electorate voted in its droves – many people with a heavy heart – for Mrs Thatcher. Tory central office was vindicated. Norman Tebbit had been correct early on in setting out to destroy the Alliance, and it's not too difficult to see how on all the major issues the Alliance gave him the openings for his many attacks and challenges on where the Alliance stood in terms of economic and social policies. Unfortunately, the Alliance was unable to project many of its excellent policies into the campaign at all. The rational approach lacked the passion and conviction of the two parties, whose differences were as wide as they had ever been in living memory.

In spite of this, David Owen, with a weak hand, still managed to dominate the campaign. This led to a lot of criticism from those who were not given the opportunity to shine so brightly; Roy Jenkins and Shirley Williams came across very well but their views were somehow reminiscent of the politics of the 1960s. Roy Jenkins in particular had a problem, as the Tories heaped much of the blame for the permissive society on him. Perhaps the Alliance should have allowed Shirley Williams a bigger share, instead of William Wallace who came across as well-intentioned and well-informed but below the standard normally required of a front-bench spokesman. (Mrs Williams displayed her charms in Cambridge against a strong Labour challenge and an even more formidable threat from the sitting member, the Tory Robert Rhodes-James.)

All this was to lead to the belief that the performance would have been better under one leader and indeed one united party. Therefore, before the election was over, David Steel had resolved to face this problem by working for an early merger of the two disparate parties.

This idea was not mistaken in principle: it was, in the event, badly executed, however. It resulted in the personal negation of David Owen, who was the one politician capable of providing the merged party with the kind of co-ordination it might well require. The merger proposal also appeared as a device to eliminate David Owen as a national politician; some old scores were settled. Was there more than a scintilla of a desire here to remove him from his leadership role and to deny him his natural stage? David Steel appeared to regard his former co-leader of the Alliance as the real impediment to the achievement of parliamentary power. David Steel also came to regard Owen as a threat to the realignment of the centre. His conviction grew that a merger between the two parties would resolve both issues by removing Owen and the SDP from contention.

It was clear that preparations for this event had been made prior to the election. Indeed, on the Wednesday before polling day, Dick Newby, a senior official at SDP headquarters, a leading figure in the election campaign and close to the Liberals, rang David Sainsbury to enquire whether he could rely on David Sainsbury's support for a merger after the election. This was an error on his part, as David Sainsbury refused point-blank and relayed the conversation to David Owen.

At that time also, the members of the election campaign committee, including John Pardoe, John Harris and Dick Newby, actually sat down and discussed the fact that a merger was inevitable. David Owen had known for a long time that they had been discussing having a merged party with Shirley Williams as the leader.

While Dick Newby's phonecall to David Sainsbury was more than a little surprising, David Steel's move didn't come as a surprise except in the manner in which it was done.

It appears that Paddy Ashdown made a speech calling for a merger immediately after the election on 11 June, which was little noticed except by David Steel, whose aides encouraged *The Observer* to give it prominence that Sunday. Thus, on 14 June 1987 David Steel was forced into calling for a merger by his own people.[8]

On the Saturday, Roy Jenkins came out in favour of a merger, which was entirely in line with his long-held belief that this was inevitable and desirable. Then on the Monday, both Shirley Williams and Bill Rodgers came out in favour of the merger, too. David Owen had talked to Shirley Williams on the Saturday and they had agreed to discuss the matter in the National Committee – something David Owen had decided should happen before the election – and that it would have to go to a members' ballot and couldn't be decided by the Council for Social Democracy. Shirley Williams proposed to David Owen that there should be a discussion in the CSD to get the backing for a ballot. David Owen was agreeable to this process.

However, on the Monday, 15 June, Shirley Williams proposed a form of words which David Owen found unacceptable. He did not participate much in the National Committee meeting held that day.

Also that day, David Steel rang David Owen to say that he was putting out a memo which he wanted David Owen to see before it went out to his colleagues. This telephone call was immediately followed by one from Chris Moncrieff of the Press Association, who wanted David Owen's comments on this memo before he had even seen it!

David Owen's document that was put out on the Wednesday following the election called for an 'amicable settlement'.[9] He argued that since the issue of merger had been with the SDP for so long and was leading to a split within the party, that a ballot of the members should be held. Those members that wished to merge would not be obliged to merge if they didn't agree with the negotiated terms. At the time, David Owen claims, all four of the MPs were against this, as the suggestion implied the party was irrevocably split – something they refused to accept at that stage.

Option One, of which Bob Maclennan was the architect, proposed evolving together under an over-arching constitutional framework; however, David Steel brutally rejected that option in favour of a choice of merger or bust. At this time it was hoped that David Owen could remain leader of the party, but when asked at a fringe meeting whether he was prepared to continue as leader, Owen declared that there would have to be a movement from the grass roots of the party.

Following this meeting the Grass Roots Uprising campaign was founded.

In the event Bob Maclennan was a reluctant candidate for the leadership, since he was in favour of the option for the parties to evolve together gradually and, as the draughtsman of the SDP's constitution and a lawyer, looked for a constitutional resolution regarding the merging of the parties in a kind of federal constitutional framework. He appeared on television arguing against Russell Johnson, the Liberal MP, who was in favour of merger. He was surprised when Charles Kennedy, his protégé, came out in favour of joining a merged party. Since he was the senior of the two pro-merger MPs he felt obliged to take on the leadership. He did.

He is fiercely objective about himself, openly recognising that he doesn't have the necessary extrovert personality and charisma of a leader. He is self-effacing and an intellectual who is neither an abstract theoriser nor a word-spinner, but a softly spoken Scottish lawyer who speaks with great accuracy, occasionally displaying a dry sense of humour. He is sensitive but tough-minded, a man of few illusions about politics or himself. As a junior minister, he was in the Department of Consumer Affairs answering adjournment debates with great patience and detail.

At parliamentary question time he could always be relied upon never to sparkle. His quiet manner often led him to be ridiculed by his fellow Scottish Labour MPs known for their backbiting. However, as an administrator he was strong, and had his admirers in the civil service. He is a man who is clearly not afraid to take risks, and this quality was recognised by the SDP Conference in September 1987 when his first speech as leader was extremely well received, having the right mixture of toughness and flexibility in his approach to the Liberals. His speech was rather better received than that of the veteran Roy Jenkins when he admitted that he regretted perhaps not intervening as elder statesman on the whole question of merger immediately following the general election, which could have prevented the debate being conducted in such a destructive manner. A number of delegates indicated that they thought that Roy Jenkins was one of the sources of the problem, whereas Bob Maclennan's hands were completely clean. Bob Maclennan's patent honesty of purpose appealed to the delegates, most of whom were sick and tired of the sectarianism and emotionalism displayed by Shirley Williams and other members of the Gang of Four, including David Owen. As leader, he addressed himself boldly and thoughtfully to issues which a leader of a party is expected to have views on.

Unlike his fellow Scotsman, David Steel, who possessed a lucid mind but perhaps lacking depth, the reverse is true of Bob Maclennan.

The negotiating team on the SDP side was composed of Bob Maclennan, Frances David, William Goodhart, Lindsay Granshaw, John Grant, Charles Kennedy MP, Clive Lindley, Dickson Mabon, Jane Padget, Anne Sofer, John Strak, Ian Wrigglesworth, Shirley Williams, Will Fitzgerald, Tom McNally, Ben Stoneham and Dick Newby. For the Liberals, Alan Beith, Tim Clement-Jones, Andrew Ellis, Philip Goldenberg, Tony Greaves, Gwyn Griffiths, Peter Knowlson, John Macdonald, Christopher Mason, Michael Meadowcroft, Rachael Pitchford, Adrian Slade, Andrew Stunell, Donald Crook, Des Wilson and Jim Wallace, and was led nominally by David Steel. Bob Maclennan kept a sharp eye on the negotiations and played a major part in the detail throughout, no doubt always looking over his shoulder in anticipation of what David Owen might think of the package when it was completed. David Steel, never a man to concern himself with detail, kept himself aloof from the process, even finding time to travel abroad, giving the impression he was bored with the whole business, and this was later confirmed when he joined Bob Maclennan for the final drafting of the policy statement.

The joint document *Voices and Choices* which was later to receive the rebuff of the entire parliamentary Liberal Party, was drafted under the leadership of Bob Maclennan with the detailed work undertaken by Hugo Dixon, the former *Financial Times* journalist, and the policy analysis provided by Andrew Gilmour. It was Alan Beith who had the watching brief for the Liberals, overseeing the broad sweep of policy as well as the detail. Throughout the process, specialists from both parties were kept informed by telephone, almost as it was being compiled. The weakness of this arrangement was that they were only informed about policy ideas when they fell in their area of specialism, because both leaders were of the opinion that the document as a whole should not be leaked, which would dampen the impact of the launch. Well, this did not in the event turn out to be much of a problem. Curiously, the Liberal spokesmen did make objections about the passages that they thought would be unacceptable, but the overall document was not made available for their inspection until the penultimate day of the negotiations. In true

Liberal party tradition, few actually read the document, presumably thinking that their earlier drafting criticisms had been assimilated. However, the Liberals do not appear to have been involved in the detail of the policy document, so it is true to say it was very much a Bob Maclennan statement, characteristically straightforward and presented without fudge. Mr Maclennan's courage was admirable: people of both parties were very impressed with his performance during this difficult period.

The final document contained controversial proposals for the means-testing of child benefit, extending VAT to children's clothes and food, and indicated strong support for the continuation of the British independent nuclear deterrent and the commitment to NATO. The policy statement, together with the preamble to the joint constitution, reflected social democratic principles at the expense of what has been up until now a Liberal approach to policy.

This, however, didn't prevent David Owen's allies from attacking the draft as an activist constitution rather than one for ordinary members. Danny Finkelstein, a youth member of the party's National Committee, in a circular addressed to young members of the SDP said that the balance of the draft differed significantly from the SDP's constitution. For example, there was an important shift towards activist power in the selection of parliamentary candidates because ballot papers would only be given to members who attended selection meetings or who made a specific request for them, whereas SDP members are entitled automatically to receive ballot papers. Secondly, the draft gave 'massive power to interest groups' which he presumably felt would include all the Liberal-related fringe bodies like the Greens that would have votes in the conference. Thirdly, he claimed, the 'vastly increased powers' being proposed for the annual conference 'that led to poor Liberal party decisions in the past are embodied, albeit in a slightly different form, in the merged constitution'.[10]

What is surprising is the curious way in which David Steel dealt with this episode. After all, it was he who proposed the merger negotiations after the general election and now he appeared not to apply fully his mind either to the tone or flavour of the statement or to the policy details, although he readily signed it and equally as readily repudiated it when he was rebuffed by his parliamentary colleagues. Mr Steel was in an unenviable position when challenged by his colleagues who were not known for either their consistency or loyalty.

Bob Maclennan's approach was, from the beginning, serious, meticulous and thoughtful, his quiet manner hiding an intellectual toughness and rigour sharpened by his lawyer's training. There could not have been two more contasting approaches.

Bob Maclennan had every right to be aggrieved by the reaction to the document since it clearly had his personal imprint and presumably represented his credo. He had taken a close look at his Liberal colleagues and discovered that his worst fears were fully justified. The fact that the policy statement had to be so detailed was a measure of the distrust between the two negotiating parties; however, it must have been difficult for Bob Maclennan to accept that the policy statement was now politically dead and to concede that new negotiations should be undertaken. It must have been even more difficult to stomach what Edmond Dell, from the SDP's side, and Des Wilson, from the Liberal side, produced in the end: a bland document.[11]

It perhaps would have been better not to have had a statement at all, or to have had just the constitution, a document which is difficult to fault from the SDP point of view as it contained more SDP philosophy and ideas about how the party should be organised and run than the Liberal philosophy and ideas about organisation.

However, whichever way you look at it, it was a humiliating climbdown for Bob Maclennan who had to accept it for what he considered to be the greater good of the party. When he first saw the agreed statement, he apparently thought of rejecting it, and according to the account by John Grant in *The Observer*, which he has not challenged, it does appear that Bob Maclennan changed his mind within perhaps one hour, finally describing the document as 'magnificent'. Clearly the success of the constitution was enough to make up for the disappointment of the second policy statement, and yet it was really a triumph of technique over purpose.[12]

Following the Sheffield conference (discussed later), in late January 1988, the membership of both parties was sent statements by both the pro- and the anti-merger groups together with the constitution of the SLD. The ballot, which took place in March 1988, was what really amounts to a sad end to the high hopes of 1981, as far as the SDP was concerned, and marked the ostensible end of the Liberal Party as it had been for the last century. The original SDP was dead: the new SLDP was about to emerge into a hostile world.

It was apparent that the Liberal Party would become the senior partner, and therefore the SLD was likely to be seen as a continuation of the Liberal Party. As David Steel made clear, many of the Liberals would call themselves Liberal social democrats and the party might be dominated by Liberal activists who could alienate the SDP element. Of course, whilst David Steel had no wish to isolate former SDP members who opted to join the new merged party, he was naturally more concerned that the totally unavoidable relegation of the word Liberal threatened to alienate the Liberal majority in the newly formed party.

Of the 100 000 Liberals, only 52 per cent voted at all in the ballot; 87.9 per cent voted in favour, 12.1 per cent voted against, and there were 126 abstentions. Of the 59 000 members of the SDP, 55 per cent voted; 65.3 per cent voted in favour, while 34 per cent voted against; there were 125 abstentions and 132 spoilt papers.[13]

This result was interpreted by political commentators as a merger without passion or strong commitment.

An outstanding issue remained: who was going to lead the new party? The certainty was that it would not be Robert Maclennan nor in all probability David Steel.

It was significant that in 1988 the contest was between two former Liberals. This confirmed the impression that the merger between the two parties amounted to a takeover by the Liberals of the SDP.

The merged party was divided over whether to seek to form coalitions with Labour in the future because of the leadership's increasing dislike and distaste for what had become known as Thatcherism. It was not only Thatcherite policies but a personal dislike for Mrs Thatcher and her obvious lack of respect for the moderate centre that fuelled these feelings.

Any electoral pact in the future between the SLD and the continuing SDP will be made all the more difficult by the open conflict that has arisen since the call for merger by David Steel. It remains to be seen whether this conflict will be resolved.

David Steel and the Liberals have achieved what they set out to do, which was to isolate David Owen from Roy Jenkins and Shirley Williams taking the majority of the Liberals and a sizeable number of the SDP with them.

What was apparent was how far the Gang of Four became incompatible with each other. Roy Jenkins, the elder statesman of the four, brought with him to the SDP a parliamentary career of distinction, having been a reasonable Home Secretary and an outstanding Chancellor of the Exchequer, and although he was a disappointment as President of the European Commission, there is no doubt he is the intellectual heavyweight of the original Gang of Four. But he had a fundamental flaw, which in the age of television politics proved to be his great handicap: despite having outstanding parliamentary powers of eloquence, he never had an effective platform manner outside the House of Commons, and was handicapped too by the judgement of some of his closest advisers which on occasions influenced him to make unwise decisions. Personally, he is warm, generous and loyal to his friends to a fault, and when replaced by David Owen, accepted the situation with grace. His criticism of the style of David Owen's leadership became more apparent when there were clashes over presentation and policy between Shirley Williams, the President, and Bill Rodgers the Vice President.

Bill Rodgers's track record, in the Labour Party, of fighting the left was second to none; he was a seasoned campaigner long before David Owen was elected to parliament. He was general secretary of the Fabian society and the organising genius behind the campaign for social democracy which was the praetorian guard of the late Hugh Gaitskell. He has a good brain but is a dour, sound speaker. His performances never fell below or rose above a certain standard.

He must have been disappointed by the meteoric rise of David Owen into the Cabinet as Foreign Secretary, particularly since he had long been interested in the area of defence and had emerged as a specialist himself. Losing his seat was a tremendous blow to him and to the party. It had the effect of making him less emollient and gradually more hostile towards David Owen's autocratic leadership. He was a disappointed man who possibly felt himself to be a failure.

However, it was Shirley Williams who was to prove the most difficult of colleagues (see Chapter 11). She had been seen as the golden girl of the Labour Party: personable, sincere and passionate, a convert to Roman Catholicism who could inspire audiences and loyalty from party supporters. Her personality allowed her to make more than her fair share of mistakes and still be forgiven. She has the quality of being able to give the impression to whomsoever she speaks that they are the most important person in the room. Her obvious sincerity gained her many admirers: she was often compared with Mrs Thatcher, whose hectoring manner she never sought to emulate. As one colleague remarked: 'Who would you prefer to sit next to at a dinner party – Shirley or Margaret?' He was himself in no doubt about whom he would prefer!

The Sheffield Conference of the Council for Social Democracy which met on 30 January 1988 marked the end of the original SDP. The conference was held in the Octagon building of the University of Sheffield. The feelings between the pro-mergerites and the anti-mergerites were so intense that weekend that the two groups had their own separate hotels which they used as their headquarters. The tension between the two groups was about to explode into violent controversy.

The night before the conference there was a public argument between Shirley Williams and Mike Thomas about the use of the hall by the Campaign for Social Democracy, after which the Campaign for Social Democracy threatened legal proceedings. This set the tone for the conference.

The conference itself had all the depressing flavour of the old-style politics. The personal animosity expressed was just what characterised Labour Party conferences, and what was alarming and supremely disappointing for the observer was that these feelings of bitterness between colleagues became more important than the merits of the arguments. The Gang of Four were now engaged in gang warfare with no holds barred.

The conference was pure theatre, with a standard of debating no higher than that of most party conferences which become disfigured by personal animus.

Dr David Owen and his anti-merger supporters, including Rosie Barnes and John Cartwright, boycotted the conference; only John Cartwright the Vice-President spoke from the floor putting the case against merger in reply to Roy Jenkins.[14]

The debate was unenlightened and acrimonious. Even Roy Jenkins who is normally balanced and urbane was bitter and confused, and as a result was barracked by a good section of the conference.

It seemed that the main reason for merging for most of the delegates was to defeat Mrs Thatcher's government. A merged party, in the view of most delegates, stood a better chance of defeating the government than the parties would separately. In other words, the new merged party would seek to define itself in relation to Thatcherism. The original principles or philosophies of the individual parties and their *raison d'être* seemed to be of less relevance. In fact it was unclear what the new party would really stand for, and there was the danger that it would become a party of and for the extremists of the centre.

The result of the vote was conclusive for the pro-mergerites: 273

voted for merger, 28 voted against and 49 abstained. However, 443 council members were registered to vote and 93 members were absent from the conference.

It remains unanswered as to how many of those 93 were acting on David Owen's advice to boycott the conference so that the merger could go through unblocked. Among those who voted against the merger, there was the feeling that Owen and his supporters should not have boycotted the conference and should have actively fought against the merger.

The SDP of 1981 was effectively killed in 1988. Will its successor succeed where the original party failed? Dr David Owen remains confident. Why?

Well, he has constantly reiterated that since the 1950s voting behaviour in Britain has changed radically. We have witnessed the breakup of the traditional vote and rigid party loyalties. Whereas thirty years ago the working class nearly always voted Labour, now we find that about 40 per cent of trade-unionists vote Conservative. Similarly, the professional classes cannot be counted upon now to vote Conservative, unlike thirty years ago. Teachers, social workers and civil servants have tended to vote Labour. In addition to this, rather than voting for one party all their lives, people are now likely to vote for different parties. So fluidity in the class system has given rise to new and often shifting political loyalties.

Regional factors and the effect of the television age have influenced voting behaviour. The political party has declined while the importance of the political personality has increased.

Another trend of the last twenty years or so is the growth of populism, fuelled by single issue pressure groups and opinion polling.

We no longer think in terms of the ideologues' blueprints of perfect policies for the perfect society but have a more pragmatic approach to policy-making for the imperfect world. Politics has nonetheless become more ideological and less pragmatically based in the UK since the Conservative victory of 1979. Paradoxically, it was in these circumstances that Thatcherism found such fertile ground, appealing to self-interest, and self-reliance at the expense of collective provision, by the state.

However, the new leader of the SLDP, Mr Paddy Ashdown, will try to produce policies that will appeal to disillusioned former Labour Party voters. This will require him to try and occupy the centre-left ground, and as a matter of tactics he will concentrate on Mrs Thatcher and her policies in relation to social and welfare provisions, intellectually defending the Beveridge principle of universal provision. Since Beveridge himself was a lifelong Liberal, clearly there is a historic logic which will give the party the opportunity to create the impression that it is the caring party, and claim the welfare state to be a creation of the Asquith/Lloyd George administration before the First World War. The SLDP will accept those aspects of the so-called enterprise philosophy so strongly emphasised by the three Thatcher administrations, which have forced the trade unions to accept new work practices and British industry, particularly the Confederation of British Industry (CBI), to be more in favour of competition and presumably attack head-on the belief that it's only the aggressive entrepreneur in industry and commerce that must be nurtured, even if it is at the expense of the less successful.

Since the Labour Party will be shifting its policy in the same direction, the SLDP will need to develop something distinctive or at least appear to be saying something different from the Labour Party if it is to survive. The new party soon to be popularly called the Democrats prepared for an election contest once it was clear that David Steel had decided against standing for the leadership. Mr Steel only remained leader for a short period: he was replaced by Paddy Ashdown who has the necessary charisma for television and is an engaging speaker but who lacks experience and probably depth.

Clearly if David Owen had adopted different tactics he would now be leader of the SLDP, but the resentment this would have caused among many leading Liberals and grass-roots supporters on the Liberal side of the new party, keen to push 'Green policy' with its anti-nuclear philosophy, would eventually have divided the party anyway.

The original SDP is dead: long live the SDP. It may yet have an important if marginal role to play in British politics in the mid-to-late 1990s.

Th extremists of the centre can still be saved from their own folly by the example of the loyalist SDP under David Owen. It would be a disaster for British politics if the dissident radical elements of the Liberals did to the SLD what the Militant Tendency has done to the image of the Labour Party. The parallel is striking: but is it entirely valid? Evidence suggests that such a parallel is overdrawn and exaggerated. There could be a realignment or even convergence between the newly formed SLD and the born-again SDP in the mid-to-late 1990s. Labour is, however, certain to continue its long decline which the 1988 leadership struggle confirmed. Mr Tony

Benn's bid for the party leadership damaged Labour only slightly less than his attempt to defeat Denis Healey's candidature for the deputy leadership in the early 1980s. The emergence of Paddy Ashdown, as the first leader of the SLDP initially, however, gave a lift to the flagging fortunes of the centre. But the law of diminishing returns ensured that the SLDP's rise was short-lived. For unless and until it comes to terms with David Owen's Social Democratic Party the future for the centre looks increasingly bleak.

11 From Alliance to Misalliance?

As the late T. E. Uttley wrote in *The Times* on 26 January 1988 in a piece entitled 'This Unattractive Alliance' with reference to the then on–off Liberal-SDP negotiations for a merger:

> It is the Alliance which stands out as representing the highest degree of cultural homogeneity in British politics. Nor is the homogeneity purely cultural; the Alliance, in respect of its leading figures, is a predominantly professional middle-class party.
>
> In the absence of the 'unifying single issue' which will make an impact on a large and widely distributed enough section of the electorate, what can these poor people now do? Well, like Asquith, they can 'wait and see'.
>
> It is still possible that with some conjunction of events – something which put the Thatcher ascendancy in danger or a degree of listening on the part of Mr Kinnock which destroyed the Labour Party – they might find themselves in a position to extort from a minority government a radical measure of electoral reform. That, most assuredly, would change the face of British politics.[1]

'The SLD and SDP both possess a vested interest in electoral reform but in order to achieve it a *modus vivendi* between the respective party leaders must be achieved if success at the polls is to be guaranteed.' Electoral reform can only come after electoral success by both parties as measured in the popular vote and in the number of seats won.

The continuing viability of the SDP is therefore a prior condition for the electoral success of the SLDP itself at the next general election. In the words of David Sainsbury and Leslie Murphy (both Trustees of the Social Democratic Party), the new party (SLDP):

> would lack the coherent and realistic policies which have evolved inside the SDP. It was generally accepted that the manifesto for the last general election lacked conviction because these policies had to be watered down to reach a compromise within the Alliance. One of the strengths of the SDP in recent years, and one of the things that has made it an exciting political force, is the fact that David

Owen had pushed the party into confronting difficult decisions and into looking for new solutions. Thus the SDP has moved from a position of opposing any change to the boundary between the public and private sector, to one where the main criterion for judging proposals for privatization is the scope for introducing competition and consumer choice.[2]

It is obvious that strong and principled leadership in Britain counts for something, as Mrs Thatcher has shown. Dr David Owen is therefore probably the only real alternative national leader to Mrs Thatcher, but as Brian Walden contends:

Owen is not a Thatcherite, simply a man who understands the moving forces in present society and knows that they cannot be reversed by nostalgia, sentimentality or snobbery. He occupies one of the three honest positions in British politics. The other two are taken by the prime minister and the Marxist left.

To write off Owen is to suppose that the British people are dolts who cannot tell a hawk from a handsaw. Are they really going to swallow the yarn that the Labour party has an enthusiastic belief in private ownership? Or that the Social and Liberal Democratic party has discovered a formula for bringing back Lord Keynes, Shirley Temple, and happy communities dancing round the village maypole?

Owen's strategy should be based upon a recognition of the good sense of the British voter. He must give up these tactical ruminations about pacts and deals. They sound sordid and are incomprehensible to ordinary voters. The role that awaits him is that of moral spokesman for the new society.

He should say what he thinks about every issue of the day without worrying about where he stands on the political spectrum. Voters are not interested in what is left, right or centre. They desire a truthful voice that gives their lives a moral dimension.

They want an analysis which squares with their experience. What that means is that though they want fearless criticism of our social and economic failings, they also want an acknowledgement that, for most people, Britain is a better place to live in than it has ever been before.

The truth is odious to all reactionaries. If he proclaims this loud and clear, Owen need fear neither obscurity nor rejection.[3]

The crucial point is that the traditions as well as the attitudes and ethos of the old Liberal Party and the SDP brought to the alliance differing perspectives which served it well. As David Owen himself wrote:

> Without the SDP the Alliance would never have been able to maintain the policy stance that we did over the Falklands, over the miners' dispute, over the right-to-buy council house legislation, over the market economy, over the Prevention of Terrorism Act, over deployment of cruise missiles that has led to the imminent INF agreement, over the integration of tax and social security and over maintaining the minimum deterrent. There are a host of other policy areas where the SDP voice has been crucial.[4]

None of this would have been possible but for David Owen's dominant influence. As John Grigg rightly observed *vis-à-vis* David Owen:

> Politically he appeals, as Eden did, to the middle ground, and he has acquired a reputation for moral courage at least equally well deserved. But he may also share the streak of vanity, and the tendency to monomania, which in the end were Eden's undoing.
>
> As a minister he showed decisiveness and imagination, though his achievements were limited by the relatively short time he spent in each post. In official quarters, however, and more especially in the Foreign Office, there was considerable muttering about his arrogance. Some of this may have been due to resentment of a young man with a mind of his own; but not all.
>
> His contribution to the reshaping of British politics since 1981 has been brilliant in many ways, but also bedevilled by his obsessive attitude to the Liberals, which in turn has been complicated, if not caused, by his rather tortured relationship with Roy Jenkins (another expatriate Welshman).[5]

This alleged obsession with the Liberals led, of course, to David Owen's resignation as leader of the old SDP after members had voted for a closer-than-expected 57 per cent to 43 to reject his advice and open merger talks with Liberals in August 1987. Having declared, when the SDP was formed in 1981, that it would be 'the most democratic party', Dr Owen felt he had little choice but to stand down as leader after four years when the result of the ballot of its 58 500 members was declared early in 1988.

'The members have decided, as they have every right to do, to seek a merger with the Liberals against my advice and, in the circumstances, I do not believe I should continue as their leader during the period of the negotiation,' he said in a statement.[6]

Dr Owen at first left the impression that he was simply putting his leadership in cold storage and might reactivate it if a second ballot in February rejected the merger terms.   .

But as the days wore on, it became clear that he was now setting his sights on leading a 'Mark II SDP' comprising all those party members he could persuade to hold on to the faith – working if possible in alliance with the merged party.

Mr Steel voiced regret that Dr Owen was setting off into the 'semi-wilderness' when he could have helped shape a more effective third force. Yet David Steel was determined that in no circumstances should Owen lead that third force.

Dr Owen, however, pressed ahead with keeping the rump of the SDP intact, but came under strong attack from those once very close to him for his negative attitude towards the Liberals. They feared he was heading for the wilderness. According to Peter Jenkins there was not enough scope for a fourth party in the British two-party system:

> The Owenite claim to be the exponents of a 'new politics' is nonsense. There is no possibility of practising 'multi-party politics' under the British system.
>
> The claim to be the one true voice of social democracy is also bogus. Social democracy is not a sectarian creed. It is a broad approach to politics, one shared by some in the Labour Party and more in the Liberal Party. The Liberals may be unsound on defence, maverick in other respects, but the decision was to see what could be done in uniting the two parties. Those who do not like the result must shop elsewhere.
>
> Dr Owen has no title to the SDP. The result of the ballot cannot reasonably be construed as a vote for 'amicable separation'. SDP members were asked whether they favoured the idea of merger or not and a majority said they did. They were not asked if they would support Dr Owen splitting the party to set up one of his own.
>
> He hasn't a leg to stand on in his bunker. But there he is, surrounded by a last-ditch entourage, inventing new schemes for the confounding of his enemies and moving imaginary armies on the map. The bitterness of defeat seems to have got the better of his judgement. The virtuoso one-man band performance which in the last parliament made him the most impressive politician in the

country after Margaret Thatcher has degenerated into a display of megalomania.[7]

Dismissive words indeed from a man married to a leading light in the SDP, Ms Polly Toynbee, *Guardian* writer and SDP candidate.

However, in maintaining the new SDP Owen elected to bide his time, in the expectation that the newly formed SLDP would soon vacate the middle ground and opt for a deal with Labour in a bid to construct an anti-Thatcherite coalition. Then in those more propitious circumstances the loyalist SDP could step forward to seize the middle ground. This approach was not deemed to be mere opportunism but a clear challenge, for, as *The Times* editorialised on 31 August 1987:

> Social democracy – though originally a term to denote a species of Marxist – has shown itself throughout post-war Europe to be a position distinct from Liberalism. Its heyday was reached in the West Germany of Herr Helmut Schmidt, whose party went into a coalition with the country's Liberals – not into a merger with them. It is perfectly reasonable for Dr Owen to want to hold on to the title.
>
> Some of the reviews of Dr Owen's recent book of interviews with Mr Kenneth Harris have tried to make out that there are no great differences of principle involved in the merger, and that all the trouble is caused by Dr Owen's notorious vanity. The most entertaining and abusive of these reviews, in the current London Review of Books, is by Mr Richard Holme – a close associate of Mr David Steel. There speak men who do not really believe that, say, keeping Britain a nuclear power, like France, at a time when American nuclear protection is steadily being withdrawn from Europe, is a real issue of principle. For that reason alone, it would be a good thing if Dr Owen – against all the present odds – manages to remain a force in British politics, whatever he and his followers have to call themselves.[8]

But as David Owen made clear at the SDP Conference in Sheffield in February 1988, where the party finally voted in favour of merger by a decisive majority, the SDP could still be seen as closer to the heartbeat of the nation than any other political party:

> We did not risk all in 1981 to create this party, to sustain this party, to carry its banner, to win seats in Parliament and in the council chamber in the name of this party only to see it dismembered.[9]

He was pretty certain that a majority of SDP members, of their own free will, would decide to remain members of the party. Thousands of people who had never been SDP members had said that they wanted to join the party. 'But they want the clarity, the consistency, the conviction of the SDP, which will continue.'[10]

An amazing start had been made. Well over 20,000 people were now committed to continue the SDP. 'We will need many thousands more. We who love this party will not be forced into a loveless marriage. We will not be told "There is no alternative". We resented the cry that it was merger or bust. Friends are parting company. But one can differ in politics without committing hara kiri. You may be quite clear that the SDP is and will remain an independent party but we shall always be ready to work with like-minded politicians in all parties.

There is no need to cut each others' throats, no need to fuel a family feud. We should go our separate ways, respecting, but not exaggerating our differences, and ready, one day, perhaps when wiser counsel prevails, to work, although in a different way, with former friends and colleagues.[11]

Sensible partnerships would continue to be established at grassroots. It would be done by people who championed the politics of proportional representation.

David Owen had listened that day to the personal comments, the gladiatorial language, the antagonistic and adversarial politics which he thought they had all put behind them.

'Let it be clear. The SDP will neither provoke, nor shirk a fight. We will remain what we are – a national party.

If need be, we are prepared to fight every seat at the next election. We are not fools. We know that it would be wiser for a different counsel to prevail, but if it does not, no one should doubt our resolve or our commitment.

After what we have done to ourselves over the past few months, we cannot expect to scale those heady heights until all of us earn again the trust of the British people. It will not be easy, but I predict that the day will come when the SDP is seen to be closer to the heartbeat of this nation than any other political party.'

In 1985 the party's message had been clear. There had been no equivocation about the need for conventional and nuclear disarmament. Dr David Owen concluded: 'We can return to those days.'[12]

This speech can, of course, be dismissed as conference rhetoric, but it was entirely conceivable that by 1990–1 the SDP could once again become the second pillar within a reconstituted alliance. And yet as *The Times* suggested in its leader the next day:

> The New Social and Liberal Democrats clearly hold the electoral advantage however. They benefit from the Liberal grass roots organization, its flair for local issues and the harvesting of protest votes. They are also strengthened by the leaven of former Social Democrats who were schooled in the politics of power in the Labour Party. Moreover, the new party will have a more centralist constitution than that of the Liberals, even though the power over policy to be given to the elected sovereign conference could create problems for the leadership. Although principles have been fudged so far, there is at least the possibility for the merged party of a more solid edifice than the Liberals had built on their own. [13]

This argument was compelling, and David Owen quickly recognised the need for an electoral deal with the SLDP once it had chosen its first leader. Such a deal would at first be ruled out by any leader of the SLDP, and indeed upon his election to the post of party leader Paddy Ashdown brutally dismissed any talk of a deal with the SDP under Dr David Owen. Yet that was only to be expected. In the fullness of time, attitudes, Owen surmised, would change. But will they? The Kensington by-election in the summer of 1988 provided a possible answer, because it was already clear that the two parties could only harm each other by splitting the vote in favour of the incumbent party, which resulted in the Conservatives holding the seat with a reduced majority. As Geoffrey Smith observed in a percipient piece in *The Times* written some four months before the by-election in Kensington:

> For both sections of the old Alliance, however, where the first by-elections come is at least as important as when. The trial of strength between them will come partly in the local government elections, partly in opinion polls, but above all in parliamentary by-elections.
>
> The SLDP will need not only to come ahead of the Owenite candidate, but also to demonstrate before the next general election that the Owenites are not strong enough to stop the SLDP capturing an otherwise winnable seat.
>
> If the Owenites could show that their intervention meant the

difference between the SLDP winning or losing in its stronger constituencies, they would be able to threaten the SLDP with the loss of most of its sitting MPs if it refused to have some kind of electoral pact.

But the strength of the Owenites is likely to vary sharply from one constituency to another. So the fortunes of the two parties may hang on whether the early contests come in seats which an Owenite candidate fought last June.[14]

The contest for the leadership of the SLDP centred less on policy than on personality. The leadership battle was keenly fought between the stolid Alan Beith MP and the somewhat meretricious Paddy Ashdown MP who apparently agreed both on substantive issues and on the fact that they had no desire to work with the remnants of the SDP.

However, the scale of Ashdown's victory over Beith was greater than either man had predicted. This could prove to be significant, because Ashdown was thought to be the candidate of those identified with a post-Liberal position which stood closest to the Owenite analysis of the political issues. Alan Beith was a Liberal; Paddy Ashdown a reconstructed Social Democrat. Thus his victory potentially threatened the cohesion of the SLDP which remained largely the old Liberal Party incarnate. Hence his need to denounce Owen in the strongest possible terms. Yet his election pleased David Owen because the SLDP members, by electing Mr Ashdown, have opted for charismatic leadership, although their desire for a balanced ticket was reflected in the other election results. The result of the leadership election declared on 28 July 1988 also included the outcome of the contest for the party presidency. Mr Ian Wrigglesworth, the former Labour and Social Democrat MP, gained 28 638 votes to beat the former Liberal president, Mr Des Wilson, with 21 906, and the former Welsh SDP chairman, Mr Gwynoro Jones, with 6479. It was clear that the election of Des Wilson to the party presidency would have outraged those former Social Democrats who still believed that they were taking part in a merger and not a takeover by the Liberals.

Mr Ashdown said that Labour had had its chances, but had muffed them. He ruled out deals with Labour or Dr Owen's party, saying: 'I have made it clear that the period of coalitions, necessary though it was, is now over.' Labour was not about to recover as a major political force. According to Paddy Ashdown: 'Labour will continue to muff it. I can see no reason at all why we should now be talking about coalitions, pacts and alliances. We are on our own, and we are going to make it on our own.'[15]

He made it clear – though this was rather predictable – that the new party's strategy for dealing with Dr Owen's organization would be to ignore it as an irrelevance. He was scathing in his dismissal of Dr Owen, who issued a statement congratulating Mr Ashdown on his victory and expressing the hope that it would not be too long before they co-operated to promote the cause of multi-party politics and proportional representation.[16]

Mr Ashdown simply ignored Owen's message.

Mr Ashdown, however, did concede that Dr Owen was a force to be reckoned with, but only as a man and not as the leader of a party, because 'I don't believe, with 2 per cent of the votes, I can perceive a time in the future when an electoral pact would be considered by this party.'[17] So spoke the new leader on the morrow of his victory. More crucially he refused to say when he believed the SLDP could replace Labour as the main opposition to the Conservatives. It is clear that in order to displace Labour as the chief opposition party the support of the Social Democratic party would be essential. Thus David Owen foresaw the need for a new alliance between the SLDP and SDP. Mr Ashdown did not: then that was to be expected. He obviously fears Dr Owen personally, as was made plain at his post-election press conference. His fear can be explained rationally: his own party lacks clear definition. He attempted to define its purpose at his press conference which gave a frightening insight into its vacuity:

> 'our party', he declared, 'can be defined as a) "an open and debating party" b) "a participative party" c) "a party that remembers we can't attack Mrs Thatcher by defending the past" d) "a party distinct and different"'.[18]

This was not a good start: however, it would be expecting too much too soon for greater clarity from a leader who has yet to establish his own personal style. His intellectual weight appears to be on the thin side but there is no doubting the degree of support he enjoys among the grass-roots of the SLDP. As Ian McIntyre wrote (admittedly rather tongue in cheek):

> Some of Mr Ashdown's more enthusiastic followers obviously regard him as a cross between the Duke of Wellington and Richard Hannay – the sort of chap who could bound up the Thirty-Nine

Steps two at a time and still breathe quietly at the top. The opposite camp sees it rather differently, depicting him as a sort of reconstituted Mad Mitch of the Argylls with a couple of A levels thrown in. He would certainly lead from the front, though his followers might not always be there when he looked round. He sounds a bit like the cavalry subaltern of whom his colonel once wrote laconically: 'The men will follow this officer anywhere, if only out of curiosity.'[19]

This at least appeared to be an improvement on David Steel, whose leadership of the Liberals rarely aroused curiosity, only a growing sense of despair. But was the new party ready for 'action man' leadership? How would this new party respond to positive leadership on the question of defence, given the unilateralist majority of the SLD?

The SLDP therefore has a credibility problem. However, this credibility problem does not arise simply from equivocation over defence, or indeed because of Paddy Ashdown's modest political experience and lack of sufficient *gravitas* in the House of Commons where his reputation is not very high. It arises much less from his slender parliamentary experience – which started in 1983 when he was elected as the Liberal MP for his Somerset constituency – than from the nature of the Social Liberal Democratic Party itself, which, despite its new appearance, is basically the old Liberal Party under new management. Its principal task is to become the main opposition party and at the same time establish a definite identity in British politics. The plain truth is that only one man – David Owen – could effectively lead such a party with those aims. The task is beyond Mr Ashdown, just as it overtaxed his predecessor David Steel. In order to move towards displacing Labour and towards achieving a bigger share of the popular vote, the SLDP needs to convey the impression of being a united party on good terms with a party like the SDP, which, though small, could, as we have argued, split the vote that the Alliance in the past has enjoyed. To relinquish this asset by attempting to ignore or even confront the SDP, under David Owen, will gravely reduce the appeal of the centre in British politics.

Yet the prospects for such unity are slender given the history of the Liberal Party whose members comprise the vast majority of the SLDP. The Liberal element of the new party are the problem. They have proved to be undisciplined and self-destructive at the grass-roots level in the past. They have been prepared to humiliate their 'leaders' at the Liberal assembly over crucial policy issues, especially over defence where the unilateralists within the party are a force to be reckoned with (Mr Ashdown was once one of their number). They have also, at the parliamentary level, been openly fractious and disloyal to their leader (Sir Cyril Smith virtually declared open warfare on his leader David Steel, and refused to attend the annual assembly because of his dislike of his colleagues!). This is the party that Mr Ashdown inherits and which he seeks to lead. He can only provide effective leadership if he recognises, sooner rather than later, that the unity of the SLDP cannot be achieved by seeking to destroy Owen's SDP. The sad fact is that both parties can only destroy each other. Mr Kinnock would welcome this; Mrs Thatcher would become the chief beneficiary.

The true situation was well expressed by Michael Jones, the perceptive political editor of *The Sunday Times*, who, in his weekly column, following Paddy Ashdown's first press conferences as leader of the SLDP (the tenth anti-Tory leader in the preceding 161 months of Thatcherite Toryism), concluded that:

> When Mr Ashdown writes of the SDP as 'insignificant', he endorses an approach that owes more to pique than prudence. The hard fact is that the SDP is still there with a national figure at its head, a parliamentary presence in both houses, 30,000 paid-up members and a Mori rating of 4%.

> The SLD has 80,000 members, a much bigger parliamentary presence but a Mori rating of only 8%. What does that say about the damaging effect of the SLD–SDP rift? And what is Mr Ashdown going to do to end it? Wage civil war on the centre-ground of British politics, it seems. Mrs Thatcher will be delighted.[20]

12 The Breakup or the Breakout?

The original SDP has failed; this book described its birth and final demise. Beyond seeking to evaluate the unique set of circumstances which led to its brilliant rise and to its unfortunate decline, we have identified the more fundamental reasons for its failure to break the mould of British politics. These have much to do with an ideology which was not perceived as distinctive enough to set the SDP apart from the Liberals and Labour. The chief rivals for the role of the opposition party most likely to be bidding for power either with a parliamentary majority of their own or as a partner in a coalition government were lacking in a distinctive ideology, associated with one capable of mobilising mass support. But to whom should the Social Democrats appeal for support?

The Conservatives could always appeal to middle-class opinion and expect it to sustain them electorally when the trial of strength came in a general election. They could appeal to dominant middle-class values reflecting respect for existing institutions and the virtues of personal growth based upon rising expectations. Upward social mobility itself depended upon a growing economy in which young, ambitious men and women could expect steady incremental advance in a political environment freed from the total stalemate of a corporate society which, as always, threatened to destroy the basis of British enterprise in the post-war period.

Labour could appeal to its working-class vote which, however, is a declining asset. But, as we have argued, the ideology of Labourism is specific and uniquely functional to Labour because it helps to distinguish the party from its opponents. Crudely expressed, capital and labour are historically associated with the Conservative and Labour parties.

The SDP had no such advantage or perspective: it sought to appeal to the middle ground of British politics but not on the basis of a vested interest in the corporate state. For the party recognised that the question of liberty was indissolubly intertwined with the economic problem.

The SDP never did succeed in acquiring a clear ideological position: for it lacked a defined doctrine or a basic core interest;

human spontaneity and empiricism were not enough. Its commitment to a social market economy was never properly defined or seriously advanced (except by David Owen who soon lost interest in it). A strong commitment to a social market economy was never pressed home with the warmth, limpidity and richness that the concept deserved. The party never acquired a radical stance complementary to or consistent with the Thatcherite revolution.

The lack of ideology was not fatal, but it blurred the SDP's image, which was further weakened by the nature of the alliance with the Liberals. This was an unavoidable weakness because the Liberals were the natural allies for the SDP in bidding for the centre of British politics. The only other alternative would be the Labour Party under John Smith or even, perhaps, Bryan Gould, but neither man would be allowed to form a centre grouping with David Owen. The Labour Party would fight them to the death.

The very notion of alliance at the centre of British politics, of course, presents a weak image. Moreover the Liberals had the dubious reputation of being the natural 'extremists of the centre'.

The two general elections undid the SDP as a rising force in British politics. This was the supreme test and the party failed it. It need not have done so – failure was not inevitable, defeat was not certain.

The 1983 campaign produced a mediocre result for the SDP; 1987 produced a disaster. This was because from the outset the Alliance had targeted the wrong enemy, Mrs Thatcher's government.

Dr Owen's instincts were better; he wanted to attack – and displace – Labour as the principal opposition party. His wisdom was ignored; Mr Steel's folly followed. The electorate became confused. Where did the Alliance stand – to the left or right of Mr Kinnock? No doubt some Liberals were to the left, others to the right. The SDP under Owen's tough centrist stance alone saw that unless and until Labour was displaced as a major political force in the country, the SDP could not assume its historic task of forming a non-socialist opposition (the alternative government) in a post-socialist Britain (as well as in a post-Thatcherite Britain).

Viewing the 1987 general election campaign it can now be seen in retrospect that the alliance between the SDP and the Liberals was not a genuine alliance at all: there was no real cohesive campaign strategy. This was not an alliance: it was co-belligerency. In fact, Steel and Owen were political adversaries whose mutual dislike even overshadowed their intense personal ambition.

Once the Alliance no longer faced the electorate, disintegration

was certain to follow. Mrs Thatcher got her second stunning parliamentary majority (even if not of the popular vote); Dr Owen got
his deserts; Mr Steel his revenge for the real and imagined slights that
he had suffered at the hands of David Owen.

Yet this was not so much the end of a formal marriage – because it
was never consummated – between the two like-minded leaders and
parties, as the end of a common-law marriage – with a touch of sin
about it. It had always been a bit too shallow: it simply lacked
substance and genuine mutual respect. Failure was inevitable.

David Owen was not blameless: he is contemptuous of fools and
impatient with friends. He was an awkward leader of his own party
and a pretty trying partner for David Steel, who despite his faults,
struggled long to establish some rapport with Owen.

Dr David Owen was a better parliamentary leader than he was an
extra-parliamentary leader. He would have made a better prime
minister than a leader of the opposition. He was and is a man of
power.

He was, in fact, a less-than-great leader of a fledgling party. But he
towered over his contemporaries as a political figure. Indeed the
smaller Gang of Three were never his equal in providing the
high-profile leadership which modern party politics require in a
media-dominated environment.

Mr Roy Jenkins (as he then was) was never an effective leader of
either the SDP or of the Alliance. Mr Jenkins possessed personal
gravitas yet possessed surprisingly little weight as a politician. Even in
parliament Roy Jenkins proved less effective than David Owen.
Statesmen make poor politicians and Mr Jenkins had become too
grand.

Mrs Shirley Williams was a better speaker than either Jenkins or
Owen, though an unoriginal thinker, when compared with Owen who
was not himself an intellectual. His personal arrogance destroyed her
respect for him. She possessed admirable personal qualities and high
moral virtue. She evoked love and admiration from both friend and
foe alike. She was something of a legend; her patent honesty and
modesty were there for all to see. She was also quite astute. But there
was another side to her personality as well, which played a significant
part in destroying her relationship with Owen. Her periodic dis-
appearances to recharge her waning spirits were rather an embarrass-
ment to her colleagues, who expected her to be constantly available
as a leading figure in the party. David Owen came to view her with
marked disfavour, and, from his perspective, with good reason. She

possessed strong convictions, which were derived from her earlier commitment to democratic socialism, and yet apart from disavowing her membership of the Labour Party her intellectual attitudes had changed very little.

It was clear to Dr Owen that he had overestimated her flexibility and capacity to ruthlessly re-think her basic political beliefs. She was not much attracted by the so-called social market strategy; she could not shake off the dirigisme which so impressed her in the 1950s and 1960s. Yet she had much to contribute to the SDP because she possessed a flair for analysis and could extrapolate trends, especially when thinking on her feet. She was the thinking man's feminist. David Owen depended upon her to begin with, for she possessed ministerial experience with a good parliamentary record as well as an impressive platform manner.

She quickly tired of Owen's style of leadership once he took over the party. It is tempting to think that they very probably disagreed over policy issues, but it is much more likely that temperamental differences were more important in explaining their growing alienation. His decisive and authoritarian leadership contrasted with her hesitant and, at times, indecisive approach to both policy and organisational issues. Yet her seminar approach to public issues inspired admiration for its lucidity and compassion. She had the spontaneous gifts and stylistic inclinations of an American politician seeking pragmatic solutions to complex issues.

We stress Shirley Williams's attractive personality and complex character because she was an important figure in British politics. We wish also to emphasise how the split over merger was not just a disagreement over tactics or methods.

Lord Jenkins's position was also pivotal, but he was less ambivalent about David Owen. However, it is difficult to determine his influence over policy.

To write about Roy Jenkins is a pleasure: his views appear so reasonable and compelling. His writing – like his beautifully crafted speeches – are eloquent and penetrating. And yet, is he just the elegant advocate of distilled conventional wisdom which has more style than content? His preference for style is well known: he often appeared irritated by David Owen's poor syntax. Roy Jenkins is as magisterial as befits the Chancellor of Oxford University. He is a distinguished biographer and gentleman essayist in the best amateur tradition. His writings never had the influence they deserved. He compels respect from those who know him best but he is not a man of the people.

Mr Jenkins (as he then was) was the real star of the SDP and its first leader. He carried enormous weight and prestige that helped raise the SDP to the quite dizzy heights described in this book. However, he did not share the Owenite belief in a four-party system and therefore presupposed that the SDP and the Liberals would one day merge. To him, the centre of British politics needed just one party structure, though in the short term there was a place for a party seeking to attract former Labour ministers, MPs and party members as well as Labour voters.

He also appealed to non-doctrinaire conservatives. His defection to the SDP was not unexpected: it was a courageous and calculated move. As a former deputy leader of the Labour Party, and EEC commissioner, this defection was impressive, given his lifelong commitment to the Labour Movement. His credentials were beyond dispute, and only Denis Healey's defection to the SDP could have produced a more impressive recruit. Jenkins was not, however, an unalloyed asset to the SDP, for he symbolised the past, and a failed one at that. His image lacked mass appeal, but he did appeal to so-called 'wet' opinion whose liberal sympathies were now passé. His presidency of the EEC hitched his star to a respected institution among SDP members, but one to which popular opinion was largely hostile or indifferent. Of course, David Owen shared Jenkins's Europeanist sympathies, but Owen was identified more strongly with defence, about which both elite and popular opinion were far from indifferent or hostile. It was clear that Jenkins represented a facet of the SDP thinking which Owen later decided to repudiate.

This was the 'soft' centre which confused moderation with a litany of liberal causes. David Owen and Roy Jenkins became incompatible, because one was a hard-nosed social democrat and the other an urbane liberal with a small 'l'. Roy Jenkins was deeply affronted by the nature of Thatcherism. His sensibilities were outraged by the value-system of the tradesman's daughter. He remained wedded to the values of Oxbridge.

Support for the SDP at the outset indicated acute anxieties about the new thinking which the Thatcher government represented between 1979 and 1981 (pre-Falklands) – and which caused many Conservatives to desert to the centre ground occupied by Jenkins and his friends who longed for a return to the post-war consensus. David

Owen alone stood defiantly opposed to this line. He was beginning to see the much vaunted Limehouse Declaration as an appeal to the past.

The Limehouse manifesto had quickly dated because Britain was moving into a very different ideological milieu in which statist solutions, so beloved of post-war elites, could no longer provide relevant prescriptions. The welfare state had been purchased at a frightful economic cost to the nation by institutionalising stagnation and its vicious off-spring, 'stagflation'. The nanny state had become a cripple. The welfare state was demand-driven and demand for services had become insatiable as people's expectations of the state reached unprecedented levels.

Mr Jenkins's prescriptions for the SDP were steeped in 'corporatism' and 'interventionism', which were not made any less contradictory by his stressing a diminution in the latter. Dr Owen saw Jenkins as a liberal who was intellectually closer to David Steel than to himself, and as an old-fashioned radical although not a liberal economist. Thus he was regarded by Owen with increasing irritation, because he (Owen) wished to expound the new radicalism consistent with the social market economy. To David Owen, Roy was not radical enough when it came to reassessing the role and purpose of the publicly financed welfare state.

However, it is clear that Roy Jenkins, Shirley Williams and Bill Rodgers, because they probably disapproved of Owen's shift to the right, were quick to seize upon David Steel's merger initiative, suggesting an element of collusion with Steel to depose Owen as the front-runner for the leadership of the parties of the centre. They (the Gang of Four) subconsciously preferred a deal with Labour rather than a *modus vivendi* with Thatcher.

They did not deliberately seek his personal destruction but they acquiesced in a process that had precisely that result. There was something decidedly ungenerous about the behaviour of David Steel, both before and after his merger proposal, with regard to his conduct towards David Owen. The relish with which he predicted his political oblivion, and his lurid accusation that Dr Owen was a 'hijacker' who had removed a couple of coaches from the SDP train only to take it into a siding, was a tacit admission of the damage that David Steel had caused Owen personally and the SDP in particular. Whether David Steel's move against the SDP in 1987 reflected a well-thought-out and planned putsch to remove David Owen from contention as a national political leader, or whether it was just further evidence of

Steel's curious inability to grasp the essentials of a finely balanced political situation, will be endlessly debated. But in his speech to the annual conference of the Scottish Liberal Party on 5 March 1988, which after forty-three years' separate existence was about to become part of the Social and Liberal Democrats, David Steel drew a tenuous analogy with the fate of the so-called Liberal Nationals who had broken away from mainstream liberalism in 1946. He pointedly recalled that this breakaway group had sided with the Tories. 'The lesson is clear,' he said. 'We hear nothing today of the Liberal Nationals and our liberal tradition is stronger than ever.' This was, however, a false and facile comparison to draw. The SDP had, of course, never been a part of the Liberal Party nor was it derived from the liberal tradition (whatever that was supposed to convey). It was and is an autonomous party which after seven years short existence was narrowly manoeuvred into agreeing to merge with the Liberals. This actually split the party in two, with David Owen and his loyalists declaring themselves to be the true exponents of the social democratic tradition with a separate organisation and political programme. If, as Dr Owen admits, he wept uncontrollably in the privacy of his hotel room when the SDP's Portsmouth Conference decided in favour of merger with the liberals, then his tears were justified. Yet this was not the end of the SDP, but another beginning. At the re-launch of the Social Democratic Party, under Owen's leadership, it was announced that he had a £25 000 war chest. This cash had flooded in from nearly 15 000 individual donors in the first six months after the merger row split the old SDP. Thus, by March 1988, the Owenite group had attracted an average income of £6682 in gifts from supporters; the average individual donation was more than £13. Moreover, David Sainsbury, the supermarket millionaire made it plain that he too would be contributing to the finances of the party.

Mr David Steel's reference to the fate of the Liberal Nationals was therefore hardly apposite, given that the SDP could still boast three MPs and more than twenty peers taking its whip in parliament. Moreover, the SDP still retained a large membership, reliably put at 30 000.

On Tuesday 8 March 1988, the new SDP was re-established at a meeting of its national committee just five days after the Liberals and the pro-merger Social Democrats launched themselves as the new Social and Liberal Democrats. Dr Owen therefore leads a party which has more substance than the former Liberal Nationals, who were never much more than a few disgruntled liberals clustered around David Lloyd-George's errant son.

Yet, of course, the split between Steel and Owen was never just a trivial disagreement but it was a disagreement between two equally ambitious men seeking power and influence. They clashed over objectives and tactics. David Steel, for example, claimed that the values of Thatcherism were in direct conflict with those of liberal democracy. David Owen took the view that such a blanket critique of Thatcherism ignored the positive gains that had resulted from some – by no means all – of Mrs Thatcher's policies since 1979, and that the beliefs underpinning Thatcherism were not all bad and therefore there was no inherent conflict between the values of Thatcherism and those of liberal democracy. For David Owen the real conflict was between the values of social democracy and 'Bennite' socialism. David Steel and David Owen were therefore in a state of disagreement but it was a disagreement which could have been reduced if not resolved given goodwill. David Steel foolishly chose to confront or even possibly to deflate David Owen, whom he personally disliked and transparently feared in equal measure. But his challenge to Owen was not solely personal. David Steel was to some extent a man of principle though of limited vision. His dislike of David Owen was not entirely irrational – Owen was heartily disliked by the vast majority of Liberals because of his arrogance. But in truth there could be no future for either the newly created SLDP or the born-again-SDP, which had the result of emasculating David Owen.

It could be maintained that nothing was gained and much was lost by the isolation of Mr Enoch Powell by the official Conservative leadership under Mr Edward Heath because of his alleged views on race relations. Likewise, nothing was gained and much was lost when Mrs Thatcher excluded Edward Heath from her government. So with David Owen: nothing was to be gained and much was to be lost by his political death. David Steel's attempted political isolation of David Owen did not succeed. But there was and is a real risk that the harm done to him electorally will damage irreparably the future of both parties as they struggle to gain legitimacy. Mr Steel acted unwisely, to put it no higher, by raising the merger issue in the way that he did. Of course there was a plausible and compelling case for a merger between the Social Democrats and the Liberals just as there is a strong case for a merger between the new Social and Liberal Democrats and the Social Democrats once political conditions have matured. But a merger must not become a takeover, as was substantially to be the case when the two parties merged in 1988. The paradox remains, however, that if the newly formed Social and Liberal Democrats were to succeed at the next election in securing more seats in the House of Commons than the Social Democrats (SDP), then the need for a new merger collapses. But one thing is clear, if both parties continue to confront each other, they will fail to win sufficient seats in the Commons to displace Labour as the principal opposition party. This is catch-22 for both parties, and this absurd situation should have been foreseen by David Steel when he first raised the merger issue following the last general election.

This interpretation of events should, of course, be accepted with caution. Perhaps David Steel could not have predicted that Owen would reject unconditionally his merger proposal. Therefore the subsequent isolation of David Owen was not inevitable because such a response was likely to be an act of self-laceration, which even Owen was not capable of perpetrating. Indeed it is arguable that David Steel thought that Owen would make a bid for the leadership of the new party. Perhaps Owen should have made such a bid, but nothing was more obvious than that such a bid would have failed. The Liberals would have nominated Steel, or more probably, Ashdown to oppose him. David Owen's defeat in such a context was therefore foreseeable and was probably foreseen by David Steel. It is clear that in either case, whether Owen stuck to his own party or sought to lead the new one, he personally faced a massive setback to his plans to be a leading figure in remoulding British politics.

We have no doubt that the demise of David Owen, should that in fact be the case, would deny Britain the services of one of the most able politicians of his generation. His political eclipse would probably mark the end of an attempt to build upon the new right-of-centre Thatcherite consensus in the years that lie ahead.

His potential for effective leadership could be lost. This occurs when the principal opposition party – the Labour Party – is led by a far-from-harmless but nonetheless genial personality who was the most lightweight leader of his party since George Lansbury in the 1930s. For Labour, in present circumstances, is simply not a viable opposition party, and unfortunately the future prospects for the post-1988 SDP are also poor, if not hopeless. And yet there is scope for a fourth party given the volatile electoral situation. This fourth party will need, of course, to stand apart from the newly formed Social and Liberal Democrats (SLDP) and seek to attract disaffected Conservative and Labour voters. Such voters are unlikely to find Mr Kinnock's Labour Party nor Mr Ashdown's SLD to their liking, but they will equally feel repelled by Mrs Thatcher's doctrinaire approach to the nation's problems.

There is much truth in Brian Walden's oft-repeated assertion that Britain needs a party of popular capitalism. The successor SDP should try and tap that strain of populist opinion in Britain, which is just as likely to be found on the council estates as in the areas now being gentrified by the 'yuppies' and their ilk.

It might even be possible to imagine the following scenario in the years that lie ahead, say by 1991/2.

The Conservative government faces a general election under Mrs Thatcher in the wake of the poll tax legislation controversy as the nation divides over the uneven distribution of economic growth between North and South. The economic prosperity favours the high-growth South East, but the trickle-down theory is beginning to generate wider economic effects, as measured by the falling number of unemployed. With the rate of inflation around 6 per cent – still higher than the government would wish and still higher than the European average – high-tech industries begin to generate an increasing number of graduate-calibre jobs.

Conservative standing in public opinion polls puts them 5 to 10 points ahead of Labour – a party which remains deeply divided under Kinnock's rather chequered leadership as he faces successive hard-left attacks for his more 'realistic' policies. Mr Ashdown's Social and Liberal Democrats (SLD) have made few electoral inroads in intervening by-elections, though their standing in public opinion surveys reveals potential support from around 20 per cent of the electorate. The successor SDP has got stuck at 6 per cent of the popular vote, according to the surveys. As the election approaches it is clear that Mrs Thatcher is all set for her fourth term as Prime Minister, with a manifesto committed to more radical policies, including the privatisation of coal and the railways and an implied dismemberment of the NHS. Interest centres on the implications of the completion of a single market in goods and services which the European community is due to complete by 1992. This has excited some interest fuelled by rising economic expectations. Mrs Thatcher's personal standing is rather higher than that of her government. Neil Kinnock's own standing in popular esteem lags behind Paddy Ashdown. Dr David Owen registers slightly more support than Mr Ashdown. But taken together, the SLD and SDP could displace Labour as the principal opposition party as measured by their joint share of the popular vote. Thus the forthcoming election is about the possible demise of Labour rather than an election offering the inevitability of a Conservative defeat. It is clear, though, that the SLD/SDP have agreed to a *de facto* alliance during the campaign while still conducting separate strategies with David Owen stressing his fourth party status.

The underlying macroeconomic situation is not as satisfactory as in the two preceding years, so that the pressure to join the European Monetary System (EMS) has reached crisis point in the cabinet. Mrs Thatcher remains adamantly opposed to joining. There is some Conservative disquiet that Mrs Thatcher's decision to seek a fourth term has frustrated the ambitions of Sir Geoffrey Howe and Mr Nigel Lawson (not to say Mr Tebbit's). Mr Cecil Parkinson is seen as *de facto* heir-apparent to Margaret Thatcher, which further divides Conservative opinion.

Since the end of 1988 the British economy has been manifestly in trouble, with its adverse trade balance, inflationary tendencies as reflected in house prices, and high interest rates which threatened to squeeze Britain's promising economic growth rate. This, together with growing disquiet about the competitiveness of British industry as 1992 approaches, creates increasing electoral volatility.

Mrs Thatcher becomes increasingly isolated from her Treasury ministers (with Nigel Lawson possibly preferring life in the city to soldiering on at the Treasury). Mr Parkinson goes to the Treasury. The rise of Cecil Parkinson as Thatcher's potential heir-apparent demoralises the Tory party both in the House of Commons and outside. Yet speculation centres on Margaret Thatcher's determination to push on for another five years if she gets a decisive parliamentary majority.

The election campaign proves to be no mere re-run of 1987, and with the early collapse of Labour – as its campaign strategy buckles under the combined weight of the Tory onslaught on Mr Kinnock, and the contradictions within Labour's more realistic manifesto which lacks credibility and substance – the SLD/SDP quickly gain support.

The SLD and SDP exceeds Labour in its share of the popular vote going to the opposition parties. Labour trails with less than 20 per cent of the popular vote, according to public opinion surveys published on the eve-of-poll.

Labour in any event finishes with fewer seats than those held in combination by the SLD/SDP. The return of a surprising number of Scottish National Party (SNP) members who support the SLP/SDP rather than Labour further tips the balance. Mr Ashdown becomes leader of HM opposition, with David Owen being invited to play his part in the role of loyal opposition.

Mrs Thatcher's majority of twenty+ seats or so ensures her a fourth successive victory. Labour is, however, finished. Mr Kinnock is swiftly replaced by Mr Robin Cook, an abler man and far more acerbic than his predecessor.

Where does this leave the SDP and David Owen in particular? Well, two things are obvious: his separate party did not really harm the SLDP and the SLDP did not seriously harm the SDP in those constituencies where a local truce agreement was struck.

The time for a proper merger has now truly arrived. This time a merger follows from success at the polls and not from a sense of futility and failure. The new merger negotiation produces a party more to the liking of David Owen, with activist 'Liberals', however, indicating their sympathy for the left wing of the Labour Party. The Ashdown–Owenite populist pro-enterprise party stands ready to humanise the face of Thatcherite Britain.

Thus in the following general election – say, around 1995/6, or so – a non-socialist party under Paddy Ashdown and David Owen assumes office to steer the country into the new European dimension of British politics which then commands the support of the British people. Mrs Thatcher's revolution is complete and will probably stand for an entire generation as an example of renewed British enterprise and self-confidence. Dr Owen becomes prime minister in succession to Paddy Ashdown – Owen being the Lloyd-George to Ashdown's Asquith – in 1998, at the age of 60 (still younger than Churchill in 1940 when he became prime minister!). Mr Ashdown's failure as prime minister arises from his overall failure to stamp his personality on his cabinet and from the standing challenge from his strong-minded chancellor David Owen.

This 'prediction' is not sheer fantasy but a reasoned i.e. remote possibility in the long term. Manifestly, in the medium term the 'revolution' which Mrs Thatcher is bent upon achieving by destroying all vestiges of socialism, will have run its course. She will have done inestimable service to the nation but her lack of interest in and regard for the victims of this revolution could prove to be her final undoing. Lord Acton's dictum that all power corrupts and absolute power corrupts absolutely, may be the final comment on the career of Britain's strongest peacetime prime minister this century. Her personal egotism may yet overwhelm her commonsense and intuitive wisdom in the heady wake of a fourth successive electoral victory as she projects the image of a quasi-monarch destined to enjoy political longevity and unprecedented power.

However, this is a rather optimistic scenario. It could be that we may have witnessed the rise and fall of SDP which amounts in historical terms to little more than an epiphenomenon in British politics, its rise being simply a consequence of the collapse of Labour's old coalition and the disaffection of those who regarded themselves as social democrats. The 1988 merger therefore between the Liberals and SDP marks the end of the latter as an autonomous force in British politics.

Dr David Owen would have no political future: the 'new' SDP having an even shorter history then the old one between 1981 and 1988. The nation will, of course, be all the poorer for such an outcome, since the Conservatives will then govern the country until the turn of the century. Britain would then have enjoyed one-party rule for over twenty years. Would Britain in those circumstances be spared the corruption and misuse of power which other one-party systems inherently encourage? Perhaps.

Yet if the merger negotiated in 1988 between the Liberals and SDP had been achieved differently, namely with Owen's support, then the newly formed SLD would have carried even greater credibility than was likely without his support. Mr Steel therefore recklessly launched the merger proposal without due regard to the need to achieve a *modus vivendi* with David Owen, which was not impossible, although the actual merger would have come later, say, in 1990 or so.

Mr Steel's bad timing, combined with his apparent myopia, had therefore destroyed the centre of British politics for probably a generation. This may appear to be a harsh judgement, but timing is everything in politics; his move to promote merger was maladroit to say the least. He must have calculated its probable outcome. His intentions were no doubt mixed and therefore not all bad, but the swiftness of his move was perceived by Owen as a coup in which he (Owen) was to be given no real choice but to accept a *fait accompli*.

David Owen did not see how he could have behaved otherwise than he did: to reject merger and defend his party to the end. It was his determination to resist the merger which contrasts with the supine acceptance of the timing of it by the remainder of the Gang of Four. In the final analysis they lacked the courage of their convictions (or, to be kinder to them, they simply lacked judgement).

The launch – or rather relaunch – of the SDP in 1988 was a

courageous if not desperate act by David Owen and his loyalists, backed strongly by the steadfast John Cartwright and the indefatigable Rosie Barnes. Those who stayed with the SDP were doing more than sticking to Owen, they were ensuring to the best of their ability the integrity of what they knew to be the essential character of the SDP, which they suspected would be overwhelmed by the weight of Liberal preferences and prejudices if a total merger ensued. Were they right to take that view?

The option to soldier on as the fourth party occupying a distinctive political and ideological position in British politics was the inevitable decision, even though it was likely to end in failure. The future is not predetermined, and given the continued decline in Labour's position which had in the early 1980s made the rise of the SDP seem possible, we may yet see once again the ascent of a non-socialist opposition. But the survival of the SDP could be essential to the survival of a credible opposition itself. This is not to assert that the newly formed SLDP cannot or will not constitute a viable challenge to Labour. It is merely to assert that the British political system needs a party to the right of Labour and which displaces Labour as the principal opposition party. This party should not be a re-run of Labour, as some Liberal activists would doubtlessly prefer, but an avowedly non-socialist radical party dedicated to the promotion of popular capitalism, a party willing to challenge Mrs Thatcher at her own game and committed to pushing the frontiers of the social market economy towards a genuinely meritocratic society where the strategy of backing the strong brings succour and hope to the weak. David Owen has in particular always distinguished very clearly between personal self-expression and social action in the pursuit of an harmonious social order.

The pluralist society with its capitalist economy still remains the best hope for mankind. The SDP and the SLDP must at first separately, and later together, push the fulcrum of British politics firmly back to the centre, in order to balance the counter-revolution that Mrs Thatcher has so courageously initiated since 1979. Socialism, surely the greatest myth of the nineteenth and twentieth centuries, would have been removed from the political agenda.

The SDP and its ally the SLDP have in theory their part to play in a post-collectivist Britain. In spite of all these hopes concerning an SLD/SDP electoral alliance there is sufficient evidence to suggest that the SDP can secure just enough votes to wreck both parties' meagre prospects. Thus the collapse of Labour as a party of government could be accompanied by the collapse of the Social Liberal Democrats (SLD) and of the Social Democrats (SDP) as measured in votes cast and seats won. The result must be that the Conservatives continue to govern the country indefinitely until they themselves split into two, rather like the split between the 'free traders' and the 'protectionists' in the last century. It could be well into the twenty-first century before the party of Mrs Thatcher – though not under her personal leadership – is removed from power. British democracy itself would be imperilled by such a bleak prospect.

We conclude that it is perceived to be in the national interest that a viable opposition party should emerge in the interregnum which is capable of winning power. Preferably that opposition party should be a properly merged SLDP and SDP, but not on the present basis as established in 1988, which was, in fact, a device to destroy the SDP and was to prove, ironically enough, equally debilitating to the Liberals.

A merger must be a means to an end and *not* an end in itself. The SDP may yet save the SLDP by its example. The historic task of the SDP is to be a catalyst for other opposition parties and extra-parliamentary actors who feel that British democracy is endangered by the absence of a strong opposition to the most powerful peacetime prime minister this century. There must be an attractive alternative government waiting in the wings, and since it cannot be Labour, for all the reasons discussed in this book, then it must be the Social Democratic Party and the Social and Liberal Democrats working together in coalition. Of course it is remotely possible that Labour, say, under John Smith or Bryan Gould, could stage a political and electoral recovery which could then be seen as a victory for the centre. But to believe that, you have to disregard the history of the Labour Party since 1979, or believe in miracles.

Yet by the end of 1988 with the Thatcher government in trouble over its running of the economy some commentators were beginning to believe that Labour could stage a credible recovery sufficient to prevent the Democrats or the SDP from emerging from the political shadows and thereby pushing Labour aside. It is certainly unwise to write Labour off as an electoral force incapable of being regarded as the alternative government. Mr Kinnock and his Shadow Cabinet colleagues are beginning to appear a formidable force in British politics despite the disaster of the Govan by-election in mid-November 1988 which saw a stunning victory for the Scottish Nationalist Party (SNP) over Labour. Perhaps Mr Kinnock has been

as much underestimated as once Mr Clement Attlee was in his time
when Labour was struggling to gain political ascendency? And yet the
doubt persists in Britain that Labour can regain its credibility. The
Labour Party as a whole – leaving aside the parliamentary leadership
– will still probably insist on socialist doctrine and policies which the
electors do not want. As Professor David Marquand rightly contends
even in the wider context of Europe the Labour Party stands for an
obsolescent doctrine:

> Yet, in the increasingly bourgeois family of late 20th-century
> European Socialism, one poor relation stands apart. The Labour
> Party once prided itself on its bluff, Anglo-Saxon common sense
> and its pragmatic distaste for continental theorising. Now, even
> with its new Gordon Browns and Tony Blairs, it is far less
> pragmatic than its continental counterparts, and far more encum-
> bered by theoretical baggage.
>
> It is also far more prone to spouting the slogans of a class war
> which scarcely anyone wants to fight, and far more deeply entren-
> ched in the shrinking proletarian ghettoes plastered around the
> shrinking smokestack industries.
>
> That, of course, is why it lost the last three general elections.
> Neil Kinnock would dearly love to bring his party up to date, but
> he does not know how to. His head tells him that he should talk the
> new language of the 1980s and 1990s. His heart belongs to the old
> world of the 1930s and 1940s.[1]

This explains the tragic decline of Labour very clearly but equally
makes it obvious that should that decline be reversed the country
could slide into a protracted political crisis. However a solution is to
hand: electoral reform through proportional representation. Such a
reform of the electoral system would ensure coalition government
which would push Labour into opposition on a permanent basis. Thus
the priority for the progressive non-left is to work for a coalition
against Labour in order to displace it as the leading opposition party
and then to work for coalition government in the post-Thatcher era
which will come sooner or later. A sensible Conservative government
should lose no time in introducing some form of PR in the next
parliament but it would be too much to expect a triumphalist Mrs
Thatcher to possess the incentive to accomplish this.

The agenda, then, for a coalition against Labour which ultimately
seeks to displace them as the principal opposition party and which
itself seeks a parliamentary role within a coalition government, has

begun to take shape. The alternative strategy of working towards a coalition with Labour against the Conservatives under Margaret Thatcher can be regarded as a non-starter, despite David Owen's suggestion at the SDP's 1987 Torquay conference that an opposition coalition with Labour was now possible. His lapse of logic has more to do with an attempt to get proportional representation off the ground than with a new-found respect for Labour under Mr Kinnock. Labour would have to disavow socialism before such an anti-Thatcherite coalition proved possible, and that would involve the renunciation of Clause 4 by Labour and the complete expulsion of the hard left. Such a prospect must be reckoned remote.

Clearly on the issue of attempting to displace Labour, rather than making a desperate bid to remove the Conservatives, Mr Ashdown's Democrats (née SLDP) are much closer to the position of the SDP than Dr Owen's surprising speech appears to indicate. The potential coalition against Labour must be based on Mr Alton's premise that a reconciliation between the SDP and the Democrats consitutes the first step towards such an objective. There appears little alternative to this strategy for either party, because as things stand they merely possess a capacity for mutual assured destruction. What both parties possess in common is a desire to eclipse the Labour Party, just as the old Labour Party wished to eclipse the Liberals. This requires something more constructive than the continued vilification of David Owen, as Lord Jenkins of Hillhead no doubt fully realises in his more reflective moments.

The road to achieving a new alliance between two like-minded parties need not prove complex nor difficult, as both David Alton, the dissident Democrat MP, and John Cartwright, the SDP President, have maintained. The will to achieve this does not yet exist, but it will develop as two facts become ever more apparent: that Labour is a broken reed, and that another Conservative victory will prove certain if the SDP and the Democrats fight each other. Their irrational dislike of each other is the rage of Caliban at seeing his face in the glass; the SDP and the Democrats have more worthwhile features in common than the ugly disagreements they have with their adversaries.

Notes and References

Introduction

1. Hugh Thomas, *John Strachey*, Eyre Methuen, 1973, p. 98.
2. Ibid.

1 Labour's Traditional Image: Support for a World Role

1. Erenest Bevin reiterated the continuity of British foreign policy when he argued with the Conservative spokesman that, in the coalition government during the war, he never differed on any important issue of foreign policy. Vol. 413, H. of C., 20 August 1945, Col. 312.
2. *Keep Left*, 1947, p. 42.
3. Geoffrey Lee Williams, *The Permanent Alliance: The European–American Partnership 1945–1984*, Sijthoff, Leyden, 1977, p. 227.
4. *Keep Left*, p. 42.
5. Geoffrey Lee Williams and Bruce Reed, *Denis Healey and the Policies of Power*, p. 97.
6. Ibid.
7. R. H. S. Crossman, *Socialist Foreign Policy 1951*, Socialist Union Publication, p. 15.
8. Geoffrey Lee Williams, *The Neutralist Tendency*, p. 39.
9. Ibid.
10. Foreword by Philip Noel-Baker, in R. H. S. Crossman, *Socialism and Foreign Policy*, 1953, p. 31.
11. Ibid.
12. *Keep Left*, 1947, p. 30.
13. Ibid.
14. Paul Foot, *The Politics of Harold Wilson*, Penguin, Harmondsworth, 1968, p. 203.
15. Ibid.
16. *Keep Left*, 1947, p. 35.
17. Ibid.
18. Ibid.
19. A. Bevan, *In Place of Fear*, Davis-Poynte, 1952, p. 123.
20. Ibid.
21. Ibid.
22. *Keep Left*, 1947, p. 45.
23. A. Bevan, *In Place of Fear*, p. 124.
24. Noel-Baker, *Socialism and Foreign Policy*, p. 22.
25. *Problems of Foreign Policy*, 1952, p. 13.
26. Ibid.
27. Ibid.
28. Noel-Baker, *Socialism and Foreign Policy*, Socialist Union, 1951, p. 7.

29. Ibid.
30. Ibid.
31. Ibid.
32. Geoffrey Lee Williams and Alan Lee Williams, *Crisis in European Defence*, p. 228.
33. Ibid.
34. Williams and Reed, *Policies of Power*, p. 231.
35. Ibid.
36. Ibid.
37. Geoffrey Lee Williams, *The Neutralist Tendency*, op. cit. p. 37.
38. Ibid.
39. *The Labour Party Conference Report*, Scarborough 1960, p. 47.
40. Williams and Reed, *Policies of Power*, p. 252.
41. Ibid.
42. Ibid.
43. Ibid.
44. Williams and Williams, *Crisis in European Defence*, p. 229.
45. Ibid.
46. Geoffrey Lee Williams and Alan Lee Williams, *The European Defence Initiative*, p. 39.
47. Geoffrey Lee Williams, *The Permanent Alliance*, pp. 328–9.
48. Ibid.
49. Ibid.
50. Ibid.
51. Ibid.
52. Ibid.
53. Ibid.
54. Ibid.
55. Williams, *The Permanent Alliance*, p. 330.
56. Ibid.

2 Labour and the Defence of the Realm: The Abandonment of Britain's World Role

1. In his book, *A Record of the Labour Government*, he does provide some evidence of considered retrospection, though not much. Mr Wilson's second book, *The Governance of Britain*, is more analytical and for the student of politics more useful.
2. The trade-union 'bloc vote' elects the twelve members of the trade-union section of the NEC; it also effectively determines who are elected as the five members of the 'women's section', and the Party Treasurer.
3. The populist/socialist approach is, strictly speaking, a post-1970 development. Professor MacKintosh is surely right in asserting that the populist/socialist approach is not genuine. As MacKintosh contended, this populist approach consisted of lending support 'to the best organized and most defiant groups, presumably because they are showing most working-class vigour'. See 'Problems of the Labour

Party', *The Political Quarterly*, Oct/Dec 1972.
4. Robert Thompson, *Defeating Communist Insurgency*, Chatto & Windus, 1966.
5. Royal United Services Institute Lecture, 22 October 1964.
6. The phrase 'of the first rank' was a splendid invention of the Foreign and Commonwealth Office.
7. The opposition to Barbara Castle's *In Place of Strife* which was promulgated in 1969 in a belated bid to control prices and incomes through statutory means, ran into considerable trade-union opposition. This played some part in radicalising the trade-union leadership at both plant and national level. See Peter Jenkins, *The Battle of Downing Street*.
8. Ibid.
9. This phrase crept into Denis Healey's robust defence of his Defence Review of February 1966. In March he described his policy as 'an exercise in political and military realism'.
10. See David Greenwood, 'The 1974 Defence Review in Perspective', *Survival*, vol. 17, no. 5, Sept/Oct 1975, for a comparison between the 1974 revision of the planned defence effort and that of 1966.
11. See Hedley Bull, *Anarchical Society*, Macmillan, 1976, p. 24. Professor Bull says that 'a society of states (or international society) exists when a group of states, conscious of certain common interests and common values, form a society in the sense that they conceive themselves to be bound by a common set of rules in their relations with one another and share in the working of common instructions'.
12. Ibid, p. 41.

3 The Nature of Labour's Historic Coalition

1. G. D. H. Cole, 'What is Socialism?', in *Ideologies of Politics*, ed. Anthony De Grespigny and Jeremy Cronin, OUP, 1975, p. 16.
2. Tom Nairn, *The Left Against Europe*, Lawrence & Wishart, 19??, p. 87.
3. Evan Durbin, *The Politics of Democratic Socialism*, Routledge, 1940.
4. Stephen Hasler, *The Gaitskellites*, Macmillan, 1969.
5. G. D. H. Cole, 'What is Socialism?'.
6. Henry Pelling, *The Origins of the Labour Party*, Clarendon, 1954.
7. Anthony Crosland, *The Future of Socialism*, Cape, 1956.
8. Henry Pelling, *The Origins of the Labour Party*.
9. Eric Heffer, *The Class Struggle in Parliament*, Lawrence & Wishart, 1973.
10. G. D. H. Cole, *A Short History of the British Working-Class Movement*, Allen & Unwin, 1948.
11. Ibid.
12. The history of Poland's *Solidarity* seems to support this interpretation.
13. Stephen Hasler, *The Death of British Democracy*, Elek, 1973.
14. Ibid.
15. Margaret Cole, *The Story of Fabian Socialism*, Macmillan, 1961.

16. Ibid.
17. Alan Bullock, *Ernest Bevin*, vol. 1.
18. Ibid.
19. Ralph Miliband, *Parliamentary Socialism*, OUP, 1973.
20. G. D. H. Cole, *A Short History*.
21. Ibid.
22. Alan Bullock, *Ernest Bevin*.
23. Anthony Crosland, *The Future of Socialism*.
24. Williams and Reed, *The Policies of Power*.
25. Geoffrey Lee Williams, *The Neutralist Tendency*.
26. Ibid.
27. Bullock, *Ernest Bevin*.
28. G. D. H. Cole, *A Short History*.
29. Ibid.
30. Ibid.
31. Ibid.
32. Ibid.
33. Ibid.
34. Bullock, *Ernest Bevin*.
35. Ibid.
36. Williams and Reid, *Policies of Power*.
37. Ibid.
38. Ibid.
39. Ibid.
40. G. D. H. Cole, *A History of the Labour Party*, Routledge, 1948.
41. Miliband, *Parliamentary Socialism*.
42. A. Bevan, *In Place of Fear*, pp. 118–19.
43. We do not imply that Richard Crossman was a marxist. He was merely over-impressed by marxist achievements. This trait may be regarded as endemic among left-wing intellectuals.
44. Richard Crossman, *Socialism and the New Despotism*, pp. 16–17.
45. Ibid.
46. Stephen Hasler, *Death of British Democracy*, p. 137.
47. Joseph Frankel, *National Interest*, OUP, 1963.
48. Bullock, *Ernest Bevin*.
49. Ibid.
50. Hasler, *Death of British Democracy*, p. 137.
51. Peter Wiles, *Populism*.
52. Anthony Crosland, *The Future of Socialism*, Jonathan Cape, 1956; and John Strachey, *Contemporary Capitalism*, Gollanccz, 1956.
53. Quoted in Hasler, *The Death of British Democracy*, p. 47.
54. Hedley Bull, *The Anarchical Society*, p. 246.
55. Quoted in Hasler, *The Death of British Democracy*, Williams, p. 47.
56. Ibid.
57. Williams and Reed, *Policies of Power*.
58. Ibid.
59. Hasler, *Death of British Democracy*.
60. Ibid.
61. Williams, *The Neutralist Tendency*.

62. Ibid.
63. Ibid.
64. Ibid.
65. John Strachey, *In Pursuit of Peace*, Fabian Society, 1961, p. 18.
66. Ibid.
67. Williams, *The Permanent Alliance*.
68. Williams and Reed, *The Policies of Power*.
69. Williams, *The Neutralist Tendency*.

4 The Split

1. Geoffrey Lee Williams, *The Neutralist Tendency*, p. 56.
2. Ibid.
3. Ibid.
4. Ibid, p. 24.
5. Ibid.
6. Ibid.
7. Ibid.
8. Ibid.
9. Ibid.
10. Ibid.
11. Ibid.
12. Ibid.
13. Ibid.
14. Ibid.
15. Ibid.
16. Ibid.
17. Peter Byrd, *Social Democracy and Defence: The British Labour Party*, British Atlantic Publications, 1984.
18. Ibid.
19. Ibid.
20. Geoffrey Lee Williams, *Global Defence: Motivations and Policy in a Nuclear Age*, Vikas, 1984, p. 222.
21. Peter Byrd, *Social Democracy*.
22. Ibid.
23. Ibid.
24. Geoffrey Lee Williams, *The Neutralist Tendency*, p. 32.
25. Ibid.
26. Ibid.
27. Williams and Reed, *The Policies of Power*, p. 239.
28. Williams, *The Neutralist Tendency*.
29. Ibid.
30. Geoffrey Lee Williams, *Neutralist Tendency*, p. 9.
31. Ibid.
32. Ibid.
33. Ibid.
34. Ibid.

35. Ibid.
36. Ibid.
37. Ibid.
38. Ibid.
39. Ibid.
40. Peter Byrd, *Social Democracy*, p. 17.
41. Ibid.
42. Ibid.
43. Ibid.
44. Ibid.
45. Geoffrey Lee Williams, *Neutralist Tendency*.
46. Ibid.
47. Ibid.
48. Byrd, *Social Democracy*.
49. Ibid.
50. *Fourth Report from Defence Committee*, H. of C. 36, 1980–1.
51. Byrd, *Social Democracy*.
52. Ibid.
53. Ibid.
54. Ibid.
55. Ibid.
56. Ibid.
57. Ibid.
58. Ibid.
59. Ibid.
60. Ibid.
61. Williams, *Neutralist Tendency*, p. 33.
62. Byrd, *Social Democracy*.
63. Ibid.
64. Ibid.
65. Williams, *Neutralist Tendency*.
66. Williams and Williams, *The European Defence Initiative*, p. 67.
67. Byrd, *Social Democracy*, p. 19.
68. Ibid.
69. Ibid.
70. Williams, *The Neutralist Tendency*.
71. Ibid.
72. Ibid.
73. Ibid.
74. Ibid.
75. Byrd, *Social Democracy*.
76. Paul Mercer, *Peace of the Dead: The Truth Behind the Nuclear Disarmers*, Policy Research Publications, 1986.
77. Williams, *The Neutralist Tendency*.
78. Mercer, *Peace of the Dead*.
79. Ibid.
80. Ibid.
81. Peter Byrd, *Social Democracy*.
82. Ibid.

83. Ibid.
84. Ibid.
85. *Defence Without the Bomb, the Report of the Alternative Defence Commission*, Taylor & Francis, 1985.
86. Ibid.
87. Ibid.
88. Ibid.
89. Ibid.
90. Ibid.
91. Ibid.
92. Ibid.
93. *Campaigning for a Fairer Britain*, Labour Party Publication, 1982.
94. Ibid.
95. Ibid.
96. Williams, *The Neutralist Tendency*, p. 62.
97. Ibid.
98. Ibid.
99. Coral Bell, *The Debatable Alliance*, p. 52.
100. Hasler, *Death of British Democracy*.
101. Williams, *The Neutralist Tendency*.
102. Ibid.
103. Ibid.
104. This was made clear by both men in numerous speeches.
105. Byrd, *Social Democracy*.
106. *The Times*, 30 September 1985.
107. Ibid.
108. Ibid.

5 The Triumph of the Left over Defence

1. Coral Bell, *The Debatable Alliance*.
2. Williams, *The Neutralist Tendency*, p. 26.
3. *The Military Balance 1982*, IISS.
4. Williams, *Global Defence*, p. 32.
5. Williams, *The Neutralist Tendency*, p. 17.
6. Ibid., p. 49.
7. Ibid.
8. Ibid.
9. Ibid.
10. Ibid.
11. Ibid.
12. Ibid.
13. *Labour Party Annual Report*, 1982.
14. Byrd, *Social Democracy*.
15. Ibid.
16. Williams, *The Neutralist Tendency*, p. 32.
17. Clear from speeches and interviews given by the so-called 'Gang of Three'.

18. Williams, *The Neutralist Tendency*, p. 33.
19. Ibid.
20. Ibid.
21. *Labour's Programme 1982*; Labour Party Publications, 1982.
22. Ibid.
23. Ibid.
24. Ibid.
25. Christopher Coker, 'Naked Emperors: The British Labour Party and Defence', in *Strategic Review*, vol. 12, no. 4, Fall 1984.
26. *Labour's Programme 1982*.
27. Ibid.
28. Ibid.
29. Ibid.
30. Ibid.
31. Ibid.
32. Ibid.
33. See speeches by Dr Owen *et al.*
34. The state of opinion on these issues is examined in Bruce George and Curt Pawlisch 'Defence and the British Election', in ADIU *Report*, vol. 5, no. 4, 1983. See also Ivor Evan's analysis of the election results, in the *Guardian*, 14 June 1983.
35. John MacKintosh, *Political Quarterly*, vol. 43, no. 4, Oct/Dec 1972, p. 47.
36. See William Paterson and Ian Campbell, *Social Democracy in Post-war Europe*, Macmillan.
37. Williams and Reed, *The Policies of Power*, p. 227.
38. See Tony Crosland's monumental study, *The Future of Socialism*.
39. Williams, *The Neutralist Tendency*.
40. Ibid.
41. See Geoffrey Lee Williams, 'The Ideology of Labourism', unpublished Ph.D. thesis, Open University, 1978.
42. Williams, *The Neutralist Tendency*.
43. Ibid.
44. Ibid.
45. Ibid.
46. Geoffrey Lee Williams, *The Natural Alliance for the West*, Atlantic Trade Publications, 1979.
47. Mr Scargill's leadership of the NUM has decidedly syndicalist tendencies.
48. Mr Hatton's policies were subject to disapproval by the Labour leadership under Mr Callaghan and by his successors. The extent of *Militant* penetration of the Labour Party was examined in the *Underhill Report 1978* which was never officially published.

6 The British Political Tradition in Crisis

1. Peter Zentner, *Social Democracy in Britain: Must Labour Lose?*, John Martin, 1982, p. 7.

2. Alfred Sherman, 'Why the Mould is Still Intact', *The Times*, 28 August 1984, p. 10.
3. Ian Bradley, *Breaking the Mould*, 1981, p. 19.
4. David Rees, *Lugano Review* 1975, 'A letter from Britain'.
5. David Marquand, 'Inquest on a Movement: Labour's Defeat and its Consequences', *Encounter*, 1979.
6. David Rees, *Lugano Review*.
7. Zentner, *Social Democracy*, p. 9.
8. David Rees, *Lugano Review*.
9. Denis Kavanagh and Bill Jones, *British Politics Today*, 1983, p. 29.
10. David Rees, *Lugano Review*.
11. Ibid.
12. See Bo Sarlvik and Ivor Crewe, *Decade of Dealignment*, CUP, p. 30.
13. David Rees, *Lugano Review*.
14. Ibid.
15. Ibid.
16. Ibid.
17. Ibid.
18. Kavanagh and Jones, *British Politics Today*, p. 29.
19. David Butler and Donald Stokes, *Political Change in Britain*, Macmillan, 1974, p. 30.
20. Kavanagh and Jones, *British Politics Today*, p. 29.
21. David Rees, *Lugano Review*.
22. Ibid.
23. Ibid.
24. David Marquand, 'Inquest on a Movement'.
25. David Rees, *Lugano Review*.
26. Ibid.
27. Ibid.
28. Ibid.
29. Ibid.
30. *World Marxist Review*, Nov. 1973.
31. Betty Matthews, *Britain and The Socialist Revolution*, C.P. Publications, 1973.
32. David Rees, *Lugano Review*.
33. *The Underhill Report*, 1978.
34. John P. Mackintosh, 'The Future of the Labour Party', *The Political Quarterly*, Dec. 1972.
35. Kavanagh and Jones, *British Politics Today*, p. 29.
36. Ibid.
37. Hugh Stephenson, *Claret and Chips – The Rise of the SDP*, p. 7.
38. Ibid.
39. Ibid.
40. Bradley, *Breaking the Mould*, p. 43.
41. Ibid, p. 8.
42. Butler and Stokes, *Political Change in Britain*.
43. Ibid.
44. Bradley, *Breaking the Mould*, p. 16.

7   Straws in the Wind: The 1979 Vote of No Confidence

1. Bradley, *Breaking the Mould*, p. 17.
2. Ibid.
3. Marquand, 'Inquest on a Movement'.
4. Ibid.
5. Ibid.
6. Hansard H. of C. debates.
7. Ibid.
8. Steven Strasser and Tony Clipton, 'Lady in Waiting', *Newsweek*, 9 April 1979.
9. Impressions from Alan Lee Williams, then a Labour Member of Parliament.
10. Ibid.
11. Ibid.
12. Ibid.
13. Ibid.
14. Ibid.
15. Ibid.
16. Marquand, 'Inquest on a Movement'.
17. Ibid.
18. Bradley, *Breaking the Mould*, p. 45.
19. Ibid.
20. Crosland, *Future of Socialism*, p. 17.
21. Hasler, *Death of British Democracy*.
22. Ibid.
23. Ibid.
24. Dick Taverne, interviewed 17 April 1985.
25. Ibid.
26. Ibid.
27. Ibid.
28. Ibid.
29. Dick Taverne, *The Future of the Left*, Cape, 1974.
30. Ibid.
31. Ibid.
32. Ibid.
33. Ibid.
34. Ibid.
35. Bradley, *Breaking the Mould*, p. 59.
36. Ibid.
37. Ibid.
38. Williams, *The Neutralist Tendency*.
39. William Rodgers, vice president of the Social Democratic Party, interviewed 29 March 1985.
40. Ibid.

8 The Birth of the SDP

1. Bradley, *Breaking the Mould?* p. 27.
2. Roy Jenkins, 'Home Thoughts from Abroad', in BBC Dimbleby Lecture *The Rebirth of Britain*, 3 Nov. 1979, pp. 13–14.
3. Ibid, p. 26.
4. Zentner, *Social Democracy*, p. 130.
5. Ibid.
6. Noel Tracey, *The Origins of the Social Democratic Party*, Croom Helm, 1983, p. 38.
7. David Owen, William Rodgers and Shirley Williams, 'Open letter to their fellow members of the Labour Party', in the *Guardian*, 1 August 1980, p. 11.
8. Tracey, *The Origins of the Social Democratic Party*, Croom Helm, 1983, p. 38.
9. Ibid.
10. Bradley, *Breaking the Mould*, p. 95.
11. Ibid.
12. Taverne (interview).
13. Geoffrey Smith, 'Why a Liberal Alliance is So Critical for the New Party', *The Times*, 20 March 1981, p. 14.
14. Stephenson, *Claret and Chips – the Rise of the SDP*, Michael Joseph, 1982, p. 29.
15. Wayland Kennet, ed., *The Rebirth of Britain*, p. 4.
16. Ibid.
17. Rodgers (interview).
18. David Owen, 'The Enabling Society', in Wayland Kennet, *The Rebirth of Britain*, London, Weidenfeld & Nicolson, pp. 241–2.
19. Ian Bradley, 'Socially Distinguished People', *The Times*, 30 Nov. 1981, p. 10.
20. Bradley, *Breaking the Mould*, p. 104.
21. Ibid.
22. Shirley Williams, 'Why People Are Hungry for the New Beginning', *The Times*, 26 March 1981, p. 14.
23. Alan Lee Williams, speaking at the English Speaking Union, 28 March 1981.
24. Bradley, *Breaking the Mould*, p. 104.
25. Stephenson, *Claret and Chips*, p. 24.
26. 'Anger as Public Are Left Outside', *The Times*, 27 March 1981.
27. SDP Policy statement.
28. Ibid.
29. Ibid.
30. Alan Lee Williams, speech, Labour Club, Hornchurch, 27 Nov. 1981.
31. Ibid.
32. Rodgers (interview).
33. Ibid.
34. Dick Taverne, 'Unite or Die: The Alliance Choice', *The Times*, 12 Jan. 1982, p. 2.
35. *The Sun*, 17 July 1982.

36. Alan Lee Williams, speech.
37. Stephenson, *Claret and Chips*, p. 63.
38. Ibid.
39. Zentner, *Social Democracy*, p. 183.
40. Ibid.
41. Zentner, *Social Democracy*, p. 59.
42. David Butler and Denis Kavanagh, *The British General Election of 1983*, p. 26.
43. Ibid.
44. Kavanagh and Jones, *British Politics Today*, p. 184.
45. Ibid, p. 185.
46. Butler and Kavanagh, *The British General Election of 1983* p. 291.
47. Ibid.
48. Ibid.
49. *New Statesman*, 17 June 1983, p. 1.

9 The Chimera of Electoral Reform

1. Kennet, p. 246.
2. Jeremy Joseph, *Inside the Alliance: An Inside Account of the Development and Prospects of the Liberal–SDP Alliance*, 1983, p. 216.
3. This system was much approved by many members of the SDP.
4. Vernon Bogdaneor, *What is Proportional Representation?*, 1984, p. 27.
5. Ibid.
6. Ibid.
7. Ibid.
8. Taverne (interview).
9. Joseph, *Inside the Alliance*, p. xvi.
10. Taverne, *The Future of the Left: Lincoln and After*, Cape, 1976.
11. Zentner, *Social Democracy*, p. 917.
12. Dr Owen has never encouraged the idea of merger as a feasible one and has always preferred the notion of an alliance with the Liberals.
13. Joseph, *Inside the Alliance*, p. xvi.
14. Alan Watson, President of the Liberal Party, interviewed 23 April 1985.
15. Ibid.
16. Ibid, p. 243.
17. Philip Webster, 'Alliance Cannot Go On in Present Form, Says Liberals', *The Times*, 17 August 1984, p. 1.
18. Rodgers (interview).
19. Taverne (interview).
20. Rodgers (interview).
21. Ibid.
22. Taverne (interview).
23. Austin Mitchell, *Four Years in the Death of the Labour Party*.
24. Bo Sarlvik and Ivor Crewe, *Decade of Dealignment*, pp. 340–1.
25. Ibid.
26. Ibid.

27. 'A Long, Long Way From Limehouse', the *Guardian*, 10 April 1984, p. 21.
28. Crewe and Sarlvik, *Decade of Dealignment*, p. 343.
29. Sherman, 'Why the mould is still intact', *The Times*, 28 August 1984, p. 10.
30. Rodgers (interview).
31. Ibid.
32. Ibid.

10 The Beginning of the End

1. Rosie Barnes enjoyed a meteoric rise to fame which seemed to mimic the history of the SDP. What she lacked in political experience she made up for in her extraordinary capacity to project common sense into politics.
2. The split with the Liberals over the Trident D5 system illustrated that the agreement over the future of Britain's deterrent was far from assured. Even the SDP was divided over Trident, but Owen realised that though he would have preferred a cheaper system, there was no real alternative to Trident if Britain was to remain an effective nuclear power.
3. The Alliance's stand on defence was both contradictory and counter-productive. It confused both supporters and voters.
4. David Owen's realism on this issue can be contrasted with the response to this suggestion from the Liberal members of the Alliance during the election campaign.
5. Mrs Thatcher threw David Owen onto the defensive in an area of policy where he was a master of his subject. This tended to blunt his personal impact on the defence issue throughout the election.
6. The Alliance's joint commission on defence produced a classic fudge and mudge, to quote David Owen.
7. Following the 1987 general election Mr Kinnock tried to reassess defence in the light of the intermediate nuclear missile treaty of December 1987. He merely created further confusion.
8. We found evidence that David Steel faced enormous pressure from his colleagues to broach the issue of a merger as soon as the election was over. There is also some evidence that the matter had been raised by Steel's aides *before* the election.
9. David Owen anticipated that the split within the SDP was inevitable.
10. Finkelstein circular address, December 1987. Danny Finkelstein is a stout supporter of David Owen, and his analytic skills have often been used to support his leader.
11. Bob Maclennan's tough stance involved by definition *detailed* policy issues because of his distrust of the Liberals.
12. It was indeed a pyrrhic victory.
13. The Liberal vote was disappointing but even the SDP vote was not overwhelming.
14. John Cartwright's speech was an effective debating speech but

appeared to have little impact on Roy Jenkins. The SDP Sheffield vote marked the end of the first SDP. See the *Guardian*, 'A New Third Party With Plenty to Do', 1 Feb. 1988.

11 From Alliance to Misalliance?

1. T. E. Uttley, 'This Unattractive Alliance', *The Times*, 26 January 1988.
2. David Sainsbury and Leslie Murphy, 'This Murder of Ideals by Merger', *The Times*, 9 July 1987.
3. Brian Walden, *The Sunday Times*, 3 January 1987.
4. David Owen, letter to colleagues, December 1987.
5. John Grigg, *The Sunday Times*, 19 January 1987.
6. David Owen, 23 December 1988.
7. Peter Jenkins, 'From One-Man Band to Megalomania', *The Independent*, 31 August 1987.
8. *The Times*, 'Social Democracy's Name', 31 August 1987.
9. *The Times*, David Owen speaking at SDP Sheffield Conference, 31 Jan. 1988.
10. Ibid.
11. Ibid.
12. Ibid.
13. *The Times*, 1 Feb. 1988.
14. *The Times*, Geoffrey Smith, 7 Feb. 1988.
15. *The Times*, 'No Deals with Labour Party or Owenites', report by Richard Ford, 29 July 1988.
16. Ibid.
17. Ibid.
18. Ibid.
19. *The Times*, SLD election sketch, 'Squinting at the Distant Horizon', by Craig Brown, 29 July 1988.
20. *The Sunday Times*, 'Razzmatazz Falls Flat on the Centre Ground', Michael Jones, 31 July 1988.

12 The Breakup or the Breakout

1. Professor David Marquand, 'Socialism lives . . . but only in Britain', 2 Dec. 1988, *London Evening Standard*.

Select Bibliography

Bogdanor, Vernon, *What is Proportional Representation?*, Oxford: Martin Robertson, 1984.

Bradley, Ian, *Breaking the Mould*, Oxford: Martin Robertson, 1981.

Butler, David and Dennis Kavanagh, *The British General Election of 1983*, London: Macmillan, 1980.

Butler, David and Donald Stokes, *Political Change in Britain: Forces Shaping Electoral Choice*, Harmondsworth: Penguin, 1971.

Correlli, Barrett, *The Collapse of British Power*, London: Eyre Methuen, 1972.

Eden, Douglas, 'Crosland: An Alternative View', *Encounter*, June 1979.

Harris, K. and David Owen, *David Owen: An Autobiography*, London: Pan Books 1988.

Hasler, Stephen (ed.), *Tragedy of Labour*, Oxford: Basil Blackwell, 1980.

Jenkins, Roy, 'Home Thoughts from Abroad', in *The Rebirth of Britain*, London: Weidenfeld & Nicolson, 1982.

Joseph, Jeremy, *Inside the Alliance – an Inside Account of the Development and Prospects of the Liberal–SDP Alliance*, London: John Martin Publishing Ltd, 1983.

Kavanagh, Denis and Bill Jones, *British Politics Today*, 2nd edn, Manchester: Manchester University Press, 1983.

Kennett, Wayland (ed.), *The Rebirth of Britain*, London: Weidenfeld & Nicolson, 1982.

Marquand, David, 'Is There New Hope for the Social Democrats', *Encounter*, April 1983.

Mitchell, Austin, *Four Years in the Death of the Labour Party*, London: Hodder & Stoughton Ltd, 1982.

Owen, David, 'Enabling Society', in *The Rebirth of Britain*, ed. Wayland Kennett, London: Weidenfeld & Nicolson, 1982.

Owen, David, *Face the Future*, Oxford University Press, 1981.

Rodgers, William, Vice-President of the SDP. Interview conducted by Terri Sewell, 20 March 1985.

Rodgers, William, *The Politics of Change*, London: Secker & Warburg, 1982.

Sampson, Anthony, *The Changing Anatomy of Britain*, London: Hodder & Stoughton Ltd, 1982.

Sarlvik, Bo and Ivor Crewe, *Decade of Dealignment*, Cambridge: Cambridge University Press, 1983.

Stephenson, Hugh, *Claret and Chips – The Rise of the SDLP*, London: Michael Joseph Ltd, 1982.

Tracey, Noel, *The Origins of the Social Democratic Party*, London: Croom Helm Ltd, 1983.

Williams, Geoffrey Lee and Bruce Reed, *Denis Healey: The Policies of Power*, Sidgwick & Jackson, 1971.

Williams, Geoffrey Lee and Alan Lee Williams, *The European Defence Iniative*, London: Macmillan, 1986.

Williams, Geoffrey Lee, *The Neutralist Tendency: Defence and the Left in Britain and Germany*, Institute for European Defence and Strategic Studies, 1987.

Williams, Geoffrey Lee, *Global Defence: Motivation and Policy in a Nuclear Age*, New Delhi: Vikas, 1984.

Williams, Shirley, *Politics is for People*, Harmondsworth: Penguin, 1981.

Zentner, Peter, *Social Democracy in Britain: Must Labour Lose?*, London: John Martin Publishing, 1982.

Index